Uproarious

How Feminists and Other Subversive Comics Speak Truth

Cynthia Willett and Julie Willett

University of Minnesota Press
Minneapolis
London

This book is freely available in an open-access edition thanks to TOME (Toward an Open Monograph Ecosystem)—a collaboration of the Association of American Universities, the Association of University Presses, and the Association of Research Libraries—and the generous support of Emory University and the Andrew W. Mellon Foundation. Learn more at the TOME website, available at openmonographs.org.

Different versions of chapter 1 were previously published as Cynthia Willett, Julie Willett, and Yael D. Sherman, "The Seriously Erotic Politics of Feminist Laughter," *Social Research* 79, no. 1 (2012): 217–46; Copyright New School University; reprinted by permission of The Johns Hopkins University Press; and as Cynthia Willett and Julie Willett, "The Seriously Erotic Politics of Laughter: Bitches, Whores, and Other Fumerists," in *Philosophical Feminism and Popular Culture*, ed. Sharon Crasnow and Joanne Waugh (Plymouth, U.K.: Lexington Books, 2013): 15–36. A different version of chapter 2 was published as "Going to Bed White and Waking Up Arab: On Xenophobia, Affect Theories of Laughter, and the Social Contagion of the Comic Stage," *Critical Philosophy of Race* 2, no. 1 (2014): 84–105; copyright 2014 The Pennsylvania State University; reprinted by permission of The Pennsylvania State University Press. A different version of chapter 3 was published as Cynthia Willett with Julie Willett, "Can the Subaltern Animal Laugh? Neoliberal Inversions, Cross-Species Solidarities, and Other Challenges to Human Exceptionalism," in *Interspecies Ethics*, by Cynthia Willett (New York: Columbia University Press, 2014), 29–59; copyright 2014 Columbia University Press; reprinted with permission of Columbia University Press.

Published by the University of Minnesota Press
111 Third Avenue South, Suite 290
Minneapolis, MN 55401-2520
http://www.upress.umn.edu

Printed in the United States of America on acid-free paper

The University of Minnesota is an equal-opportunity educator and employer.

Library of Congress Cataloging-in-Publication Data
Names: Willett, Cynthia, author. | Willett, Julie, author.
Title: Uproarious : how feminists and other subversive comics speak truth /
    Cynthia Willett and Julie Willett.
Description: Minneapolis : University of Minnesota Press, 2019. | Includes
    bibliographical references and index. |
Identifiers: LCCN 2018061115 (print) | ISBN 978-1-5179-0828-7 (hc) |
    ISBN 978-1-5179-0829-4 (pb)
Subjects: LCSH: Wit and humor—Social aspects.
Classification: LCC PN6149.S62 .W55 2020 (print) | DDC 306.4/81—dc23
LC record available at https://lccn.loc.gov/2018061115

UMP BmB 2019

In Sisterhood

Contents

Introduction

Revamping the Four Major Theories on Humor

> There does have to be a revolution of form in order to
> accommodate different voices.
> —Hannah Gadsby, *New York Times*

The "out and outspoken" queen of comedy, Wanda Sykes, has no problem speaking truth even in the face of a difficult crowd.[1] After the election of Donald Trump, she quipped, "I am certain this is not the first time we've elected a racist, sexist, homophobic president. He's just the first confirmed one."[2] Like Sykes, we understand what is funny to some is not funny to others, but we also see how once marginalized game-changing comedians have come to center stage to reveal the profound relevance of humor in American politics. As Sykes puts it, "My comedy is speaking truth to power and speaking up for people who don't have a voice because those are the kinds of comics I grew up with." After all, she continues, "That was their style: Richard Pryor, George Carlin, Dick Gregory and Moms Mabley."[3]

By the early twentieth-first century across the U.S. cultural and political landscape, the comic, building on a rich legacy, has become our truth teller.[4] From late-night television shows such as those hosted by Stephen Colbert and Trevor Noah to stand-up performances at New York's Muslim Funny Fest, humor is not merely for escape but also a way to handle our gut instincts and to get to the guts of an issue. Yet we know that conventionally audiences expect laughter to serve as mere amusement. We also know that under the cover of amusement, toxic jokes turning on race, Islamophobia, homophobia, or misogyny and rape are used as a tool of oppression and a form of cruelty. But what of humor turned around and aimed at the abuse of power? This book is about how humor from below can serve as a source of empowerment, a strategy for outrage and truth telling, a counter to fear, a source of joy and friendship, a cathartic treatment against unmerited shame, and even a means of empathetic connection and alliance. In so doing, we challenge the philosophical foundation of humor as a simple device for debasement or for detaching ourselves from messy situations and their emotions. Instead, we offer a humor that connects body and soul, and that connects us with each other. This humor of connection is what self-described neurodivergent comic Hannah Gadsby claims when she strives to "break comedy in order to rebuild it."[5]

Since the time of Plato, philosophers and critics have treated the comedic as of lesser worth than serious art, and of little value compared to rational discourse.[6] Those with an appreciation for high art tend to dismiss comedy as lowbrow, fueled as it often is by raw emotion. Laughter and ridicule are said to expose how the body, with its animal instincts, rattles the brain and weighs down the soul. When humor has been appreciated by intellectual elites, it is most valued as a cerebral game and an elevated skill of true wit that rational minds play. Because women and others who are socially disempowered are viewed as closer to animals and ruled by emotion, they have been perceived as less capable of true humor and relegated to mockery's natural targets. Their laughter, unlike that of the assumed more logical mind, has been thought to display unseemly emotions and a body out of control. Our question is how we might shift the study of the comedic from the cerebral tease while unmasking cruelty excused as mere amusement ("it was just a joke") to expose humor's underlying power plays together with its strategies for talking truth. By embracing women, animals, and other subversive creatures as comedy's central agents rather than its targets, we aim to revamp the major theories that have for too long defined the meaning of laughter and humor.

The socially disempowered have historically found humor to be a tool of resistance in hidden (and not so hidden) transcripts that recharge the social atmosphere and body politics, yet their humor has been ignored to such a degree that they often are not even considered funny. Think about a debate that cultural critic Christopher Hitchens rekindled in 2007 when he attempted to explain "Why women aren't funny" in *Vanity Fair*.[7] Backed up by modern "science" (he cites a single study of ten men and ten women), Hitchens's answer is that Mother Nature (that "bitch") made it so that men have to find some way to appeal to women, and humor is apparently the trick. "The chief task in life that a man has to perform is that of impressing the opposite sex, and Mother Nature (as we laughingly call her) is not so kind to men. In fact, she equips so many fellows with very little armament for the struggle. An average man has just one, outside chance: he had better be able to make the lady laugh. . . . Women have no corresponding need to appeal to men in this way. They already appeal, if you get my drift." Hitchens indulges in the usual misogynist humor of the patriarch in this case by donning the mask of the underdog. Under the surface of this elevated show of wit, and arguably the science behind it, is a lowbrow tits-and-ass joke.

Debates over who is funny move beyond an ongoing battle of the sexes and its cis-gendered heteronormative subtexts. Following in the rich trajectory of intersectional theory, and aware that like Tina Fey we are white and middle class, we look not only at issues of misogyny and sexism but also at racism, mass incarceration, and Islamophobia as well as hate speech and rape jokes disguised as free speech.[8] In agreement with Patricia Hill Collins and Simra Bilge, "peoples' lives and the organization of power in a given society are better understood as being shaped not by a single axis of social division, be it race or gender or class, but by many axes that work together and influence each other."[9] Keeping in mind the "intersecting systems of power," we see that when not only women but also other targeted groups, including Muslims in a post-9/11 world and prisoners locked up under a policy of mass incarceration, mock those with inflated cultural or social authority, comedy along with belly laughs can cut deep into our gut feelings and shake up oppressive tropes and all too traditional narratives.[10] We include nonhuman animal species within our understanding of subversive agents of laughter and power, thus broadening the intersectional lens. Often unpredictable and sometimes more readily felt than explained, waves of laughter amplified through social media can alter the political landscape, forge new identities and alliances, subvert long-held assumptions built on hierarchy, and exuberantly reveal, as Tina Fey put it, that "women are just as funny as monkeys,"[11] but only because, as we insist, our nonhuman kin turn out to be comics as well.

Of course, far too often an oppressive culture either silences or reabsorbs subversive monkey laughs, reinscribing the socially disempowered as simply targets of ridicule. The stakes of who is allowed to laugh, or who is even perceived to be capable of genuine laughter and humor, are high. The erasure of the socially disempowered from the status of the comic, and thus the agent of true humor, is part of a persistent historical narrative and a master game plan that has come to define the construct of the rational man. This manly trope in turn defines others as humorless as he constructs his own self as civilized. In so doing, humor is neutered such that it mitigates laughter's radical potential, leaving a measured enjoyment of humor as at best a cerebral interlude amid serious matters. Or, in Hitchens's pithy reformulation of what women lack: "You will see what Nietzsche meant when he described a witticism as an epitaph on the death of feeling. Male humor . . . understands that life is quite possibly a joke. . . . Humor is part of the armor-plate" to deal with that "farcical bitch": life gendered female.[12] Indeed, for various elites, humor devolves into a refined mental act, an existential detachment from life or a dry intellectual enjoyment of puzzles far from the depths of the belly laugh. Just consider gallows humor as displayed in the frequent citation of Oscar Wilde's deathbed words: "This wallpaper is atrocious. One of us has to go."[13] At its most profound, cerebral wit is said to offer a moment of transcendence before one's fate. At its worst, such humor, as found in a tits-and-ass joke, reinforces oppositional dualisms through the kind of ridicule designed to keep those deemed other in their place. When the laughter of marginalized social groups is recognized, it is dismissed as comic relief, a distraction from the real matters at hand, and possibly on the verge of being out of control. Disregarding the other's laughter as mere relief reassures dominant social groups that they still hold the reins of power. The refusal to register the social power of subaltern laughter marks a central bias in standard philosophical conceptions of what humor is.

This bias is systemic and requires a full frontal attack on the very foundations of comic theory. Challenging cultural dualisms as well as human–nonhuman hierarchies, we revisit the four dominant theories that have explained laughter and comedy across disciplines—superiority theory, relief, incongruity, and play—through the multiple lenses of feminist and other game-changing comedians. Superiority theory, often understood through the critiques of humor prevalent in ancient and early modern thinkers, exposes the pleasure found in mocking others. This pleasure arises as a reinforcement of the other's inferior social status or as a means to reaffirm and enhance one's own social standing.[14] In the eighteenth century, two alternative theories gained prominence. Relief theory argued that a comic venting of emotions through a hearty laugh offers a physical release of tensions. The Western mind–body split also sported a cerebral theory of laughter's source in the perception of incongruities—that is, in the jack-in-the-box violation of mental patterns or anything that offers surprise. Various versions of this cerebral theory continue to anchor dominant approaches to humor, sometimes with a secondary appeal to humor's capacity for momentary physical relief or to its calming effect. A fourth significant theory of laughter emerged in the early twentieth century from animal studies and evolutionary speculations investigating the playful shenanigans of chimpanzees.[15] Around the same time, animal-like antics suspending hierarchical rank and privileges turned up in a prominent literary history of subversive folk carnivals.[16]

Just like the mind and body, these theories have often been understood as separate and distinct, but our philosophical approach establishes an interconnectedness that reaches deep down to the naughty parts. This alternative approach owes a debt to more than two decades of groundbreaking work from feminists, philosophers, and historians as well as social and natural scientists insisting that humans, along a continuum with other animal species, are emotionally driven, social, and embodied creatures.[17] In other words, far from an aloof mind perceiving the world at a distance, the self is a process, one both relational and porous, with various levels of consciousness and felt awareness throughout the body. Think about why doctors might inquire about the well-being of our loved ones to gauge our own physical symptoms. At the center of our lives are not just our inner thoughts but also reflections as they are entangled with emotions and networks of relationships with others. More than just perceiving and thinking subjects, we are also affective agents extended into a biosocial field of often mysterious forces.

The term "affect" indicates a significant visceral component of our multilayered selves that roots much of felt experience in the preverbal, unconscious right brain and in the gut. The gut, or enteric nervous system, is also known as the second brain and has more than thirty neurotransmitters and 95 percent of the body's serotonin. In contrast, the term "emotion" points to a significant role for the semiautonomous left brain's capacities for verbal articulation and reflection. Given the difficulty of disconnecting one part of the body from another, we do not treat the distinction between these terms as hard and fast. Nor are they meant to reinvoke a mind–body binary. Often contagious, affects are not, as in the case of the feeling of the heartbeat, merely physical sensations; rather, they are more of an emotional vibe that is easier to feel than define. Ranging from racialized fear to laughter's revitalizing energy, affects carry culturally imbued meanings across porous borders. They travel through discrete and even precise tones, gestures, and rhythms, but they also spread like waves through biosocial networks, and they thus can define the mood of a crowd. Affects like fear or laughter's pleasure might stir up a crowd and sometimes provide genuine comic relief.[18] Consider how a stand-up comedian reads a room to alter its collective vibes.

By bringing viscerally felt emotions and the gut brain into play, comedy and satire as much as any of the other arts can call us back to our animal selves. From among the most ancient literary productions—a fart joke penned around 1900 BCE during the Bronze Age in Sumeria[19]—to the contagious memes and comedy sketches that populate social platforms, no other style of communication exposes the stakes of the body and the social sphere more insistently than the denigrated genre of comedy. Perhaps this is also the reason that it has been dismissed. Taking on the caricatured figure of the rational man, our topsy-turvy approach elevates the belly laugh and frees the comical as a vehicle of communication with often unstoppable social and political momentum. In the end, we offer through the comedic not a philosophical definition of what makes us laugh but a vision of life. Such an approach, however, demands a holistic reworking of the theoretical foundations of humor. Thus, we begin our bottom-up venture into comedy by first turning superiority theory on its head.

Superiority theory is thought to offer the oldest approach to laughter. Hitchens exploits superiority theory in his just-so story of why women can't be funny: "Male humor prefers to laugh at someone's expense. . . . Whereas women, bless their tender hearts, would prefer that life be fair." Superiority theory focuses on the pleasure experienced when one is the agent rather than the target of laughter. This pleasure, the theory maintains, stems from an increase of one's power, status, or reputation at the expense of others; those others are either perceived to have been diminished or are confirmed to be of an inferior status by a humorous verbal attack, slight, or insult.[20] That some caution is due in any use of this mode of humor is signaled by comic Hari Kondabolu's warning that "there's a lot of things people find funny that are really just bullying."[21] To be sure, this was the concern of traditional philosophers who have been suspicious of laughter. Plato, immersed in a rigidly hierarchal culture, saw this problematic form of humor as the gratuitous enjoyment of weaknesses or flaws of those deemed social inferiors.[22] Centuries later, Thomas Hobbes famously explained laughter as the ego-satisfying pleasure of a "sudden glory," or a felt superiority over others.[23] In contrast to Plato, this early modern thinker believed that laughter registers not social inferiors in a static social world but rather relative changes of social position in a field that we collectively inhabit. The superfluous nastiness of ridicule that punches down continues to motivate some to argue, along with Plato and Hobbes, that ridicule should be frowned upon or even censored. Such nastiness is why the Puritans, with their rigid moral culture, banned the comedic as "evil speaking."[24]

Since the modern revolutions that followed Hobbes and the establishment of free speech as a basic right, evil speaking from charged slurs to outright racist, misogynist, and sacrilegious jokes has been vehemently defended while too often ignoring—if not playing ignorant of—the dynamics of power. Indeed, many comics assert their right to make others laugh as their first obligation, even marking among their targets the politically correct who would challenge their freedom. Think about the French journalists at the satiric rag *Charlie Hebdo* and their defense of cartoonists' depictions of the Islamic prophet Mohammed as a terrorist.[25] Backed by appeals to free speech, there are those who argue along with these cartoonists that ridicule has no limits and all is fair game. Yet that avowal is punctured with an uneasiness over where and when fuzzy lines can be crossed. Indeed, satire is hardly an innocent affair. It can be a high-stakes game of power, and as the French rag itself discloses on its website, one typically fueled by anger and politics.[26] Satire is not a toy for those who would bury their heads in the sand.

While the 2015 Paris massacre was a tragic overreaction to the cartoons, the derogatory portrayal of a revered figure for a devalued racialized minority may register as an act of hubris and humiliation.[27] An insult can feel like sticks and stones, and thus might result in significant harm. Modern liberal defenses of free speech as an absolute right ignore the degree to which speech is inextricably bound to power dynamics and social positions. These liberal conceptions of autonomy and self-ownership view the individual as detached from others at their core. In this excessively abstract view of the self and its liberty, free speech means simply expressing one's own opinions. Speech and its relation to power was more clearly understood in ancient Greek democracy than in excessively abstract and individualistic modern theories. For the Greeks, acts of humiliation performed by the powerful damage the target's social position and thereby wound their core sense of self. Too often today we misunderstand the ancient concept of hubris as a mere attitude of arrogance rather than as a relational breach that harms the vulnerable. In the ancient democracy, hubris was an act of violation, not a personality trait, and a charge directed exclusively against the entitled and privileged by those who suffered from abuse. Such abuse—for example, the hubris of a tyrant—would call forth truth telling as standing up to power, or what the Greeks termed parrhesia.[28]

Tragically, acts of laughter and insult can elicit as reactions from their targets the stereotypically violent or erratic behavior that they would claim to expose. Consequences of such reactions inevitably threaten to spiral out of control, suggesting the need for some shared sense of justice and fair play. But where to draw the line remains highly contested, with claims regarding who is the victim and who the perpetrator depending on perceptions of social positionality. The humorless—including the figure of the politically correct feminist as well as the holier-than-thou pedant, who declare some topics forever off limits—set themselves up for the irresistible ridicule typically aimed at the entitled and morally rigid. They all too readily corner themselves into the role of the straight man—those positioned on the comic stage for a fall. Yet there remains among many some nagging sense that in laughter, things can go too far.

Weighing in such considerations as the tragic impact of persistent patterns of insult and humiliation suggest that no single right, including free speech, should be treated in the abstract, removed from our lives and thus as an absolute. Like ancient acts of hubris, ridicule and insult need to be understood and evaluated in terms of their context—and this means with particular attention to the intersectional relations of power and status that they enact and the violations they risk. Antiblack slurs are not appropriate in the context of white supremacy, nor are misogynistic rape jokes in patriarchal cultures.[29] Of course, it is easy in our comic age to stake a claim against rigid absolutes, and indeed we offer no unyielding principles or universal laws. Yet along with Collins and Bilge, our intersectional lens is focused on a path toward social equality.[30] Keeping in mind that individuals can be powerful based on one category of identity but relatively less powerful based on another (e.g., as a white woman or as a gay man), we reject any static binary reading of power as up/down or dominant/resistant. Yet still we find across much of the political spectrum a principled agreement on the golden rule of comedy: one punches up, not down. Accordingly, laughter would target the ignorance and arrogance, or more to the point the hubris, of powerful elites and dominant social groups. A barb directed at arrogance is rightly perceived to take the culprit down a notch, but only because the target claims a status that is more than deserved, often displaying an unwarranted sense of entitlement. Shaming through laughter has long been thought to offer a social corrective[31] for such abuses of power, exposing through ridicule the entitled and hubristic[32] or, more colloquially, the "pig" or "asshole."[33]

While many might agree that those who suffer harm from positions at the margins of society deserve compassion if not respect, the tacit rule of comedy—punching up, not down—is not an easy call. Recall the culprit who takes more than he deserves yet thinks he is the victim. A look at the 2016 U.S. presidential election season (staged as Donald "Pussy Grabber" Trump vs. "Crooked Hillary" Clinton) underscores that who is culpable remains bitterly contested terrain. Mockers set up targets for a fall through images or stereotypes that portray their victim as having it coming. Think of Hitchens, who plays up the role of the underdog, and, threatened by the perceived demasculinization of culture, blames bitchy Mother Nature. Political correctness and its critics reveal cultural divides and media bubbles, making it difficult to determine who is on top. For a moment, let's pretend that Hitchens is right and women do prefer to be fair. That sensibility does not necessarily annihilate humor; sometimes it fuels it. Alert to buried social subtexts of laughter, we do not set aside but instead rebrand superiority theory as leveling humor, reclaiming for ridicule egalitarian methods and aims against entrenched hierarchies and biases.

Our approach assumes that ridicule operates on a multilayered field of affect and power where agents and their targets possess varying sources of status and social capital. On this biosocial field, laughter is hardly a neutral source of pleasure. It impacts how we are viewed, who we are, and our range of agency in everyday politics. Its visceral force alters the images, norms, and habits of affect and cognition that diminish or enhance identities and social positions.

Artists and theorists, in their distinct ways, have observed that comedy is bound to the mechanisms of power. When an interviewer for the *Philadelphia Gay News* inquires about the relevance of humor during "uncertain times," Wanda Sykes avers that her followers "need someone to come out and make some jokes and at least try to make sense of everything that is happening and laugh at it."[34] Speaking in front of the Senate's subcommittee on a wide-ranging discussion about "the terrorism problem," U2 front man Bono insists that "comedy should be deployed. It's like, you speak violence, you speak their language. But . . . you laugh at them, when they're goose-stepping down the street, and it takes away their power."[35] The

Russian theorist of carnival, Mikhail Bakhtin, writing during the era of Soviet totalitarianism, also did not want to speak the enemy's language. He too thought that sending in the clowns could undermine authoritarian elites by treating them to a feast of fools and setting off a laugh riot. Taking away social power is more than a mere gesture. Laughter's uproar exposes hypocrisy, unjustified privilege, and lies. It can be the scourge of the sociopath and the narcissist. This exposure is not always malice; sometimes it is righteous anger seeking some degree of social justice. For centuries, folk cultures orchestrated subversive political events such as carnivals that threatened to turn the world or dimensions of it upside down, overturn bodily hierarchies, and dissolve social inequalities. As Bakhtin explores, these festivities trace back to ancient saturnalias where the "fool or clown is the king of the upside-down world."[36] In this topsy-turvy-dom, unlikely bedfellows would come together in equal dialogue and leveling humor, all for the purpose of laying bare some naked truths—if, all too often in some folk traditions, on the backs of women. No doubt a John Belushi–style *Animal House*,[37] from fraternities to Hollywood to Congress, can be as much a festival of jerks as of wise fools. Our point is that carnival foolery from the ancient festivals to contemporary memes is hardly innocent.

However, there remains a persistent suspicion that comic laughter is politically irrelevant or ineffective. This suspicion is partly due to misunderstanding where much of its political force resides. The politics of humor is not solely in the commentary or perspective that it may verbalize. Much of the politics resides in a gut-level affective register of humor's impact on social positions. Yet often if attention is paid to the visceral affects of humor, these affects are understood too narrowly as transitory comic relief. Indeed, a common critique is that carnival humor and ridicule produce little more than a temporary respite from an oppressive situation. Employees relieve tension through mocking the boss instead of engaging in organized action that could change their working conditions. This view is reflected in traditional accounts of comic relief. Relief theory, tracing back to Lord Shaftsbury in the eighteenth century,[38] Herbert Spencer in the nineteenth century,[39] and Freud in the twentieth century,[40] explains laughter as a physical process, one typically viewed as mere venting that offers little more than a feel-good moment. In fact, laughter alters physiology and allows for a fuller sense of life and sustained vitality. Complex processes barely captured by the simple term "relief" can be glimpsed through an older term, "catharsis," which refers to both the healing component in ritual and a measure of infrapolitics. Comic catharsis, more than just physical relief, invokes ancient social practices of working through emotions and altering social identities. When relief theorists treat catharsis as merely synonymous with getting something off your chest, they hardly do it justice.[41]

We don't rebrand relief theory, but we do recast it as a cathartic, biosocial catalyst, and thus as a major player in an easily unsettled political terrain. The energy and power that subversive comics reclaim from repressive and authoritarian climates can decolonize our selves while strengthening our social and political force. Turning mockery around from victims to the oppressors can heat up and refocus the energies of social movements with their demands for change. Through the propagation of laughter, feminist stand-ups—Wanda Sykes, Ali Wong, and Samantha Bee, as well as the midcareer work of Roseanne Barr—confront the continual war on nasty women to reappropriate a public culture and a public space that is marked as all too male. If a physiological politics can demonstrate how laughter may well be the best medicine, this is because cathartic venting can be much more than an emotional or physical release and return to a calm neutral state of normalcy. Cathartic processes can transform shame and fear by serving as a catalyst for social change. Such a power dynamic on a fraught landscape plays a critical role for the well-being of our porous, relational selves. We cannot heal and regenerate apart from a rechanneling of the flows of affect and power on this biosocial field.

As a biosocial event, cathartic laughter reshapes the contours of social space, influences our affects and emotions, and offers both a reimagined social life and a catalyst for it. Comic levelers like Amber Rose and other tricksters who have converted the shame of women defined against our own bodies as tits and ass into a SlutWalk movement demonstrate how laughter can allow us to take back our lives, and fuel biosocial and psychosocial transformation.[42] Similarly, Dean

Obeidallah has taken on post-9/11 mass anxieties in both his Axis of Evil Comedy Tour and Muslim Funny Fest with the aim of combating the social contagion that infects ideas of race and nationalism for positive social change.[43] At an immediate level of felt affect, laughter's contagion, no less than that of anxiety or hate, demonstrates how affects can function as a network-like phenomena, influencing masses of people to absorb the moods of those whom they may not even know.[44] Comic relief has been miscast as a palliative or a pleasure pill, little more than a bit player in social politics, when in fact a good belly laugh has the potential to alter the vectors of affect and power on a volatile political field.

Incongruity theory, unlike relief theory, has retained its prominence over the past several centuries. This theory locates humor not primarily in bodily and emotional relief but rather in the pleasant surprise that occurs through the violation of normal mental patterns and expectations.[45] While much of the intellectual elite continue to view out-of-control laughter as vulgar, as they have for eons, cerebral puzzles are seen as different. These mental jolts produce a whimsical smile, giving the rational mind its own sense of satisfaction and elevation that keeps emotions at a distance. The philosophical impetus for this intellectual take on humor traces back at least as far as Kant and continues to influence current understandings of humor, including those of Noel Carroll, Matthew Hurley, Daniel Dennett, and Reginald Adams's use of cognitive science[46] as well as Simon Critchley's exposition of Freud's Stoic musings on humor.[47] For example, Critchley offers that what draws a smile is the existential incongruity of a human mind stuck in an animal body, with its humiliations and mortal fate. Such a Stoic take captures a dominant strand of thinking throughout the late nineteenth and twentieth centuries, and it recurs in Hitchens's rebuke of female humor. Before "blessing" women for a crippling sense of fairness, Hitchens doubles down on his neo-Freudian claim that humor is an intellectual defense against "life itself"—what men, "battered as they are by motherfucking nature . . . tend to refer to . . . as a bitch."[48]

Feminists are also aware of life's absurdities. In fact, unmasking the unexpected social and political stakes that lurk behind the cerebral turn, with its mental machinery, is one more task for those raucous belly laughs in league with Elizabeth Wilson's gut feminism.[49] Rather than cultivating mind–body separations, feminist laughs offer the chance to process injuries and punch back the patriarch not by detaching but by reconnecting the head with the belly. The mockery that converts despair into hope or diffuse anger into indignant outrage gives a jolt not just to a mental apparatus but to an entire biosocial system inextricably bound to politics and power. Along with comedian, writer, and fat-positive activist Lindy West, our excitement with comedy increases when we "feel its potential to move the world."[50] Reversals and violations upset social not just cognitive expectations. Our interest is not in the incongruities of mental or existential puzzles but in everyday absurdities that call us to action.

In contrast, first-brain approaches to humor distance the mind from the body politic and its belly laughs. These approaches also collude with the assumption that because of the cerebral qualities of humor, only humans exhibit true laughter. Yet the growing scientific evidence that nonhuman animals can laugh and can even demonstrate a sense of humor punctures any assumption of human uniqueness and distance from our animal kin. Moreover, some of the most prevalent examples of animal laughter and humor underscore the larger politics, including the social and motivational context, that may well accompany the cerebral laughter presumed to be unique to humans. One popular 2015 YouTube video of a man performing a magic trick for an orangutan demonstrates how an ape can indeed appreciate intellectual puzzles, but, we note, all the more so with the jovial camaraderie that accompanies the performance.[51] The man shows the orangutan a small box with a grape in it. Then he quickly lowers the handheld box below a barrier and, unwitnessed by the orangutan, tosses out the grape and returns the lid. When he brings the box forward again to pull off the lid and display an empty box, the orangutan bursts into Kantian laughter. To be sure, this trick demonstrates the appreciative laughter on the part of the nonhuman ape for violations of mental expectations, but this ape's subsequent reaching his arm out to the human, followed by the animal's rolling on the floor with laughter, suggest something more is at stake. In another example, a notorious chimpanzee named Georgia at Emory University's Yerkes Center sprays water on intrusive human visitors to generate laughter from her fellow enclosed apes.[52] In short, incongruity as it commonly occurs in humor is found in the camaraderie of social play, if not the game of power. Our aim is not to dispense with incongruity theory but to locate the playful aspect of mental puzzles in its larger context with political oomph. In other words, we should not dismiss what monkeys do or what they see.

These animal antics point toward yet a fourth theory: that laughter and humor originate in social play. Laughter occurs rarely when we are alone; indeed, it seems to turn on the fact that humans, like many other animal species, are group-oriented creatures. Both evolutionary theory and animal studies lend credence to the idea that more than mere rest and leisure, play affords a sphere where humans and our animal kin negotiate the ins and outs of social bonds. Indeed, the social function of laughter as a bonding agent can be witnessed in response to tickling by a friendly other, a response that humans share not only with apes but also other nonhuman critters. Scientists have tuned into everything from the chirping of amused rats to the "infectious laughter" of parrots.[53] More generally, variants of laughter work pervasively and primarily as a social lubricant and an invitation to play, and thus only secondarily as a response to a joke. As John Morreall reports in his *Stanford Encyclopedia* article on humor, laughter is especially prominent in play, including in "mock-aggression such as chasing, wrestling, biting, [and] tickling" displayed by a range of species.[54] Yet this take drops the ball on laughter's social force as theorists turn back to the trope of the rational man and his enjoyment of incongruities in their search for the relevance of play for humor.

For such theorists, the intellectual tilt of incongruity theory leaves the rational man inexplicably taking pleasure from the irrational. After all, the mind should prefer to take its pleasure from the logical, not the silly or absurd. This inconsistency in the profile of the rational man prompts the inclusion of play as a theory, and it serves as a counterweight to "humor's bad reputation" among philosophers.[55] However, this formulation of play theory gives too much to the rational man and his privileged needs.

Its key response to "how playfully violating mental patterns and expectations could foster rationality" is that humor facilitates "a disinterested attitude toward something that could instead be treated seriously" scoring for the mind some well-earned mental rest.[56] This view settles for a simple binary between the serious and the playful. Humor is said to benefit higher mental functions, as does a good vacation, by disengaging the mind from a burdensome "world of good and evil."[57] A climactic moment of Morreall's presentation of the argument, relayed through Oscar Wilde's deathbed quip cited above, underscores how humor offers a calm detachment from life and its frolics. Rather than any sustained engagement with the rough-and-tumble fray, this kind of humor transcends it.

A good sense of humor can doubtless elevate us above the burdens of the world, offering good cheer in stressful conditions and wisely counseling that we might roll with the punches rather than fruitlessly challenge unalterable conditions. Freud, writing in the midst of twentieth-century atrocities, cherished for good reason the Stoic humor that could release one from excessive investment in the world and its cruelties. Sometimes, however, social change and the emotions that motivate it require such an investment. What Bakhtin characterizes as a "serio-comic" intervention in the high-stakes games of cultures and politics plays seriously with that "world of good and evil."[58] Sometimes you roll with the punches, but sometimes you have to punch back.

Recent research on animal behavior uncovers how important play may be for negotiating relationships and cultivating, along with social bonds, a sense of fairness and solidarity; it is much more than a simple escape. On the basis of observations of wolves and other carnivores in his backyard in Colorado, biologist Marc Bekoff comes to a conclusion that may well suggest that aspects of laughter and humor trace back to a sense not merely of play, but of fair play. "Social play is thus based on a 'foundation of fairness,'" Bekoff writes, having argued that play provides a training ground for neutralizing differences of rank between playmates and for garnering social expectations of reciprocity and taking turns.[59] More than just practicing for the hunt, animals engage in play fighting to learn how to interact with others and to negotiate friendships through tacit social codes. But to play fair and establish connection, animals must first learn to level an unlevel playing field, which is also a function of comedy.

Indeed, each of the key elements of social play can perform a role in verbal or gestural humor among humans and other animals. Bekoff observes that play typically begins with a start signal, such as a bow, for a dog. For humans, we suspect, the levity of laughter can similarly communicate that mock aggression and playful insults are not meant to harm. Carnivores keep the fun going by establishing the proverbial level playing field through role reversal and self-handicapping. Dominant or larger animals self-handicap by exercising care to engage in soft biting, yielding any advantage to their more vulnerable partner. So too each animal carefully exposes its underbelly to the other in a gesture of trust. This is a role reversal that is especially important for the dominant animal to perform. Humans likewise seem to expose something like their tender underbellies through self-deprecating humor. This gesture of humor generates the possibility for more genuine interactions as psychic defenses come down. Bekoff speculates, "Animal play appears to rely on the universal human value of the golden rule—do unto others as you would have them do unto you. Following this requires empathy . . . and implies reciprocity."[60] Humor too can demonstrate this ethics of empathy and reciprocity when it temporarily suspends hierarchies and predatory behavior, leveling the field as we take turns showing our underbellies and serving as the butt of the joke. Licking our wounds and those of others to deal with or even challenge the abuses of power, we learn when and when not to bite back. Harsh ridicule, like hard biting, cuts short the play and camaraderie. In short, this scientific study (in contrast to Hitchens's) strengthens the possibility that the comic can on occasion, like "women[,] . . . prefer that life be fair."

As many stand-up performances illustrate, comedy flickers uncertainly across a murky spectrum, from the harsh bites of ridicule to empathy. Ridicule creates in-groups and out-groups as well as a distancing of others by laughing at them, while empathetic humor cultivates a sense of camaraderie by laughing at others, but only as we would laugh at ourselves. Humor, broadly understood, is a nuanced play of exclusion and inclusion, a dialectic of hostility (laughing at) and joyful solidarity (laughing with), riding an emotional roller coaster of shame and pride. At stake is the vital issue of who belongs to cultural, social, and political communities, and under what terms. Placing in conversation theorists and practitioners of comedy and satire that span centuries of intellectual thought, we offer an approach that brings forward its potential impact on social change and political movements, past and present. Our rebranding and reframing of the four basic theories of comedy, and our weaving together in the chapters that follow of their inextricable links, rest on the assumption that comedy operates along with our visceral selves in a multilayered field of affect and power. Parallel to the Stoics with their legacy, we join with Wanda Sykes, Richard Pryor, George Carlin, Dick Gregory, and Moms Mabley to offer not a definition but a philosophy of life. But unlike the Stoics, our serious yet comic vision does not elevate the human mind over an incongruous body with its mortal fate. The primary aim is not to transcend life's eternal absurdities with Stoic resolve. We engage the humor of eros—that deceptively subversive Greek word for life and love—against man-made ones. We consider our investigations in this field not the final word but an opening act and an invitation to rethink the history of humor from below together with its philosophical uptake.

Overview of the Chapters

Chapter 1 asks why feminists are perceived as lacking a sense of humor. How do feminist comics use humor not only to demand their right to the public stage but also to affirm their own sense of power and joy? Despite the perception that feminists are killjoys lacking a sense of humor, women have long used ridicule and other comic tactics to express anger and subvert traditional norms. In fact, the poststructuralist exposure of the pervasive impact of power through norms that shape knowledge and discourse leads us to suspect that forms of humor and irony might offer a means of political change more effective than any appeal to reason alone. Indeed, given that social norms shape cognitive habits, the disrupting of social norms through ridicule might free our thinking as well. This chapter seeks to untangle an often hidden history of feminism featuring a range of female comics, including Wanda Sykes, Margret Cho, and the problematic Roseanne Barr. The humor of those whom feminists have dubbed the chauvinist pig eroticizes the abuse of power and a sense of entitlement. Inspired by Audre Lorde, among others, we explore how humor can upend patriarchy by instead eroticizing alternative sources of power and joy.

In chapter 2, we consider whether laughter can alter political climates of fear and hostility. On the eve of the September 11, 2001, terrorist attacks, comedian Dean Obeidallah recalls that he went to bed thinking he was white, or at least as white as his Italian neighbors. After 9/11, however, the mood changed, along with Obeidallah's race and national identity. The use of humor in social and political movements reveals that it can alter values and change perceptions by tapping a dimension of experience that eludes any narrow conception of ourselves as impermeable individuals exercising self-agency. Waves of collective affect such as Islamophobia cross porous borders, exemplifying a contagious vibe of negative energy and a troubling unpredictability at the core of political and social systems. This chapter turns to the comic stage for an antidote to mass fears. When reasoning fails, laughter holds the possibility of altering toxic affects and thus the social landscape.

Chapter 3 challenges the idea that all nonhuman animals lack humor along with other higher capacities, rendering them inferior to humans. If various nonhuman species do demonstrate a capacity for humor, what does this tell us about the comedic and about ourselves? Animals are the ultimate uncontested target of ridicule. Hardly any major theory of mockery does not align the ridiculous with the animal. Yet nonhuman animals not only suffer from mistreatment but also assert a sense of their own defiant agency that at times takes a turn toward the comedic. Gut-wrenching histories of animal communities resisting unfair labor practices expose sources of oppression but also world making outside humanist categories. This chapter speculates on the evolutionary origins of laughter and concludes that various species use ridicule against alphas to demand fair play.

Chapter 4 examines the concept of comic relief. Is it a distraction from real problems? Or can laughter spark a communal catharsis that reconnects us with ourselves while driving out toxic social norms? Recent reflections on humor for the most part keep their proper distance from any attempt to explain its cathartic power. These approaches emphasize the cerebral functions of humor while neglecting the larger social dynamic as well as the emotions, the body, and the physiology of the affects at stake. We do not deny the value of brainy humor, but with a nod to feminist materialism's interest in the gut (not the phallus) as the second brain, we turn to the deep-down relief of the belly laugh to generate social change. The feminist SlutWalk movement, along with Amber Rose and the humor of Amy Schumer and others, exemplify the cathartic power of humor to alter negative attitudes and transform the social atmosphere by literally and figuratively changing the air we breathe.

Chapter 5 looks at whether humor can enable us to bridge social and cultural divides rather than just reinforce them. What kind of empathy could do this radical work? In much the same way that an earlier era of social justice flowered with the soulful music of the 1960s and 1970s, the emotional engine of social change over the last couple of decades has grown out of the truth tellers in stand-up comedy. Yet the truth-telling function of the comic arts can be put to multiple uses. It can rally the troops and preach to the choir, or it can build bridges over sharp social divides. Comedy Central's Jeff Ross's roast of Brazos county jail inmates and the Boston police demonstrates how humor serves as a vehicle of a radical empathy that can travel across social groups to reach a larger viewing public. While straight satire and ridicule subverts or reinforces lines of power, the empathetic humor of the roast, laced with flirtatious mockery, can offer far more than just a temporary break from the harsh realities of life. This mode of humor has the potential to de-escalate tensions and reveal the humanity of mortal enemies, thus opening up across social divisions a horizontal field of solidarity. All the more in this age of mass media, when social platforms can hold anyone hostage, laughter can burst through prison walls and insulating bubbles.

In our Conclusion, we ask, along with Tig Notaro and Hannah Gadsby, if, in the midst of frightening circumstances and pressing problems, we can afford that old formula: Comedy is tragedy plus time.

1

Fumerism

Feminist Anger and Joy from Roseanne Barr to Margaret Cho and Wanda Sykes

> I have suckled the wolf's lip of anger and I have used it
> for illumination, laughter, protection, fire.
> —Audre Lorde, *Sister Outsider*

Do you know the joke about the man who couldn't find the humor section in the feminist bookstore? Probably. Because feminists don't have a sense of humor, do they? Despite Samantha Bee, Wanda Sykes, the once seemingly progressive Roseanne Barr, Margaret Cho, Ali Wong, Tina Fey, the Guerrilla Girls, and Maysoon Zayid, if asked about feminism and humor, the first thought any of us might have could easily be a perplexed, "What?" This common failure to recognize the importance of humor for feminisms might be expected, given that all too often feminists themselves have been treated as a joke while humor has seemed to be an exclusively male terrain. Scholars have indeed noted the erasure or supposed lack of feminist humor.[1] Cultural critic Susan Douglas, for example, has illuminated the ways in which the news media has transformed feminism into a dirty word through its depiction of the typical feminist as a woman with "the complete inability to smile—let alone laugh."[2] Certainly, coming of age during or soon after the second wave of feminism, it is hard for us not to be well versed in the sad facts about hostile workplace climates, statistics on violence against women, and the need for equality in a workplace for women who are primary caregivers—facts that do not have the effect they might have on some of us self-declared rational creatures. Of course, we must also wonder, if arguments for equality worked, whether that fortress of reason called philosophy would not rank near the bottom of the humanities in measures of academic workplace equality.[3] If reason as a persuasive tool is at best only indirectly effective, a weak tool on its own, might not the sting of ridicule or the contagion of joyous laughter prove to be more effective weapons for social change? Or to turn the question around, what devices are more explosive in the social sphere, more discomforting to our conventional modes of thought, more invasive of our quasiprivate store of associations, than the well-placed joke, the display of wit, or the well-honed use of ridiculing irony?

In fact, poststructuralist perspectives on power and knowledge influenced by Michel Foucault, Gilles Deleuze, and Judith Butler, among others, should give us plenty of reason to suspect that various forms of humor or irony might be a more appropriate means of philosophical suasion than fact or argument alone. Recall that Foucault, influenced like other poststructuralists by Nietzsche, turns Platonism topsy-turvy, and posits that the soul is the prison house of the body.[4] In other words, reason itself might be as much the problem as the solution. After all, culture imposes its particular set of norms on what is valued and recognized as reason. Given that social norms shape cognitive habits, the unraveling and disrupting of sexist norms through ridicule might free our thinking as well. In the first sections of this chapter, we aim to spotlight the subversive force of feminist humor on knowledge and power at two key nodes: motherhood and sexuality. Patriarchal notions of motherhood and sexuality have traditionally reduced women's identities to polarized opposites instead of understanding them through a dynamic and creative force, one that Audre Lorde terms "erotic."[5] The erotic force in feminist humor messes with oppressive networks of power, intensifying and augmenting its own sources of pleasure and joy. As we offer some key philosophical elements toward a genealogy of feminist humor arising in U.S. popular culture, we discuss the aim, figures, conception of power, and cathartic effects of an erotic politics of laughter. Future waves of feminisms should recall and reinvoke the weapons and insights of humor from earlier waves, bringing humor into the core of academic practices and social movements.

Poststructuralist legal theorist Janet Halley offers ironic, provocative remarks on the feminist movement. In her words, one of the most interesting contributions of the critical stance that has evolved out of the feminist movement reflects the degree that it has allowed us "to take a break from feminism," or at least overly self-righteous and abstract feminist theory.[6] Her claim is that the feminist romance with rigid theories of domination and identity should give way to a poststructuralist politics and hedonics—in fact, as she puts it, to an erotic politics that is "fun."[7] The central target of her neo-Nietzschean queer sensibility is "governance feminism," or those "schoolmarmish feminists" who take themselves as experts on political correctness and who play innocent to their own will to power.[8] We do endorse one aspect of Halley's remarks in our insistence on the central relevance of pleasure for the feminist movement, but we take up our project with due caution. We do not intend to take a break from feminism or dispense with theories of oppression, or even nuanced theories of identity. The aim is to shake up any stultifying moral compass (the broken one set by systems of oppression) with the kinds of laughs that knock power off its throne. Our claim is that this kind of humor will free us from oppressive norms, some of which can seep into our feminisms as well. Moreover, a touch of self-irony serves as a corrective to any moralizing, self-righteous tendencies of our own that might lead to a feminism that is toxic. While we insist that a social movement aware of domination and fueled by outrage is relevant—and warranted, given the hardships that women continue to endure—inspired by Audre Lorde, we aim to combat outrageous norms and add sources of pleasure through an erotic politics of laughter and joy.[9]

This Is Not Your Mother's Maternalism

Feminists and feminisms have often been the targets of a venomous conservative ridicule. Subtle and not so subtle waves of insult and mockery reinforce a cloud of associations that accompanies women in their working lives, creating climates that range from hostile to chilly. These biosocial clouds of image and affect diminish voices of protest before they are even heard. Consider second-wave feminist icon Gloria Steinem's interview on *Meet the Press* in 1972. Larry Spivak appears to be less an aggressive interviewer after the facts than a caricature of the male chauvinist pig as he snaps at Steinem: "[In your words] women are not taken seriously, [they] are undervalued, ridiculed and not taken seriously by a society that views white men as the norm. . . . [Yet] men are virtually controlled by women from birth onward." Thus, Spivak scoffed, "Why haven't you done a better job. . . . Well, hasn't [the mother] had an opportunity to brainwash the male during those early years. Why hasn't she done it!"[10] Steinem responds with the facts, maintaining a poise that commands seriousness and respect, and this perhaps was the best strategy. Certainly respect is the goal. But still one could see the temptation to slap back through sharper, more pointed ridicule, thus turning the master's tool against him.

Meanwhile, some decades later, after the rise and retreat of second-wave feminism, during the era of a Teflon presidency and an ascendancy of family values, a stand-up comedian and soon-to-be television icon took a new and more incisive grasp on the master's tool. Indeed, the same questions that feminists like Steinem worked hard to rebuke with careful, reasoned discourse in the 1970s, the once great Roseanne Barr dismantled with her bawdy, working-class sense of humor in the 1980s and 1990s. Barr is not the first female comic on the public stage—just think of Jackie "Moms" Mabley, Gracie Allen, Phyllis Diller, Joan Rivers, Lily Tomlin, and Whoopie Goldberg. Yet with few women to lead the way, this female comic takes her inspiration from Lenny Bruce. Barr's humor established its potential to empower a demographic of underheard women against the moralizing backdrop of trickle-down Reaganomics, reflecting traces of feminist and working-class angst. Still, this empowering, energizing humor emerged off center from the movement's concern for the harms of domination and legal protection for those perceived as weak and vulnerable. It allowed for the creative use of outrage, an emotion that, unlike sadness or nurturing warmth, women are not supposed to express.

Roseanne Barr's target was a particularly invidious form of social power: norms of the family to which she refused to be subjected.[11] In one scene from the show *Roseanne*, Roseanne's good friend, Crystal, insists that Roseanne's husband, Dan, is the ideal man. Roseanne, unimpressed, snarls back, "Do you think he came that way? . . . It's 15 years of fight'n that made him like that." After all, "A good man just don't happen," Roseanne insists. "They have to be created by us women." As she continues her tutorial on the subject, Roseanne reaches toward a plate of doughnuts, explaining to her female coworkers, "A guy is a lump . . . like this doughnut." Flicking the sprinkles off the icing, she illustrates how first "you got to get rid of all the stuff his mother did to him." After breaking the doughnut in half, she points out that "then you gotta get rid of all the macho crap they pick up from beer commercials." Finally, she gets to her "personal favorite, the male ego," symbolized by a small bite of doughnut that she happily devours.[12] Rather than playing the worshipful wife, Roseanne explains how her relationship with Dan really works—with humor that bites. Like Spivak, Roseanne blames the mother—or at least her mother-in-law—for a role, perhaps more minor (the sprinkles on the doughnut) than male culture (the beer commercials), in supporting the male ego. But her candidate for mothering, or re-mothering, is the grown man, not the son. This mothering fosters "15 years of fight'n." Comedy, it seems, is warfare by other means. This is not our mother's maternalism.

Steinem too knew how on occasion to use humor to advance the feminist cause. Yet it is hard to imagine Steinem ever emulating the crotch-scratching, off-key-anthem-singing Roseanne Barr, and this is not about their singular personalities. Instead, this difference in style reflects the fact that feminists as a whole were not seen as having much of a sense of humor. Perhaps it is Barr's working-class identity that matters most—or as we know now, her white working-class identity. Of course, we are not suggesting that if only Gloria Steinem had been on a break from a factory job and sitting in front of a plate of doughnuts, her response to her host would be have resembled Barr's. Still, a play on crass class distinctions did propel Barr's feminism to mainstream television. Meanwhile, the frequently overlooked impact of feminist humor may reflect its excessively serious aesthetic of bourgie respectability. But it remains odd, given the rich tradition of street theater that women have utilized in everything from the double entendres of early twentieth-century blues singers and burlesque along with the 1968 Miss America pageant protest and the lesser-known Harvard Yard Pee-In to protest the lack of female restrooms both masterminded by Missouri-born black lawyer and activist Florynce Kennedy, the Women's International Terrorist Conspiracy from Hell's (W.I.T.C.H.) 1968 hex on Wall Street, and the ironic cheers of Radical Cheerleaders in the late 1990s and early 2000s.[13]

At the same time, let us not ignore other already forgotten feminist humor that was front and center of the second-wave movement. Steinem too has long understood how to mess with the master's tools. In an iconic 1978 *Ms. Magazine* essay, "If Men Could Menstruate . . . ," Steinem seems to be writing for such future stand-ups as Margaret Cho. Steinem insists that "men would brag about how long and how much."[14] At that time, the association of men and menstruation was more than just humorous inversion. This use of humor accumulates political force by borrowing from the shock value of the (allegedly) obscene, a feature of feminist humor that we will return to later. As part of broad-based political movements of the 1960s and 1970s, the incendiary humor of political radicals does not simply create diversionary tactics or comic relief. By illuminating the inversions and inflaming the passions that fuel social awareness and activism, this humor can produce climate change.

Regardless of views of earlier female humor, the humor of later comics like Cho, Sykes, and Ali Wong operates quite differently. Wong, who filmed her 2016 stand-up special *Baby Cobra* while seven and a half months pregnant and wearing a tight dress, demonstrates what it might feel like to trap a white man's head between her legs in cunnilingus and then crush that colonizer.[15] When reason fails, these comics use their erotic power and male vulnerability to turn their anger outward in explosive and self-affirming joy. We will return to this cathartic element later. Here we note that the history of female comedians has moved from the subtle wit of Gracie Allen or Lucille Ball to the fiery, often enraged provocations of feminist humorists. This firebrand humor, both fuming and fun, sets the stage for a refreshed politics of feminism. Stand-up Kate Clinton nicely coins a term for this explosive mix as "fumerist" because "it captures the idea of being funny and wanting to burn the house down all at once."[16]

Fumerism does something more constructive than burn down the house, even as it exorcises any trace—perceived or real—of the schoolmarmish demeanor in what Halley calls governance feminism. We aim to pursue this corrective break from the moralizing posture that occasionally infects some strains of feminist politics. We are fully aware that this break could be disorienting, given that the role of moral guardianship has afforded generations of women the credentials to move into the male terrain of politics.[17] Nonetheless, we want to foreground a feminism that does not brood over victimhood or inadvertently perpetuate images of female suffering and sacrifice. This feminist detox would shake up oppressive norms with a good and gutsy belly laugh. We are willing to pay the price of abandoning, at least temporarily, all traces of the early nineteenth-century embrace of republican motherhood, as well as any contemporary notions that somehow mother knows best. In order to smash the normal images of motherhood, scholars turn to Barr because in the 1980s and 1990s, "her mission was simple and welcome: to take the schmaltz and hypocrisy out of media images of motherhood."[18] Consider her famous line from her stand-up routine: "If the kids are alive at five, hey, I've done my job."[19] Cho goes so far as to entirely refuse maternal destiny, insisting, "I'm not a breeder. . . . I have no maternal instincts. . . . I ovulate and . . . when I see children I feel nothing."[20] Cho, along with other female stand-ups, uses humor to critique the politics of conventional motherhood and its moral respectability that a rigidly righteous orientation rarely questions. In solidarity with Kate Clinton, Gina Barreca, Janet Halley, and others, we call on feminism to engage openly and playfully with various forms of humor and irony as weapons of choice in tribute to fumerism. After all, across the political spectrum, from left-wing radicals to those alt-right antifeminist extremists in the online "manosphere" know full well, "Ridicule is man's most potent weapon."[21] If well aimed, we insist, it can be feminists' as well.

"Famous Penises" and "Detachable Pussies"

Fanning the flames of fumerism is a long-standing problem that women face when they make that fateful transition to womanhood. All too often women have found that both on street corners and on the comic stage they are reduced not only to the butt of a joke but also to its tits and ass. A well-rehearsed tradition of stand-up male jokesters that reflects, as Catherine A. MacKinnon charges, a larger culture that not only tolerates but eroticizes male domination prompts a woman to understand herself as a woman the moment she is being objectified.[22] Call this the humor of the asshole. Its pleasures come from the excesses of entitlement and privilege. A seemingly irrepressible flow of male libido reduces women to just the parts men find funny, often making women all too vulnerable to obsession with their bodies and body parts. Fumerism, however, turns the tables and mocks the mocker with a release of female libido that eroticizes its own sources of power and joy. This tradition of humor refuses to pay tribute to acts of harassment or objectification, preferring instead, as feminist comedian Zahra Noorbakhsh explains in the context of Islamophobia and the Trump election, "not to alleviate tensions or smooth out differences," but "to heighten them," and "illuminate" moments of "crisis."[23] Fuming humor affords women the role of trickster rather than "trick" as they sort out the implications of "famous penises," "detachable pussies," and those oh-so-sensual "loaf-of-bread-size maxi pad[s]."[24]

All of this reminds us first and foremost of comedian and producer Tina Fey's salute to her own childhood memories of coming of age. In her biography, *Bossypants*, Fey recounts some of the uncomfortable common experiences that let a girl know that she is now, ready or not, a woman, such as her mother's handing a ten-year-old Fey the Modess company's "'my first period' kit" that came with a "vaguely threatening" pamphlet about "Growing Up and Liking It." Her mother was no doubt supposed to have read the prescriptive information entitled "How Shall I Tell My Daughter," but instead she just "slipped out of the room" and Fey was left to figure things out on her own.[25] Fey soon realized that she had been "misinformed from commercials that one's menstrual period was a blue liquid that you poured like laundry detergent onto maxi pads to test absorbency" (which is why she ignored, at least for the few hours, the onset of menarche). But in her defense, she recalls, "Nowhere in the pamphlet did anyone say that your period was NOT a blue liquid." As she tells it, "At that moment, two things became clear to me. I was now technically a woman, and I would never be a doctor."[26] She also recognized that the virtues of female modesty can set you up to play the fool. As head writer on *SNL*, however, she would routinely invert the expectations of who would joke about whose body parts and hence who was the fool. Repeatedly confronted with the question of what is "the actual difference between the male and female comedian writers," she retorts, as she takes a poke at the male body: "The men urinate in cups. And sometimes in jars" (so as not to disturb the genius at work).[27] Also, it seems that "they had never been handed a fifteen-year-old Kotex product by the school nurse."[28] This difference led to Fey's "proudest moment": the moment when she got her male colleagues to understand what a hit a parody skit would indeed be if it featured *SNL*'s "female dream team" living it up in their hot "'modern gal' activities while giant sanitary napkins poked out of their low-rise jeans." This humor may not have been your mother's maternalism, but, as the *SNL* skit quipped, "This *is* your mother's pad."[29]

Modesty wasn't the only female virtue that Fey had learned to avoid. Fey realized while doing research for her hit Hollywood movie, *Mean Girls*, that playing the "nice girl" is not always the smartest way to play. She discovered while attending a bullying workshop with Rosalind Wiseman (author of *Queen Bees and Wannabes* [2002], which was the basis for the film) that there were lots of women who recalled that as young girls their transformation to womanhood often had something to do with "car creepery" that is "mostly men yelling shit from cars" such as "Lick me!" or "Nice ass." Indeed, Fey wondered as she recounted all of these stories from women of diverse backgrounds if men purposely organize this ritual of harassment. "Are they a patrol sent out to let girls know they've crossed into puberty?" Her own thirteen-year-old response to a guy shouting about her "Nice tits" was to tell the creep to "Suck my dick," which she now realizes "didn't make any sense, but at least I didn't hold in my anger."[30]

Not holding in anger is what feminist comedy does best. You may be a victim, but you will have your revenge, and a clever one at that. For the woman turned comedian, her act of revenge grants a seat at the table in a kind of game with different house rules: Let's deal a new hand as we play "Who's the real victim?" To unravel this mystery, we turn now to "our Senior Women's Issues Correspondent Kristen Schaal," who several years ago on *The Daily Show* played the game while coming to terms with the latest round of Republican woes over their already bulging pocketbooks. "Hallelujah," declares Kristen Schaal, "it's about time." Finally, "Congress is redefining rape to protect us from the worst kind of rape . . . money rape." You know—the "forcible taking of taxpayers' money to pay for abortions." It seems that American taxpayers have had "no say in the matter. . . . They just have to lay back and take it while their bank accounts are violated over and over and over again." But in February 2011, our brave Republicans in Congress decided to make a change and proposed that abortions should be paid for only in cases of "rape-rape"—that is to say, "forcible rape"—"finally closing," in the words of Schaal, "the glaring rape loophole in our health care system." Our *Daily Show* correspondent can't believe "how many drugged, und-eraged, or mentally handicapped young women have been gaming the system!" What an outrage that our "hard-earned dollars should go to women who have only been rape-ished. . . . Sorry ladies, the free abortion ride is over." Getting rid of those loopholes will prevent "money rape" and protect victimized taxpayers who don't want to pay for a young woman who has been drugged or who is with limited mental capacity, let alone one who has undergone statutory rape. Roman Polanski "plying a thirteen-year-old with Quaaludes, alcohol, and a famous penis isn't rape-rape; it's just rape-esque and shouldn't be covered—only rape-rape" would get covered.[31]

If you don't agree with the twisted logic, Schaal understands why. "Clearly you've been traumatized by years of money rape," but it's "OK to talk about it." Reaching for her chauvinist piggy bank, Schaal encourages the real victims to speak out—that is, the victims of money rape to "show me on the piggy bank where Obama took your money for abortions—was it here?" It is hard to speak out loud about the kind of violation that, for example, occurred in one year alone in 2006, when a handful of women who received abortions because of rape, incest, and health risks endangering their lives took a shocking "two-tenths of a penny per taxpayer" to fund those services. Indeed, as the comedian is suggesting, one might wonder how America can sleep at night! Clearly losing your money can lead to suffering. Liberals should not overlook the fact that the violation of trust and unfair taxation are moral issues. But the underlying point of the sketch is that rape too is a moral issue. Schaal mocks those who mock the victimologists—those big, strong men in Congress who claim to speak for ordinary Americans who would never cry (notwithstanding the then Speaker of the House, John Boehner, who was notorious for his episodes of weeping). Schaal makes us wonder who the wuss is as she asks, gesturing, "Does it hurt here?" on the figure of a pig, suggesting that Congress should tell mommy what happened.

Of course, there is something women do have that is valued almost like money. This is something mothers know and girls find out. As Wanda Sykes insists, "Even as little girls we are taught . . . 'You have something that everybody wants. You gotta protect it. You gotta be careful. You gotta cherish it.'" She adds, "That's a lot of fucking pressure." But "wouldn't it be great if you could just leave your pussy at home?" In other words, what "if our pussies were detachable!" "Just think of the freedom you'd have," if, for example, you wanted to hang out with a famous penis (not a movie director this time, but, Sykes suggests, a professional ballplayer). You could detach your pussy and go to his "hotel room at 2 o'clock in the morning." If he wants you (or, rather, your thing), you just have to remind him, "Look, my pussy's not even in the building—I'm just here to talk about your jump shot." Sykes can't help but think about how convenient it would be to have a detachable vagina. You would never worry again about going places by yourself at night. Think about getting home from work late; you're contemplating going for a jog, "but it's getting too dark." Then you remember: "I'll just leave it at home." Sykes explains to her audience, "It could be pitch black" and "this old crazy guy jumps out of the bushes," but you don't have to be scared because you can let him know, "I left it at home. Sorry, I have absolutely nothing of value on me—I'm pussy-less."[32]

To be pussy-less and hence to lack anything of value seems

reminiscent of old-school male tits and ass humor—the stuff that nice girls were not supposed to talk about, and the kind of humor men have long relied on to keep women off their patriarchal playing field. Yet Sykes turns on its head this formulaic reduction of women to property that has for far too long served to erotize male domination. Humor may not stop the crime of rape, but it does joyfully and hilariously erotize women's own sources of power through shared laughter. Sykes gives us a hint about the bonds that come of this shared laughter as she ponders how leaving your pussy at home has its own setbacks. Just think of the problems you can confront if you are on an "unrespectable" hot date and need your girlfriend to help you out. According to Sykes, it gets at some "sisterhood." That occurs when you call a girlfriend in the middle of the night and say, "Look, do me a favor; run by my house and grab my pussy." It lets "you find out who your real girlfriends are."[33]

But leaving your pussy at home when you are not there to keep an eye on it can call for a return of the maternal reprimand. Imagine coming home after being out with the girls and finding your "pussy all bent out of shape." "Ladies, you know you can't trust them." In fact, Sykes suggests you can't trust them "with shit." When confronted, her man is just "standing there" with a stupid look on his face and a sorry excuse that "some of the fellows came by." As she confronts him wallowing in his misogynist mess, she finds her pussy like an old worn sock needing to be "put it in the dryer" to get it back in shape. She adds with disgust, "I better put a Bounce in there." This kind of housecleaning—the kind that might make you dread coming home—once again affords Sykes the role of the trickster and the means to bounce back against threats, both on the comic stage and on the street corner. By turning male humor inside out, she takes her own property back. With a nod, she gives back power to the pussy and erotizes that old maternal wisdom that also allows her to put her house back in order.[34]

But are there some topics that are off-limits, that even feminist ridicule cannot tap? Some issues, such as rape, that only the male chauvinist pig would turn into a joke? In the summer of 2012, Daniel Tosh found himself in the middle of a controversy after he told a Hollywood comedy club a rape joke aimed at a female audience member. "Wouldn't it be funny if that girl got raped by like five guys right now . . . like right now?"[35] To be sure, feminists struggle to avoid being pigeonholed as the ones who need to lighten up. After the Tosh controversy, the now infamous stand-up Louis C.K. misfired as he offers his own tongue-in-cheek thoughts to Jon Stewart and the *Daily Show* audience about the "fight between comedians and feminists."[36] He insinuates that these two groups "are natural enemies. Because stereotypically speaking, feminists can't take a joke" and "comedians can't take criticism." Instead of upending the stereotypes, this comic recommends women just leave the offending comedy clubs and stop universalizing their feelings.[37] Jokes defended as light entertainment offer foundational support, as the base of a pyramid, for the cruelty of rape culture.[38] Jezebel staff writer and feminist Lindy West intervened more effectively. Observing that in response to Tosh the "conversation had devolved into two polarized camps," with outraged feminists arguing that "'rape jokes are never funny' and defensive comics wailing about how the 'thought police' is 'silencing,'" she pointed out: "The world is full of terrible things, including rape, and it is okay to joke about them. But the best comics use their art to call bullshit on those terrible parts of life and make them better, not worse. . . . Don't make rape victims the butt of the joke."[39] Cameron Esposito's 2018 special *Rape Jokes* exemplified the point.[40] In this set, Esposito poignantly addresses her own personal experience of having been raped, thus bringing forward the voice of the survivor as she rechannels the laughter against the Toshes. The first rule of the comedy club is to punch up, not down.

A Genealogy of Feminist Humor

Our approach to humor as an erotic art of flipping the master's tools is profoundly inspired by Lorde's classic essays "Uses of the Erotic: The Erotic as Power," "The Master's Tools Will Never Dismantle the Master's House," "The Uses of Anger: Women Respond to Racism," and "Poetry Is Not a Luxury."[41] Like poetry, laughter is not a luxury but an "erotic" necessity. (She ungirds the ancient Greek term from its modern pornographic meaning.) In her generative terms, "The very word *erotic* comes from the Greek word *eros*, personification of love in all its aspects—born of Chaos and personifying creative power and harmony. When I speak of the erotic, then, I speak of it as an assertion of the lifeforce of women."[42] Enhancing that life force by channeling anger into heated social movements and festive joy is fumerism's foremost aim.

Yet this chapter does more than juxtapose a maternal politics of self-righteousness with an erotic politics of feminist humor. While we would agree with Halley that it is best to take a break from any moralizing pose, we would also like to propose some philosophical elements for a genealogy of feminist humor. Here we offer a genealogy for feminism because like Foucault, we too see that history—with all of its ironies, inversions, and unexpected surprises—matters, and with Lorde, we think that domination matters. Genealogy is history and its tragedies replayed through the eye of the ironist (for us the fumerist), alert to inversions in the dynamics of power. As we continue to uncover history's irresolvable contradictions and stubborn demarcations of power, we will explore the aims and functions of feminist humor by bringing forward two figures (Foucault's term) to expose what is at stake.

While humor can invert a social order only to reestablish hierarchy and identity,[43] it can also subvert this order and achieve a more democratic aim. In her classic 1966 essay "Jokes," Mary Douglas teases out relevant, if ultimately misleading, aspects regarding humor's lack of potential for a "subversive effect on the dominant structure."[44] Douglas sharply contrasts humor as a temporary holiday from the normal order with the shock value of the obscene, which calls that order into question in a way that is dangerous or otherwise subversive for the social system. Douglas mistakenly leaves the reader assuming that in contrast to the shock of the obscene that is common in high modern art, the break or "holiday" that humor provides from social norms is inevitably a temporary diversion. In other words, for Douglas, a joke is just a joke—a holiday from the normal constraints of politics and morality, not a means of social change. However, our glimpse into the history of feminist humor suggests that both the amusing joke and the shock of the obscene can under certain conditions function within a social movement to effect egalitarian social change. Thus, the aims of some humor can be democratic and not reactionary or merely for fun. Such humor would aim not to exclude but include diverse social groups and individuals. And it would not just reinforce or temporarily invert hierarchies but level them. Moreover, such humor can take a more progressive aim precisely when it refuses to sharply distinguish itself from the obscene. Recall in this context Steinem's essay on men and menstruation. By illuminating the inversions and inflaming the passions that fuel social awareness and activism, this edgy humor helped stir a political movement. To be sure, a joke can be just a joke, but the experience of pleasure in subversion is not always an illusion or a brief diversion. As we shall further argue, in the process of subversion, humor can transform a politics of anger and resentment into a politics of joy.[45] The techniques of inversion and leveling that can account for the pleasure of the joke are well suited for the central aim of our feminist ethical vision—one of social equality and inclusive belonging.

Cultural theorists provide support for our feminist account of transformative strains in humor by suggesting a source of humor's pleasure that does not stem from feelings of superiority or in-group/out-group hierarchies. Such humor instead prompts a sense of community from a loosely defined sense of mutual belonging rather than a recognized shared identity.[46] The "unity" of this felt sense of belonging—of laughing together—occurs though suspending and rendering more porous reified positions of identity. Similarly, we argue that fumerist comedy can make visible histories of identities and struggles for recognition and identification, but as moments of dislocation and transformation. In other words, the moment of laughter may jolt one out of habitual habits and cognition and open up fresh possibilities. Comedy can create a new kind of community, one based not on homogeneity or rigid identities but rather on a shared dislocation out of customary lines of identity.[47] The joy of fumerist comedy is not in having one's preconceived identity and views confirmed, but in being startled out of one's customary alignments toward a more promising future.

If the pleasures and subversions of comedy serve unconventional moral aims, it seems fair to ask what its implications for ethics are. It has been suggested that comedians' "complaints contain a critique of the gap between what is and what we believe should be."[48]

We understand this ethical "should," in contrast to the law-and-reason-bound moral "ought" that is grounded in the modern moral theories of Kant and John Stuart Mill, as opening the way toward what we propose as a postmoral ethics. The problem with the standard modern discourse of morality is that it entails interpreting the self too narrowly as a rational and/or self-interested individual, and morality too narrowly in terms of abstract rules for action. We do not reject all elements of modern moral theory, and we accept the need for both moral laws and reason. However, as many feminist theorists insist, the modern discourse of morality (whether Kantian or utilitarian) is too abstract and disconnected from the emotionally driven and both culturally and socially embedded creatures we are to help us to grasp, let alone resist, oppressive social norms with which moral codes and normal modes of identity may be complicit. In contrast, the "should" of comic discourse eschews the standard moral language, with its problematic notion of the moral person; instead of a sharp focus on rules for their own sake, it deconstructs the disciplinary matrix through a style of comportment and sociability that is egalitarian and even visionary.[49] Feminist politics requires a utopic vision, be it implicit or explicit,[50] and such a vision is what the meaning-making genre of comedy is designed to offer.[51] When fumerists joke, mock, and critique the micropractices of everyday life, their humor often generates joyous glimpses of a better world. This anger-fueled humor challenges conventional morality and the underlying codes of normalization, patriarchal oppression, and social exclusion that this morality sustains via an ethical stance and a social vision.

Of course, tragic harms, often perpetrated through structures of domination, merit a sober and impassioned expression of direct moral outrage. Our assumption is that power does not only operate through the hierarchies or inequalities located by traditional or intersectional theories of domination. It also operates through the micropractices, engrained habits, cultural stereotypes, and implicit biases of everyday life—practices that make up the normal and normalizing codes of gender and other sites of oppression. Individuals, regardless of gender, perpetuate these norms through practices that operate behind our backs and without knowledge of our complicity. Just as ridicule and humor provide an arsenal of tools that can reinforce these norms and practices, so too can this arsenal tear those conventions down.

Poststructuralists like Foucault, Deleuze, and Butler expose such conventions as invidious and pervasive practices and techniques of normalization. They argue that these practices and techniques of normalization hold us in check as administered subjects through modes of discourse and knowledge that mold the mind as well as the body. They argue that the target of the disciplinary apparatus in modern society is abnormality.[52] Foucault demonstrated how for modern society, "nonconformity was not mere eccentricity; very often it was symptomatic of disease."[53] Those classified as sexual deviants were "subject to surveillance and constraints imposed through psychiatry and other means by or on behalf of society as a whole."[54] These sexual deviants, along with hysterical women and other so-called moral monsters, cannot always and easily reason their way out of their subordinate positions and derogatory classifications in modern networks of power and knowledge. This is because moral judgments are themselves part of the power apparatus. This apparatus constructs reason as codes, standards, and habits that render some of us or some of our experiences abnormal, disgusting, or even obscene.[55]

Central for the poststructuralist, post-Nietzschean critique of reason as the ruse of power is the use of irony and ridicule as an epistemology and a methodology. It is easy to forget the twinkle in Foucault's eye that casts a certain slant over his entire project in *The Order of Things*. Yet as Halley too suggests, remembering this twinkle is key to understanding the force of his project—a project that was designed, after all, to critique reason in part through odd juxtapositions and inversions.[56] Foucault began his book, as he explains, with

a passage from [literary author Jorge Luis] Borges out of laughter that shattered, as I read the passage, all the familiar landmarks of my thought—our thought, the thought that bears the stamp of our age and our geography—breaking up all the ordered surfaces and all the planes with which we are accustomed to tame the wild profusion of existing things. . . . This passage quotes a "certain Chinese encyclopedia" in which it is written that "animals are divided into: (a) belonging to the Emperor, (b) embalmed, (c) tame, (d) sucking pigs, (e) sirens, (f) fabulous, (g) stray dogs, (h) included in the present classification . . . (n) that from a long way off look like flies" . . . and so on. In the wonderment of this taxonomy, the thing we apprehend in one great leap . . . is the limitation of our own.[57]

The ironic voice should not be viewed as a distraction from the analytic mind-set of social critique but rather as vital to the insights produced by Foucault's genealogical method and by the momentum of real social change. Thus, we aim to develop our study of feminist ridicule with the irony of Foucault's genealogical method front and center, beginning with our treatment of those normalizing micropractices. Foucault uses what he terms figures to map nodal points in the matrices of power. In the first volume of the *History of Sexuality,* perhaps his most ironic book, Foucault highlights the figures of the hysterical woman, the masturbating child, and the sexual adult in order to locate the ways in which sexuality is controlled through biopower in the nineteenth century.[58] Other philosophers too have located figures in matrices so that we might better understand the basis for social power. For example, a genealogy of neoliberalism might foreground the figures of the consumer and the entrepreneur.[59] Feminist movements have also exposed various figures to mark nodes in networks of power. These movements, during one of their fumerist moments, countered one of these figures—the Playboy bunny—with a figure of its own—the male chauvinist pig. To understand the role of these figures in everyday practices of power, we must look back to their emergence in the context of the rising second wave of feminism of the early 1960s. In the previous decade, Hugh Hefner had invented the Playboy bunny as the newest toy for what Barbara Ehrenreich and Susan Bordo describe as the movement that preceded and solicited second-wave feminism—a movement of rebellious young men who aimed to reclaim their masculinity from what they perceived to be a new domestication, the suffocating maternalism of the post–World War II era.[60]

If the male movement had its bunny, then the women's movement also produced a figure of belittlement, the male chauvinist pig, and this figure was designed to outmaneuver the tactics of the Playboy Club. While the bunny may function as a serious figure for men of male desire, the pig functions for the feminist movement as a figure of comic ridicule, if not outright disgust. Rabbits are also known for their frequent (and mindless) copulation, and so provide a degrading image for women, as Gloria Steinem's 1963 exposé revealed.[61] The pig, on the other hand, is not simply a serious figure of women's outrage. The pig is perceived to be (unfairly to this intelligent animal) a comical and even obscene creature, far from the macho predatory beast of masculine fantasy. The pig wallows in its own filth without recognizing how disgusting it is.

More recently, this pig found his way back into the spotlight in the role of pussy-grabber in chief, together with his Playboy bunny–esque first lady. Indeed, President Trump's campaign flourished thanks to bad-boy antics that made his stoic opponent, second-wave feminist Hillary Clinton, appear as the straight man. It was nearly impossible for this policy wonk, who mistakenly thought she could balance her straight side by playing up at the Democratic convention some of her traditional motherhood credentials, to prevail on the stage. Once this master of insult transformed the debate stage into a comic one, Clinton's straight discussion of political programs was guaranteed to set her up for a fall. Indeed, when Clinton entered onto that stage, she was as a woman already positioned by comic and social norms of male public space to be the butt of the joke. And when the comic genie is let out of the box, it does not easily go back in. Caricatures of "Crooked Hillary" went viral. Nonetheless, it remains to be seen who in U.S. politics will have the last laugh. The time is ripe for feminism to reclaim the erotic politics of laughter as the pussy grabs back to talk some truth to power.

This practice of speaking truth to power through ridicule or irony recalls the ancient practices of the Cynics as described by Foucault. Foucault himself in his later writings aims to emulate this ancient practice of truth telling, or what the Cynics term parrhesia.[62] The Cynics were social critics who avoided systematic philosophy and instead cultivated the art—Foucault calls it an aesthetic practice—of ridicule and improvisation to draw attention to the arbitrary aspects of social norms. For example, the Cynics would use the philosopher's technique of reductio ad absurdum, but instead of pointing out the fallacies of arguments, they exposed the absurdity of what would pass for common sense. In the process, their occasionally obscene antics would upset public mores. In effect, these philosophers were the Lenny Bruces and Richard Pryors of their day. When fumerists practice this art of speaking truth to power through irony and ridicule, they too take up in their own way the spirit of parrhesia. Their comic spirit offers a political ethic of eros that undoes the self's conventional core, igniting the fire for unlearning bad norms and habits in a way that mere reflection just can't do.[63] Anger fuels change, but personal change and social movements need creative energy and new visions too, as Lorde well knew. The emancipatory practices of truth telling through the undoing of toxic notions of identity and community generate energy and eros for personal and social transformation.

But is the queer pleasure of this cathartic force genuinely progressive and inclusive, or might this force be forgetful of race or other dimensions of power? Any genealogical study of the figure of the pig in feminist truth telling must also point out that the male chauvinist owes much to the Pig—that is, the Pig that the Student Nonviolent Coordinating Committee and the Panthers confronted in the 1960s, the Pig that caused Watts and the assassination of Fred Hampton.[64] For, as white feminists have had to learn, race certainly can fuel the desire to burn down the house.[65] Lorde, Kimberlé Crenshaw, and Patricia Hill Collins, among others, pinpoint race along with gender among multiple variables of domination, setting the stage for what is called third-wave feminism through a development of what Crenshaw terms intersectionality.[66] Theories of intersectionality focus on exposing power through various structures of domination as they tease out interrelationships between class, race, sex, gender, and other key factors in the function of power. This crucial work opens the question of whether our engagement with fumerism converges with the understanding of multiple axes of power that we find in theories of intersectionality. Recall that poststructuralist queer theory views all sources of identity, even intersectional ones, as forms of subjection and subjugation, and affirms instead fluidity. Our aim is to work within intersectional theories of domination and indeed strengthen Collins and Bilge's call for a collective identity politics and yet show how humor opens us to fluid boundaries and unexpected alliances.[67] Humor, through its use of poststructuralist fluidity, prompts coalitions or relationships across the social divisions that intersectionality theory locates.

Let's replay the achievements of intersectional theory by way of the humor of comedian Wanda Sykes to clarify where we find a use for poststructuralist fluidity. Ultimately, both of these two seemingly conflicting theories of power—an intersectional theory of domination and poststructuralist critiques of identity—have much to offer for comedy. When Sykes highlights in her stand-up routines the unexpected ironies of her experiences as a black woman who is also a lesbian, she provides to intersectionality theory some twists and turns that can multiply perspectives and identities to a dizzying degree. The resulting disturbance of any ready-made norms, whether imposed by the white community or from the self-defining black community, amplifies the insights of intersectionality theory while shifting the insights of this theory to a new and delightfully raucous terrain. In some ways, intersectionality theory locates domination on a high-powered, multidimensional, and Cartesian-like grid of precisely defined locations and hierarchies. Black lesbian women would find their points of convergence through the intersection of multiple forces of domination at particular locations in a map of power. Sykes's black gay irony certainly picks up on these multiple axes of domination, but her humor does not then proceed to redefine or relocate the self in community in any kind of bounded way. Her humor disturbs nodes of power as well as the boundaries and hierarchies that circumscribe these nodes as she mocks them. Indeed, in her humor there is a cathartic subversion of any attempt to reassert impermeable boundaries around the self or one's community without forsaking the self and its ties for an unbound or entitled identity. On the contrary, Sykes's humor works to alter specific clusters of social positions and to make possible new ones that are no longer so sternly based on rigid taxonomies of race, class, gender, or sexuality, or on the toxic fear and resentment that can reinforce their normalizing power. The result is a renewed sense of community and alliance based less on identity or self-interest than on positive energy for a visceral connection and felt solidarity.

Consider Sykes's particular way of declaring that it is "harder to be gay than it is to be black."[68] She quips that there are things she had to do being gay that she didn't have to do being black. "I didn't have to come out being black. . . . I didn't have to sit my parents down and tell them about my blackness."[69] She then imagines telling her parents, "Mom and Dad—I'm black," and her mom acting hysterical: "You know what, you've been hanging around black people. . . . They got you thinking you're black. . . . They twisted your mind. . . . I know I shouldn't have let you watch *Soul Train*."[70] Through mocking narratives of gay development, Sykes allows us to reimagine narratives of "black" development. Sykes's characteristic irony draws our attention to modes of resistance or tactics of empowerment that do not rest firmly within any given boundaries of community and family, or on any epistemic attitude that assumes for some social group a correct point of view. What Lorde, Crenshaw, and Collins among others begin as a powerful inflection of intersectionality into identity politics ends up with what the Nietzschean (mindful that the last god resides in grammar) might applaud as Sykes's grammatically incorrect "I'ma Be Me politics."[71] Sykes sidesteps the downside of the victim sweepstakes, that counterproductive game of who's on bottom. This erotic politics cuts across so many lines of identity that one is left wondering who's on bottom and who's on top. While this ironist confronts the powers that be, her challenge is less often direct than indirect; it is engaging yet subversive. The ironist's oblique politics may not map neatly and nicely onto the oppressive taxonomies or progressive redefinitions of community and selfhood in domination theories—theories that carefully locate intersectionality. But the irony does release the fervor of insubordination that converts the toxic effects of ordinary politics into an edgy kind of joy, one that neither lacks anger nor embraces innocence. Indeed, Sykes's style of humor sets in motion perpetual reversals of expectations and norms, a plurality of counterpositions and shifting ground, rather than positing codes and rigid theory. Such comedy intensifies genealogy's heightened sense of the contingent and the paradoxical. In short, queer humor treats intersectionality to the cathartic dynamic of energy and eros that Foucault, like Collins and Lorde, has called freedom.

Similarly, Margaret Cho encompasses everything that Collins understands as intersectionality, and then some. In *Notorious C.H.O.* (2002), Cho recalls that she never saw any Asian American role models as serious actors. So, she thought, "maybe I could be an extra on *M*A*S*H**. . . . Maybe I could play a hooker or something." "What I do . . . is I take a stereotype and I enlarge it to the point where it seems ridiculous."[72] This comic technique reveals how limiting the roles are for Asian Americans and how impossible it is to imagine oneself as an agent in those roles. By overplaying the stereotype, Cho asserts her agency and undermines the stereotype. Through her use of irony, she has made it big on the comic stage—so big that when asked if she is gay or straight, she throws all dichotomies out the window and insists she is neither but instead a "slut." She likes to have sex with everyone, including the "butch lesbian"—but really butch, in her words: "The kind that roll their own tampons."[73] In that year, 2002, she wants to know where her parade is—you know, the "Slut Pride Parade."[74] The street theater of gay pride festivals, featuring the pride parade, grew out of the use of the comic to convert the negative energy of shame to self-affirming pride. Cho's skit on slut pride does not simply invert the value of the whore over the mother, to invoke the classic dualism. Instead, in proposing a pride parade for sluts, Cho uses comedy to dismantle shame and generate erotic energy for us all. That's slut power.

A significant advantage of a genealogical method is that it brings history and structures of power as well as its abuses to bear on ethical and political projects. Sykes demonstrates our approach to history and remembrance with her 2009 appearance at the White House Correspondents' Dinner. In her routine, she applauded Michelle Obama for finally unveiling a bit of the past—a bust of Sojourner Truth—in the White House. Also knowing that what goes around comes around, Sykes warns the first lady to "nail it down real well" because "the next white guy to come in—they going to move it to the kitchen."[75] How easily ordinary history forgets, conceals, and hides! How easy it will be for the next president to hide the bust of Sojourner Truth! In our radically alternative history, comics function as "social interpreters"[76] and as "comic spokesmen."[77] This is not an unprecedented move. When scholars try to unearth a bit of irony in the past, they too have turned to popular culture and "organic intellectuals" to understand aspects of conflicted social identities. It has been suggested that the refrain of Bruce Springsteen's rock anthem, "Born in the U.S.A.," offers a "unified duality, jagged pieces to the puzzle of both the song and its subjects' social history."[78] So too do feminist comedians offer jagged pieces of puzzles that speak to their subjects' social history, a social history that is all too often in the kitchen, not the boardroom. This kitchen and the routines that recall its memories are an important locus for our own genealogical approach.

This history often goes missing from the public archives and censored textbooks. Just think about how the 2018 Texas board of education voted to eliminate Hillary Clinton and Helen Keller from the mandatory history curriculum.[79] This is why Sykes claims her jokes come from the fact that "people will tell me anything," insinuating that as a black comedian, she is treated like a maid, a cook, or even a stripper, and people will "tell a stripper anything."[80] As our substitute for the academic historian, Sykes is privy to sources not otherwise available. Yet from her position on the comic stage, and in contrast to the self-righteous expert or spokesman of a social group, she refuses any rigid moral or epistemic privilege to her standpoint. She admits, for example, that she is no better than any other when it comes to racial profiling, and that this is a fault that she, like other blacks, shares with whites. When she sees a black man running down the street, she wonders, "What has he been up to?" When she sees a white guy running down the street, she assumes he is just late.[81]

Indeed, Sykes's self-ironic response to the problem of racial profiling returns us to the ethical aims of fumerist comedy. Check out her response to the question, if you can't solve racial profiling what do you do? Perhaps "just treat everyone like a criminal."[82] And indeed laughter can be a great social leveler. Sykes does not take up those stories in the kitchen—stories well beyond the public archives—as straight humorless histories. Chucking moral guardianship for the ethics of queer erotics, she tells her stories with the attitude and sense of irony that draws on comedy's catalytic power to alter what we think justice is: "White men get nervous . . . when a minority or another race gets a little power" because "they scared that that race is going to do to them what they did to that race. They get nervous so they start screaming reverse racism." But that is not reverse racism. "Isn't reverse racism when a racist is nice to somebody?" What they're afraid of, she insists, is really "called karma."[83] Karma is also history, but with visions of justice in the mix.

Let's catch a glimpse into humor's cathartic powers before we yield to the larger forces of karma and bring this chapter to an end. Humor might be just the medicine for what ails us in our social norms. Consider Stanford psychologist Claude Steele's research regarding the impact of gender and race stereotypes on climate as measured by performance among stereotyped populations.[84] This research demonstrates that these stereotypical associations affect performance even among individuals who reject the stereotypes, and that a situation that renders group identities salient may suffice to trigger the associations. For example, women perform less well on math exams when they are placed into a room with men, presumably because the presence of men triggers the stereotypical associations of female inferiority in mathematics. Steele speculates that anxiety associated with various stereotypes may account for what hinders their targets' performance. If so, then humor may offer a partial remedy. Think of Sykes's attitude about racial profiling. The ridicule of stereotypes undermines these stereotypes as social norms, but humor also dissipates anxiety and other negative emotions while generating what Lorde calls life force. We return to a full-scale treatment of catharsis later in the book. But for those who suspect that identity politics exacerbates the toxic impact of stereotypes through their mere mention to the point that, like Halley, they are convinced that we should take a break from feminism, we remind our readers of alternative feminisms. Feminism as fumerism offers one way to confront and detoxify the stereotypes, to joyfully reappropriate energy and eros from systems of domination. The seriously erotic politics of laughter burns down by bringing down the house.

2

Fighting Back against Islamophobia and Post-9/11 Nationalism

Dean Obeidallah, Maysoon Zayid, Hari Kondabolu, and Others

> You cannot fear something you laugh at.
> —Bassem Youssef, National Public Radio

On the eve of 9/11, lawyer turned comedian Dean Obeidallah recalls that he went to bed thinking he was white, or at least as white as his Italian neighbors. Growing up in New Jersey, he recalls that his father was the only one who did not have an Italian accent. To be sure, he was different, but the "Jersey kids" thought of them both as American. As far as they were concerned, Palestine—his father's homeland—was in the southern part of the state and the Middle East was just a reference to Ohio. After 9/11, however, the mood changed, along with Dean's race and national identity. In his words, "I go to bed September 10th white, wake up September 11th—I'm an Arab." Now casual encounters seem to go hand in hand with remarks that range from naive to malicious. "Oh, You're Arab," someone would say, followed with a quick mention of how much they "love hummus" or some other reference to him as a bit "exotic . . . like kiwi . . . sweet, tasty, a little hairy." Sometimes making even less sense, strangers might find his "Arab" background an uncanny coincidence because they "love Indian food." However, others would not hesitate to ask him, "Why are your people so angry all the time?" or attempt a compliment: "But *you* look so nice." Instead of a heritage history month, he complained, "What do we get—orange alert," and without fail, we are always "randomly selected for extra screenings." Tragically, he realized, "we are the new enemy. We've replaced the Soviet Union. And we are stuck here till somebody replaces us."[1]

Islamophobia is a convenient tool; Middle East studies scholar Stephen Sheehi describes it as "an ideological formation of U.S. Empire" in the post–Cold War era.[2] Not an isolated phenomenon, Islamophobia is part of shifting but persistent patterns of racism in the United States that define who is and is not a citizen. After all, as Toni Morrison tragically reminds us, "In this country, American means white."[3] The motility of racial and ethnic identity has long been understood by social science scholars and professional comedians, ranging from David Roediger (in his landmark 1993 book *Wages of Whiteness*) to Dave Chappelle (for example, his 2004 television sketch "The Racial Draft"). These theorists and comedic practitioners of social change point out in their diverse ways that whiteness or degrees of whiteness as well as other racial and ethnic identities are not sheer physical or objective properties of individuals or groups but rather emerge through charged social histories, politicized spaces, and the demands of a capitalist economy. Hence, in an instant, the boy next door can be perceived as the racialized other. In this volatile world, dynamic political and economic forces alter social identities and facilitate shifts in boundaries through cultural symbols, myths, institutional practices, discourses, and habits. Affects also play a significant role in the perception of identities and seemingly impenetrable boundaries. Like other social forces, collective waves of fear and hate readily elude the Western construct of the individual, celebrated along with the rise of the nation-state for its autonomous agency and clear sense of boundaries.

In much the way that cultural anthropologist Nadine Nabor turns to the voices and ideas of Arab Americans as agents for "decolonizing methodologies" and "new forms of knowledge," we now turn to a new generation of comedians challenging the post-9/11 milieu.[4] This chapter applies affect theory to explain first how fear can racialize the other, and second how comic laughter can counter Islamophobia and other fears across social boundaries to energize progressive moments and movements, to create, in the words of comic Hari Kondabolu, a win–win situation.

Affect

The study of affect offers insights for understanding sweeping fears targeting a race, ethnicity, or religion. As a toxic vibe, fear of others readily spreads like a disease from individual to individual and across borders to define a larger political climate. Islamophobia and racism have profoundly shaped the history of nation-states and are without question central to U.S. politics. In the post-9/11 world, through enhanced airport security, orange alerts, hate crimes, land wars, collapsed states, and refugee and border crises, we are rigidly and fearfully redefining who counts as a real American as we carve away basic human rights and civil liberties. This wave of phobia precipitates not only decisions to go to war but also broad-based political and social movements like the birthers and their leader, Donald Trump, whose mission was to alert us to the terror of an alien in the White House. For the birthers, the post-9/11 climate of fear channels the diffuse anxiety prompted by Obama's racial identity as the first African American president toward his imagined status as an outsider, someone with suspicious national and religious credentials.[5] Thus, in this current topsy-turvy post-9/11 era, the extreme right has been able to shape a politics of perception that readily led to a fear of Barack Hussein Obama as our first Muslim president, thus permitting a takeover of the White House in 2016 with Donald Trump's election. This election in turn further escalated an ongoing wave of anti-immigrant fervor that even turned young children into enemies of the state.

Here we begin to see how waves of collective affect draw their political force from the fact that they readily spread across masses of people. Affect theory provides clues to the possibilities and volatility of both ridicule and humor. Affect as the felt component of emotion may be informed by a lesser degree of reflection than a full-fledged emotion, yet it functions as an insistent motivator of behavior.[6] Theorists distinguish affects from other aspects of emotional experiences in terms of two primary characteristics. First, affects are felt as visceral and thus as operating at a gut level of awareness. Second, affects are transpersonal. "Is there anyone who has not, at least once, walked into a room and 'felt the atmosphere?'" asks philosopher Teresa Brennan as she opens her inquiry into "how one feels the others' affects."[7] We inhabit atmospheres of mood and other kinds of diffuse feeling, perceiving them as dense clouds that are hard to define, that shift shape easily, that are difficult to find our way out of. Psychologist Daniel Stern distinguishes familiar affects and emotions such as fear, anger, or joy from vitality affects; vitality affects point to the manner in which an affect or emotion is felt—as in a rush of anger, a pulsing fear, or a fading happiness, or, more fundamentally, the basic feeling of being alive, and captures aspects of what Lorde calls life force.[8] Feminist scholar Sara Ahmed focuses on how affects and emotions can carry cultural meanings and a volatile political charge.[9] Islamophobia and racist or other culturally imbued fears exemplify a contagious, collective wave of energy that can point toward a troubling unpredictability at the core of political and social systems. While studies of mass hysteria and popular discourse assume that cooler heads (aka rational individuals with their logic) could and should regain control over those emotions that are deemed irrational,[10] and that boundaries are healthy only when intact, our approach to affect studies poses individuals as nodes of biosocial networks larger than themselves.[11] Thus, rather than suggesting that the individual can always prevent societal harm by gaining command and patrolling the borders of an autonomous self, we both recognize and embrace porous borders and the hope that affects such as laughter can exert a positive force that counters the fears that fail to respond to reason alone.[12]

Comic entertainers bear serious social force. Egyptian standup Bassem Youssef, who at his peak in popularity during the Arab Spring had one fourth of the country's population as a viewing audience, observes that the fear of a tyrant, whose power depends on "fake respect," can be stripped away with satire. Questioned about why authoritarians find comedy so frightening in a 2017 NPR interview, he explains: "All of these dictators basically draw their legitimacy and their status from people fearing them. . . . You cannot fear something that you laugh at. That's why they always crack down on comedians." This is the kind of humor that prompts the producer of Axis of Evil Comedy Tour Jamil Abu-Wardeh to call for a "stand-up uprising."[13] The powers that be know that satire cannot be dismissed. Youssef was forced to leave his country for the United States after an impending court case and death threats. Now residing in the United States in the precarious position of a noncitizen, he continues to use humor to challenge the narratives and misinformation that too easily dominate the media. In the NPR interview, Youssef explains, "When I was watching people talking [about] the Middle East, they always talk about the power struggle, but they don't tell you how people get to power, how people convince millions of citizens to vote against their own interests or to believe in conspiracy theories. And I think the media is a huge factor in that."[14] Of course, the media has long played an important role in games of power, but this role has recently been exponentially amplified and globalized via social platforms, which give both trolls and comics—those artists of affect—all the greater impact.

We thus turn to the comic stage for an antidote to the spread of raw emotions such as fear and hate, and their channeling into destructive forces such as Islamophobia and racism. For where political strategies of the educated elites that are directed toward reasoning with the racist fail and even risk producing backlash when perceived as condescending, humor and wit can transform negative energy and alter the social landscape through waves of cathartic laughter. "I think joking about stuff kind of, like, takes the tension out," insists Youssef. "You know . . . satire comes from a great pain and suffering, and it's very important to take what you're facing and put it out in a light matter."[15] Laughter often functions as a source of release from the normal unpleasant stresses and anxieties of the social world.

But cathartic laughter is more than mere venting. Cathartic laughter can shift perceptions and alter social reality. For example, when 9/11 law enforcement had made "Arabs . . . the new blacks," Obeidallah ironically invites his audiences to celebrate themselves in terms of the double entendre of blackness. "Sure, we are police targets," but "oh my God, we're cool," so now "white kids in the suburbs" will "start act'n Arab with their friends, dressing Arab, wearing like traditional Arab headdress, tilted to the side to be cool, open shirt, gold chain, smelling like lamb."[16] This Arab American comic who was once white is now the new black. In a world where blackness is a persistent and tragic target as well as a fetish, he ironically affirms the Arab as the new cool. This comic's reconfiguration of coolness emits affective vibes that offer the chance and hope of altering social realities.

Laughter, like fear, is a socially contagious affect. Such affects can impact a social climate, functioning like waves rather than like properties of discrete individuals. In the post-9/11 political theater of fear, comedians take center stage for political change. The border-crossing humor of such comedians comprising the Axis of Evil Comedy Tour not only jolts perspectives but also generates solidarity across identities that are now revealed to be fluid. Through laughter, white suburbanites may find their selves, having slipped through a wormhole of social space, side by side in gleeful celebration with the alleged enemy Arab. You can laugh at your enemies, but it is more difficult to laugh with someone without an incipient sense of camaraderie. Contagious laughter thus has some serious potential. Rather than acting as a salute to an elite style of political discourse, a deft combination of mockery and humor demonstrates how we might collectively dissipate fear, soothe raw nerves, and generate the laughter that weakens Islamophobic and racist postures.

Who Can't Take a Joke? Islamophobia and the First Black President

To understand the intersection of Islamophobia, racism, and affect, we offer as a case study the first African American president, who well understood the power of humor. Anxiety set off by the 2008 election of President Obama incited questions about his citizenship and loyalty, to such an extent that these false accusations overshadowed and recast pressing demands for health care as antibusiness and thus an anti-American plot. The white nationalist birther movement seemed to only gain momentum as Republican hopefuls began in the spring of 2011 to throw their hats into the ring for the next presidential election, until the dramatic Navy SEAL assassination of 9/11 mastermind Osama bin Laden. A single (but as it turned out complicated) event transformed the political discourse and the national mood. In this case, a surprisingly successful covert military operation (contrasting with Kennedy's Bay of Pigs debacle and Carter's failed rescue attempt of the Iran hostages) was nicely timed with the release of Obama's long-form Hawaiian birth certificate as well as the 2011 White House Correspondents' Dinner, in which Obama did his own bit of stand-up, giving a comic slap in the face to the birther movement and its leader, Donald Trump. Obama's all-knowing laughter at Seth Meyer's uncanny joke in which the *Saturday Night Live* comedian suggested bin Laden was hiding in plain sight aired side by side for the next few days with images of celebratory crowds and details of America's military ingenuity. These images combined to instantaneously alter the collective mood of the nation, which in turn transformed the national identity of President Obama making him one of us, not them, thus securing his reelection.

Amid this euphoria, Michael Eric Dyson critically pondered Obama's transformation. Why did it take "killing the Muslim" to make Obama American? "Why couldn't he have been American," as Dyson points out, "when he was at Harvard? Why couldn't he have been American when he was the smartest guy in the room?"[17] One could turn cynically to the haunting words of ironist and Black Power icon Malcolm X, who (in what we now typically think of as a Richard Pryor–style of rhetorical response) suggested that "Nigger" is "what white racists call black Ph.D.'s."[18] And indeed, in this case, the killing of the enemy may well have propelled another vicious wave of anti-Muslim fervor not fully realized until the outcome of the 2016 presidential campaign, which witnessed just how ridicule can backfire and fuel a shifting politics of resentment and victimhood.

Laughter and ridicule are a wild card in a high-stakes poker game that has most recently led to a joker becoming a president. At that 2011 White House Correspondents' Dinner, Seth Meyers's quip—"Donald Trump has been saying that he will run for president as a Republican, which is surprising since I just assumed he was running as a joke"—has been blamed for spurring the campaign of a brand that didn't strike many as presidential material. "Obviously you didn't see Trump's expression," notes *Meet the Press* host Chuck Todd in a 2016 interview with Meyers. "There's actually been reporting and speculation that said that the ridicule he received that night gave him more drive to prove everybody wrong and run"—a suggestion Meyers attempts to deny. Yet regardless of impetus or motive, the spurned Trump reshuffled the deck. While playing to an undercurrent of fearmongering but also a sense of vindication from those who thought, along with Trump, that they were the butt of the joke, he did his own stand-up on the campaign trail. Now, as president, he is the joker's revenge.[19]

Ridicule is a dangerous weapon to brandish. It rallies the troops. Its infectious force can even cross illicit boundaries. Yet in crossing some boundaries, it reinforces others, generating the anger and fueling backlash among those who feel—by some inchoate mix of ISIS, Muslims, and liberal elites in the Washington Beltway—under attack. No doubt ridicule depends on the indispensable enemy. The problem we see is that once this nuclear option has been released, you can't yield its power to the other side—but you can try to alter its course.

In part this hostile climate reflects a divisive ridicule that offers its own kind of logic. The logic of the bombastic right evades the contradictions of late capitalism by offering a simpler kind of math that provokes anger and resentment at easily identified targets such as immigrants. Obama's one–two punch on that memorable April 2011 weekend of the White House Correspondents' Dinner was able to volley the volatile cocktail of mockery and anger back toward the xenophobe. Recall Obama's cheeky suggestion that Donald Trump could now move onto more important issues, like "did we fake the moon landing" and "where are Biggie and Tupac?" Simultaneously Obama mocks the fear underlying the birther accusation of his imagined alien origins with a short "my official birth video" that turns out to be an opening clip from the Disney musical *The Lion King* (1994). This clip, from a film that Obama describes as a "children's cartoon," celebrates the birth of a lion cub in Africa. Getting bin Laden, public enemy number one, of course, was ultimately what elevated the mood of the country and transformed the political discourse, but his jabbing remarks against childish fears trumped up by the birther's self-appointed leader, mediated through a modest degree of self-deprecating humor, transferred energy from a wave of fear toward the celebration of victory over a real enemy and a real American president. Yet such serendipitous waves of glee, along with the borders between in-groups and out-groups, can change overnight.

Obama balances mockery with self-deprecating humor to mitigate the trope of the angry black man; so do Muslim Americans and other targets of Islamophobia as they take command of the comic stage. President Trump's political style turns on making jokes at other's expense, but it's well documented that he can't take what he dishes out. This is a luxury that Muslim Americans cannot afford. In making a documentary for Slate, Ayma Ismail tackles the stereotype that "Muslims Can't Take a Joke" and insinuates that this is part of the reason so many Americans are afraid of Muslims. After all, what happens when you mock Islam? A quick glance at popular culture, both left and right, suggests violence—think Charlie Hebdo. "Who are the people you can't make jokes about?" rhetorically asks John Cleese of Monty Python fame. Without hesitation, satirist Bill Maher quips, "Muslims! You know it's a religion of peace. There are pieces of you there, there's a piece of you over there." Ismail knows that "comedy routines like these have created a broader narrative of all Muslims, that Islam is antithetical to Western life. Partly because it smothers free speech with violence. They say that satirists, artists, and comedians are some of the most vulnerable." While it is easy to hear jokes about Muslims, such as Maher's, Ismail's quest was to find jokes from Muslims. At New York City's Comic Strip Club, he interviews comedians Maysoon Zayid and Dean Obeidallah, cofounders of the Muslim Funny Fest, created in 2015.[20] Zayid and Obeidallah make it clear that Muslims, unlike Trump, know how to use humor not just to ridicule the enemy but also to generate positive good.

One of the comedians featured at the Muslim Funny Fest made his network debut in 2017 on *The Late Show with Stephen Colbert*. Ramy Youssef introduced himself as a Muslim "like from the news. Have you guys seen our show? . . . *Fox News* or any of the news, really. They are all about us." Youssef admits, "I get why people are afraid of Muslims. Even if I watch for too long, I'm like, whoa, am I going to do something?" American news coverage "make[s] it seem inevitable. I feel like no matter what I do I'm just going to turn thirty and get a Hogwarts letter from ISIS." With a studio audience roaring with laughter, he explains, "There is just going to be a dude at my house with a beard and owl [announcing], 'You're a terrorist, Ramy. You've been one the whole time. And we start in September.'" Thinking out loud as a Harry Potter fan, Youssef exclaims "OK, cool. Do I get a wand?" Because "I would join ISIS if they gave me a wand. Like a wand is way cooler than democracies."[21]

Such stand-ups use the magic of their gentle mockery and humor to shift perspectives and to redefine what is cool; comic transformations turn on the liquidity of affects and their impact on fluid identities. Perhaps one sign of affects' volatility appears in how far we have come from the solidarity that New Yorkers experienced after the September 11, 2001, attack on the World Trade Center. In his study of empathy, psychologist Frans de Waal observes that "New Yorkers of all races" pulled together in the face of an external threat: "The postattack feeling of 'we're all in this together' had fostered unity in the city."[22] The waves of hostility over building a mosque on the site of ground zero, first proposed in 2009, indicate the ease with which the prevailing winds of a social climate can alter direction and transform into their very opposites.

In many ways, our post-9/11 world has seen a collective mood shift in multiple directions, from a fragile and tentative moment of global empathy that had French president Jacques Chirac proclaiming "We are all Americans" to what Stephen Colbert would in 2010 term "Fear for All," a phrase that signals the emotional trials and tribulations of a neoliberal free-for-all in which out-groups serve as punching bags in an extreme right-wing victimology sweepstakes. Mass anxieties directed toward out-groups thus become an impetus for emotionally closed borders.[23] With the unrelenting toxic political climate, we are reminded that a comedian's work is never done.

As a mainstream counter to the fearmongering of the post-9/11 era, *Daily Show* host Jon Stewart, together with Colbert, orchestrated their 2010 Rally to Restore Sanity and/or Fear. In a sly skit on *The Colbert Report*, Colbert, in the persona of an extreme right-wing news pundit and now-toppled pig, Bill O'Reilly, launches his own pretend campaign, "Keep Fear Alive." Giving his television audience a "refresher course in the five basic fear groups," and with "no blast shield between us, not even a sneeze guard," Colbert confronts a laundry list of phobias through their stereotypical labels. Thus, the editor of *Out Magazine*, the vice president of the United Farm Workers' Union, the Bear Project leader from the Minnesota Department of Natural Resources, a researcher in artificial intelligence, and the executive director of New York University's Islamic Center become known simply as "Gay Guy," "Mexican Guy," "the Grizzly Coddler," "Could Be a Robot" and "Muslim Guy," respectively.[24]

When NYU's Islamic Center director, Imam Khalid Latif, attempts to sidestep the Muslim Guy trope and reeducate the Colbert persona with a dose of logic, the sketch reveals the limits of a straight cognitive approach for addressing collective fears. "We can't kind of brand an entire community through the actions of a few," contends Latif, but Colbert simply points out, "I think we have. . . . I think actions have proven you wrong." For Latif, "There's an element of flawed logic to that statement." Colbert snaps back: "But it's logic." Though Latif points out that "it's flawed logic," Colbert gets another laugh when he retorts, "But it's better than no logic." Colbert, donning the mask of the Islamophobe, draws the conclusion that he is the victim. Yes, Latif admits, but with a twist. "You're losing out the most," Latif continues, "but I don't think you know why you're the victim."[25] Throughout the sketch, Colbert mocks the tools of logic and reason, those preferred weapons of the educated elite. "I know that what you call equality is an attack on me. If you get more rights, I have fewer rights. That's just math."[26] Colbert can do the math. He understands the equation as well as any logician who, much as any strategizing politician, sets the variables of fear to fit his own needs.

The underlying lesson is deeper yet. Although modern Americans claim to distinguish themselves from less culturally advanced others through a core sense of individual responsibility, and although they readily project "tribal" forms of justice onto other allegedly primitive groups, in fact, these sovereign subjects are caught up in migrating waves of affect that they may be largely unaware of. This American "fear for all" simultaneously locates and derides the logic of a national malaise, and with it the limits of reason and logic for getting to the bottom of our angst, all while bringing into sharp focus the relevance of the comic for precipitating alternative waves of affect for political culture.

Our interest here is in the catalytic role of ridicule and humor for the conversion of fear into joyful solidarity through the propagation and contagion of underlying affects. Comedy, however, is not a panacea. Racist jokes and other popular sources of ridicule can amplify social climates of prejudice and fear. Meanwhile, audiences are self-selecting, leaving comics preaching to the choir. Those who do not share the comic's perspective may find the humor offensive and fuel for their own outrage, or they may miss the irony entirely. But it is also true that ridicule and humor can rally the troops while dissipating phobias and fostering a more inclusive and hospitable climate. For susceptible audiences, the contagion of laughter loosens the hold of stereotypes and, as producer of the Axis of Evil Comedy Tour Jamil Abu-Wardeh insists, creates community through cross-border laughs.[27] As such, these laughs soften boundaries and identities while also diverting tanks and tyrants, as made clear in Youssef's nicely titled 2016 documentary, *Tickling Giants*.[28]

Social Networks

As anyone who has experienced the urge to yield to uncontrollable waves of laughter or widespread panic and fear might suppose, human beings are less the sovereign individuals—masters of ourselves—than we often like to make out to be. It is just such waves of affect as laughter and fear that theorists who study social networks set out to explore. "Superorganisms," as described by various social network theories, can regulate the affect and physical function of nodes—aka people—through a process generally mysterious yet also partly measurable.[29] Consider studies suggesting that one's friends and even one's friends' friends—including people we do not know—can affect any number of dimensions of our lives, from health conditions to levels of happiness. Two researchers have found that if a person's friend, a friend's friend, or a friend's friend's friend's weight alters, then that person's weight is likely to alter in the same direction.[30] Similarly, the prevalent mood among an association of friends is more likely to impact our mood than is a change in our individual financial situation in what researchers postulate as three degrees of influence.[31]

Affects can spread like a physical contagion across thousands of miles via waves of energy transmission. Whole epidemics of panic, fear, and even laughter can unfurl through these invisible waves. The Arab Spring not only fanned out across North Africa but also across ethnic and continental boundaries to spur on protests in Spain and Greece, then across the Atlantic to the labor protests against union bashing in states like Wisconsin. Subsequently, the fear and hatred promoted by authoritarian regimes have also spread. Youssef observes: "When racism arrives, it doesn't discriminate. It really goes and spreads the hate, and it will affect everybody."[32] Network theories of affect predict that these massive waves of influence can occur without any personal acquaintance with other nodes (people) in the network, and without anything like what we would ordinarily call personal agency or responsibility for the norms or behavior that people imitate and propagate to others. Nicholas Christakis and James Fowler portray these ripple effects as "a kind of synchrony in time and space . . . that resembles the flocking of birds or schooling of fish."[33] Psychological states, like physical diseases, emerge regardless of individual exertion simply because we inhabit a social milieu that harbors them.[34]

Who and what is responsible for racism and other panics when they sweep across the masses? Needless to say, these researchers are as perplexed as any of us would be with what becomes of the modern concept of moral responsibility. Modern moral theory (Kant's ethics of duty and Mill's utilitarianism) attributes responsibility to individuals without regard to the porous and social creatures that we are. But how do we blame individuals for behavior when we function as nodes of networks traversed by cascades of affect? Do we reinvoke the tragic ethos of ancient Greece with their so-called tribal justice, those for whom a foul air and a symbolic scapegoat carry the toxins of damage and harm? Recall that ancient Greek dramas consign the source of communal malaise to a figure like Oedipus, then purge the toxins by exiling its symbolic source. Modern-day honor killings—and even the West's own racist purges—play on similar tribal logics of punishment.

Second-generation Indian American comic Hari Kondabolu offers a mocking example of tribal justice, Western style, in his 2018 Netflix special, *Warn Your Relatives*. "Hate crimes and racial violence are like the original terrorism in this country, but there is such a high bar to prove something is a hate crime. . . . Did they say a racial slur? Can you prove its intent? Was there a video recording or was there a white witness—you know, an eye whiteness? Was whiteness present at the time?" Kondabolu mockingly inquires. "Terrorism, on the other hand, has a very low bar." For example, if you hear an explosion and "there's a falafel place" nearby, then it must be "terrorism"! Of course, Kondabolu reminds the audience, if "a white dude did the shooting, that's mental health issues. That's completely different."[35] In other words, our modern racism also functions as a twisted tribal logic.

In a search for alternatives to the age-old tribal responses to perceived social problems, yet recognizing the inadequacy of modern moral theory, with its excessive reliance on individual agency, social scientists suggest a therapeutic approach. This approach entails that social policy "target [for treatment] the hubs of the network, namely those at the center of the network or those with the most contact."[36] Foucault exposes these normalizing techniques of modern bureaucracies as horrifying for queers and anyone else thought to be deviant. Perhaps neither tragic rituals of scapegoating nor therapeutic models of discipline and punish (to borrow the Foucauldian locution) rest easily with those of us who are equally wary of forms of tribal justice and modern bureaucratic techniques of determining who is normal and who is not. Instead of combating massive waves of negative affect via tragic scapegoating or bureaucratic expertise, we turn to laughter and comedy for the promise of a more salutary medium of social change. Laughter provides a break in the stream through which the affective tides are unsettled and opened to shifts and alternative directions.

We do not by any means suggest that all comedy is the same. Even attempts to be progressive often turn out simply to be salutes to normality. Amid the controversy surrounding the building of a central New York Islamic Culture Center, and in an earnest attempt to confront anti-Muslim bigotry, television host Katie Couric suggested in December 2010 a "Muslim version of *The Cosby Show*." According to Couric, "*The Cosby Show* did so much to change attitudes about African Americans in this country, and I think sometimes people are afraid of what they don't understand."[37] Presumably this style of good-humored, middle-class ethnic sitcom would ease tensions and represent people as all basically just the same. While Couric rightly points toward the significant role that humor can play in shifting the political winds, her remarks only highlight the assimilationalism (or whitening) that Bill Cosby's brand of middle-class humor (that is, before he was outed as serial rapist) encourages, and thus a form of political transformation that doesn't challenge and in fact may contribute to the race- and class-based hierarchies of neoliberalism.[38] Cosby and Couric at best offer a holiday or temporary reprieve from social angst, not the comic punch needed to transform social norms and the climates that sustain them.

Such sugar-coated sitcom humor doesn't cure racism—certainly not when race is mixed with the politics of class that neoliberalism so viciously fuels. Neoliberalism may hold open the promise of a pass for those model minorities who attain the education, skills, and cultural demeanor that are viewed as meriting high status and income levels like the Cosby family, but it exacerbates problems for the working class even as it perpetuates racial stereotypes across class differences. Wherever older forms of biological racism might seem to wane, neoliberal racism kicks in. These race- and class-based inequities require a sharper form of comedy—not the sentimental humor of the sitcom but rather the edgy ridicule targeting late capitalism's phobic panics and racism.[39] Of course, we don't want to dismiss entirely the Couric concept. After all, Iranian American comedian Maz Jobrani effectively draws on sentimental humor, even if he does so tongue in cheek. He calls out to an imagined white audience, "We're not Arab. . . . We are white, so stop shooting" as he slyly and playfully shifts his identity away from the villainous Iranian to claim a more soothing Persian heritage. "I am not dangerous. . . . I am Persian like the cat," and "colorful" and "handwoven" like the rug.[40]

While the Axis of Evil comedians offer an alternative to the sentimental humor of the mainstream sitcom, their self-deprecatory humor adds to a range of tones and a nuanced strategy that includes the abrasive and aggressive humor that characterize "the wit of retaliation and the comedy of revenge."[41] Recall after the John F. Kennedy assassination Malcolm X's jibe at white America: "The chickens are coming home to roost."[42] Kondabolu highlights a revenge element in his updated revision of satirist Jonathan Swift's 1729 "Modest Proposal" that the Irish might solve their problem of hunger by selling their children as food for the wealthy. Kondabolu suggests that instead we eat the rich—more specifically, that we eat their organs. But of course, out of recognition of their humanity, he jests, "We will force feed them organic grains . . . then we would have them walk around their very large estates—they would be free-range." His over-the-top proposal, however, aims not for revenge but for a starting point in a negotiation process, the final aim of which is health care with a public option. Revenge humor in this case is not used simply to turn the tables on the rich. It is part of a strategy of humor that reaches for more potential allies in a bid for a greater good.

Still, the abrasive element is necessary for challenging variants of the neoliberalism that pervade all aspects of American life that sentimental humor alone would allow to stand unchallenged. Sheehi explains that the global ambitions of U.S. politics require Islamophobia to rationalize domination of Mideastern oil reserves and the necessary invasions and loss of life that this domination entails. He finds this Islamophobia across the political spectrum, from conservatives to liberals, reaching even into the Obama administration. Hence, we are not surprised that Kondabolu is even skeptical of how white liberals would handle a hate crime: does that mean that "they call an ambulance after the hate crime"? Or does a liberal hate crime mean, "I am going to be hit over the head with a bottle of kombucha." In another liberal setting, a Seattle coffee shop, he decides to confront a guy who makes a racially insensitive remark; this time Kondabolu leaves the racist feeling bad but himself feeling good, which he gleefully declares a "win–win situation." He remains skeptical of the onlookers in the coffee shop who "do what white liberals tend to do when there is a confrontation: they put their heads down and pretend like nothing is happening," or afterward say, "Don't worry, Hari . . . I'll give you a hug."[43] Sentimentality is not enough. Yet he also avails himself of a measure of self-deprecatory humor that reaches out for allies and does indeed point toward a win–win.

Pakistani American comedian Kumail Nanjiani also knows how to generate a win–win. He explains during an *SNL* monologue,

"Just because you're racist doesn't mean you have to be ignorant. An informed racist is a better racist." He heard a guy rant on that "all Muslims are sexist—the Koran says women can't drive." Nanjiani responds, "Yeah, pretty sure the Koran never said that. Because if the Koran had said that women can't drive cars 1,400 years ago, I would be a mosque right now, and so would you, because that would mean the Koran predicted cars." After Nanjiani's film *The Big Sick* appeared in 2017, "his Twitter feed became a nightmare" because a lot of people demanded that he "go back to India," a place he has never been. This is what led Nanjiani to sarcastically pronounce, "The problem with most racism . . . it's the inaccuracy. That's what bugs me. Do the research. Put in the work. You will see the benefits." He then further explains to his audience: "If someone yells at me, 'Go back to India,' I'd be like, that guy's an idiot. But if someone was like, 'Go back to Pakistan, which was part of India until 1947 and is now home to the world's oldest salt mine,' I'd be like, that guy *seems* to know what he's talking about. I'll pack my bags."[44] Like the comedians of revenge, these humorists expose hypocrisy and other social vices; but by sprinkling ridicule with self-deprecatory humor, they defuse anxiety and generate a counterwave of joy and solidarity.[45]

Hypocrisy and Critique

Derisive stereotypes and racial jokes function in a politics of domination by either pressuring out-groups to assimilate or scapegoating them altogether. In contrast, progressive humor combats the dominant culture through something like the kind of "immanent critique" that Nancy Fraser and Linda Nicholson attribute to twentieth-century traditions of critical theory.[46] The key task of the critical theorist has been to expose the contradictions in hegemonic capitalism. Capitalism claims to free workers from feudal social hierarchies when in fact it reentrenches them in unfree class-based systems of unfair labor practices. Satire and other edgy forms of humor can reveal the contradictions that afflict a society, but comedy does not rely on a strictly cognitive approach to expose and untie the knots in a system. Instead, humor turns on a more affectively engaged modality of critique, exposing not just contradictions but also hypocrisy.

Indeed, attacking hypocrisies of dominant groups may be the key strategy for comedians of immanent critique, given that their aim is partly characterized by the assertion of their own relevance and belonging. Ever undermining ethnic hierarchies in America, *Daily Show*'s Aasif Mandvi, born in Mumbai, reminds us of the hypocrisy of our immigrant country as he mockingly quips, "It wasn't easy for *our* European immigrant ancestors." After all, "They had a long arduous journey just to get here, and then they had to go out and kill a continent's worth of squatters, while still suffering from boat lag." In fact, he continues, "I think these new immigrants have it easy. Give me a choice between wiping out a nation of indigenous peoples and busing tables, it's no contest—better tips!" Mandvi points out the injustice of the in-group defining itself in this case as hardworking against an out-group as lazy when in fact that out-group's hard work renders it a perfect candidate for the characteristics that often define the American identity. For if hardworking defines the allegedly Anglo-Saxon Protestant ethic of U.S. cultural identity, as the conservative thinker Samuel Huntington and his followers continue to insist, then these comedian critical theorists prompt us to ask once again who the real Americans are.[47]

Hard work may be Americans' mantra and freedom our stated philosophy, but Mandvi uncovers instead a neoliberal calculus of who counts as American: "I'm brown but I'm from India," and thus, in his words, "I'm tech support slash cardiologist brown . . . not dishwasher slash Los Angeles parking attendant brown" as he mockingly suggests that more points have been assigned to immigrants who speak English or have technical skills. A perplexed Jon Stewart, playing it straight, responds by reminding us of our theoretically democratic principles: "But it is the antithesis of our founding. . . . What happened to the motto, the old motto, 'Give us your tired, your poor, your huddled masses, yearning to breathe free'?" Mandvi suggests that Stewart needs to get up to speed: "That was the old slogan," but America has rebranded its immigration policy. Echoing the then current United Parcel Service tagline, he proposes as the new slogan for national policy, "What can brown do for you?" Of course, the notion of "What can brown do for you?" is not new but reflects a long history of global migration and industrialization in the United States that necessitates cheap labor but also a collective response.[48]

Collective Laughter and Movement Leaders

Solidarity across social divisions and the social movements that sustain this solidarity might be assisted by recalling the malleability of race and ethnicity—something comics do especially well. The Irish, Italians, Jews, and Catholics have all been the new black, which is always at the bottom in our white supremist country, where the first immigration law in 1790 permitted only alien "free whites" to become citizens. In the context of discussing our current malaise over immigration, Colbert flashes up on a screen a perfect quote to uncover the long history of racism in this country. Colbert observes it was Republican Senator Mitch McConnell who said, "[With all these unwanted Mexicans, America will] become a colony of aliens, who will shortly be so numerous . . . [that they] will never adopt our language or customs, any more than they can acquire our complexion." Colbert offers his ironic correction as the punch line. "I'm sorry," he says, "that was not Mitch McConnell last week. That was Benjamin Franklin in 1751. And he wasn't talking about Mexicans. He was talking about Germans."[49]

There is, of course, a history of some immigrants striving to become white, but we can also find episodes of solidarity based not on striving for whiteness but rather on challenging the whiteness on which so much racism and social exclusion depends. As Vijay Prashad explains, the way forward is not through assimilation, which is after all just a ploy for white supremacy now in its neoliberal stage, nor in a reactive resurrection of boundaries to fortify some cultural nationalism.[50] Prashad notes, "In U.S. history the Irish, Italians, Jews, and—in small steps with some hesitations on the part of white America—Asians and Latinos have all tried to barter their varied cultural worlds for the privileges of whiteness."[51] But he observes as well more hopeful signs in "the interactions of the Black Panther Party with the Red Guard and the Brown Berets in the mid-twentieth century; and finally, the multiethnic working-class gathering in the new century."[52] For these ethnic groups, the choice has been clear: either the "vertical assimilation" up a ladder that leads toward "bright whiteness," or solidarity forged among those pushed back down.[53]

Alliances combating the recurrent exploitation of racialized labor depend on the fluidity of social identities. Such interactions may be among the most valuable achievements of that ironist who mixes the heat and the vision of egalitarian political movements with the savvy techniques of the comic stage. Scholars have unearthed a rich tradition of infrapolitics that links African American humor with radical reimagination.[54] Historian Manning Marable powerfully complicates our understanding of Malcolm X as not only an agent of revenge but also an agent of visionary solidarity: "What made him truly original was that he presented himself as the embodiment of the two central figures of African American folk culture, simultaneously the hustler/trickster and the preacher/minister. Janus-faced, the trickster is unpredictable, capable of outrageous transgressions; the minister saves souls, redeems shattered lives and promises a new world."[55] Malcolm X is not the only example of an ironist or satirist turned movement leader and visionary in the civil rights period. Historian Steven Estes mentions that Black Panther cofounder Bobby Seal got his start doing comedy, among other odd jobs.[56] Given this continuity between black activism and subversive comedy, we ought not be surprised by the observation that Richard Pryor, whose comedy "spoke the unspeakable . . . about white people and their racism," was given "his private tutorial under the direction of [Panther cofounder] Huey Newton."[57]

More recently, humor has also reemerged, along with Latinx- and Mexican American–led campaigns for human rights. One powerful example dates to May 1, 2006, when over a million protesters took to the streets in opposition to anti-immigrant fervor intent on criminalizing undocumented workers and militarizing the border. The protests centered on a playfully serious boycott inspired by a 2004 mockumentory, *A Day Without a Mexican,* and featured signs such as one that read, "Jose called today! Make your own taco."[58] Under the Trump administration, these protests have gained new sense of urgency, as threats of building a wall and permitting countless deportations have become a reality, not just a campaign threat.[59]

Anti-immigrant fervor turns on an old trope of what it means to be American that prizes hard work. The mockery that aims to shed light on injustice has been misdirected toward some of the hardest workers in America—an irony that gained popular and congressional attention thanks to the comic techniques of satire. The inability to see the vital importance of immigrant labor prompted the United Farm Workers of America (UFW) to play a similar game with the master's tools, or at least with definitions of who is lazy (an all-too-familiar racial slur) and who is hardworking, and hence what it means to be a real (deserving, entitled) American. More specifically, the UFW initiated the "Take Our Jobs" campaign in summer 2010, and in so doing, UFW president Arturo Rodriguez foregrounded the plight of Mexican agricultural workers, revealing the hypocrisy of immigration policies with a website that encourages unemployed American citizens to take the job of undocumented workers. Indeed, the UFW website makes getting a job just an easy click away, but there is a catch. As Rodriguez points out, the work is hard and physically demanding—and hence no one who does the work is white.[60]

Gut-wrenching ironies risk losing their charge when they are theorized as mere cognitive incongruities. Too much is at stake. The job description on the UFW website demands working outdoors in often above ninety-degree heat, being fit enough to lift fifty-plus pounds, and mastering various tools of the trade, which meant that on July 8, 2010, at the time of Rodriguez's appearance on *The Colbert Report*, only three U.S. citizens had taken on this minimum wage/piece rate opportunity.[61] Colbert committed himself to becoming the fourth citizen to sign up for the "Take Our Jobs" challenge while insisting that there must be air-conditioning. The irony of undermining basic human rights for a population that processes our poultry and harvests our crops, thus feeding our nation, and that is a tribute to the dignity of labor evokes more than a chuckle. To begin to alter the anti-immigrant waves of hate and fear demands some comic relief, but also some sharp redirection. Colbert's slapstick efforts as an agricultural laborer resulted in his fall 2011 congressional testimony, bringing yet more attention to the ironies of what it means to be a hardworking American.

Against the backdrop of the 2016 presidential election, artists and playwrights have also invoked comic irony to challenge an intense wave of anti-immigrant backlash. Lin-Manuel Miranda's hit Broadway musical, *Hamilton*, plays on the contradictions of America's ambiguous history as a nation of immigrants. In 2016, Miranda released the *Hamilton Mixtapes*, with powerful musical tracks including "Immigrants (We Get The Job Done)": "I got 1 job, 2 job 3 when I need them / I got 5 roommates in this one studio, but I never really see them," sings K'Naan. "And we all came to America trying to get a lap dance from Lady Freedom / But now Lady Liberty is acting like Hilary Banks with a prenup."[62] Similarly, Lalo Alcaraz, a prolific Chicano artist and creator of the first nationally syndicated, politically charged Latinx comic strip, *La Cucaracha*, began circulating on social media a cartoon with the caption, "Mexico built the Trump wall for free." However, the map is redrawn by the clever cartoonist to keep out the real thieves. It shifts the boundaries between the two nations decisively north, returning to Mexico those territories of the Southwestern states stolen from it after the 1846–48 U.S. invasion.[63]

Responsibility across Borders

It is remarkable how hard borders and identities are perceived to be when one is looking at people who are not considered to be sufficiently white. In response to the Islamophobia of the post-9/11 era, Obeidallah, who "went to bed white and woke up Arab," suggests, "White is not a skin color, it's status. It's the way you're treated in society." The difference between Arab, Muslim, Persian, Mideastern, and South Asian, all too readily lumped together, and white is that "white people never suffer as a group when a few people do something bad in their group," like "NASCAR," "Paris Hilton," and "country music."[64] Whiteness typically turns on a concept of individual responsibility, in contrast to the so-called primitive logic of tribal justice attributed to alien cultures. But as Obeidallah's jibe suggests, in fact white people often invoke the very logic that they aim to distance themselves from when they blame an entire group for the actions of a few. The solidarity we seek does not require that flawed logic yield to good logic, if by good logic we mean keeping our categories and identities free from confusion. Americans have long thought that their "civilizing mission" is to bring a modern culture of individual responsibility to so-called primitives, with their irrational emotions, but they too are moved by affects; they too blame and punish others on the basis of their group identity. However, during a never-ending post-9/11 crisis, humor offers the contagious laughter that can diminish collective fear and anxiety. In so doing, it demonstrates the power of affect to spread across porous borders, rendering identities, along with actions and attitudes, fluid and primed for a solidarity that building a wall can never stop.

3

Can the Animal Subaltern Laugh?

Mocking Alpha Males with Georgia and Koko

> I recently had a mind-altering experience communicating
> with a gorilla. Her name is Koko. We shared something
> extraordinary—laughter.
> —Robin Williams, The Gorilla Foundation

Monkey Business

Animals have long been seen as funny, but something to laugh at, not with. Indeed, if there has ever been a perpetual butt of a joke, it has been animals, who seem to be instinctive creatures more different from than similar to humans. Yet the big surprise is that comparative studies of nonhuman primates and other intelligent animals do not provide humans with that long-sought-after difference that makes us ontologically distinct and superior. Studies of emotions, cultures, communication skills, and even desires within nonhuman animal species have uncovered more parallel capacities than expected.[1] Stephen Colbert's spoof on a monkey experiment illustrates the humor of endeavors to reestablish human exceptionalism in the context of the post-2007 recession: "Consumer spending is down and we're in danger of a crippling double dip recession . . . but science has found the secret to getting this economy moving again: monkeys!"[2] Colbert explains that a scientist has joined forces with an advertising firm to test whether capuchin monkeys trained to understand and use money will choose an advertised bowl of Jell-O over the other brand. This is, as a *New Scientist* headline proclaims, "the first advertising campaign for nonhuman primates," which aimed to determine if commercialized images of female monkey genitalia and of alpha males would motivate consumer patterns among subapes.[3] As a member of the superior species, Colbert exclaims with mock earnestness that an advertising experiment that exploits the crass animal instincts of monkeys will teach us nothing about ourselves. Meanwhile, images of female lady parts pop up on a screen alongside a Diet Pepsi as Colbert ponders his "urgent reasons" for wanting the drink. To make sure that his human audience doesn't miss the punch line, a final image of Colbert appears with his own monkey grin, gobbling down Jell-O as the all-revealing monkey vagina flashes in the background, leaving us wondering who the real monkeys are.

When it comes to monkey see and monkey do, we turn to our own comic mix of philosophical reflection: animal studies of communication skills, emotions, and desires, as well as histories of solidarities that cross species divides. Nonhuman animals are assumed not only in Western myth but also in science and philosophy to be above all else inferior to humans, having been constructed as passive, ahistorical, unfeeling, or unthinking, but inevitably lacking Western, colonial, civilizing, or, more recently, neoliberal virtues.[4] Indeed, throughout our post-Paleolithic history, social stratification and cultural exclusion have often entailed projecting demeaning or monstrous animal imagery onto the subaltern. Rituals of humiliation that ridicule the other as a subhuman animal are primary devices for enforcing outsider or subordinate status. Clearly humans have mastered the art of ridicule, and at nonhuman animals' expense. Philosophers entrenched in Western traditions go so far as to define humor in conjunction with the human as a reflection on the gap between the physical and the psychical. Laughter is said to occur with transgressions at the site of this break, as when the animal imitates the human or vice versa.[5] But what would it mean if some of the animals assumed to be the most proper objects of ridicule have the capacity to laugh? The association of animality with the subaltern provokes the thought that perhaps like their human counterparts, animal subalterns might laugh back.[6]

Subaltern studies have established that ridicule and other forms of humor serve as accessories of cruelty and props of power;

they also provide discourses and technologies of reversal, leveling hierarchies by turning stratified structures upside down.[7] At the same time, the field of animal studies has begun to document the capacity for laughter in primates, dogs, and even rats.[8] Far from laughter's being a uniquely human characteristic, as has long been thought, primate mockery along with common forms of animal play reveal the means for an infrapolitics of cross-species outrage.[9] This cross-species defiance not only unsettles alpha male status but also provides spaces for egalitarian ecologies of inclusive belonging beyond our market-driven neoliberal consciousness. In this chapter, we speculate on the evolutionary origins of laughter, concluding that various species use humor to build solidarity and ridicule against the powerful to demand fair play.

Messing with the Missing Link

Philosophers and scientists for too long have failed to question the question of what makes us uniquely and superiorly human. A popular scientific and philosophical approach is to insist on the superior cognitive or linguistic capacities of humans. An ironically illuminating variation of this kind of a claim is offered by Svante Pääbo, the world-renowned head of the Max Planck Institute for Evolutionary Anthropology in Leipzig. Pääbo reflects on the magnitude of his current projects in evolutionary genetics, including sequencing the Neanderthal genome and engineering human protein in mice. These epoch-making exercises in what Foucauldian cynics call biopower could have sci-fi outcomes, like making pets out of Neanderthals rescued from indenture as lab animals for big pharma (Hollywood-style *Rise of the Planet of the Apes* [2011] redux).[10] In the eyes of big science, these biolicious projects are no less than "attempts to solve a single problem in evolutionary genetics, which might, rather dizzyingly, be posed as: What made us the sort of animal that could create a transgenic mouse?" This is how *New Yorker* writer Elizabeth Kolbert's essay on Pääbo's ambitions restates the philosophical question about self-knowledge that has "been kicking around since Socrates and probably a lot longer." Kolbert adds, "If it has yet to be satisfactorily resolved, then this, Pääbo suspects, is because it has never been properly framed. 'The challenge is to address the questions that are answerable,'" he informs Kolbert.[11]

If only Socrates had thought of reframing his questions to his pumped-up interlocutors so that those Socratic questions could be answered! But he was a pretty clever philosopher; asking only questions that are answerable sounds like a good strategy for scientists, but it could put philosophers out of business. Anyway, so-called stingray Socrates, master of the unanswerable question, may well have been more of a ridiculing ironist than an earnest knower—the philosopher as stand-up comic, debunking pretensions rather than proclaiming them. Such serious debunking is not, however, where Pääbo's admittedly astounding research aims to take us. If the philosophical question of what makes us human is to be framed around our allegedly unique or superior human capacities—such as language, technology, or, for that matter, humor—Pääbo's restatement of the question seems in keeping with what some of the more serious-minded philosophers and other straight-shooting seekers of knowledge have always sought to do: provide answers. Yet as we shall see, Socrates's ironic style of questioning spurs a more stimulating approach to the age-old question, "What is man?" This alternative approach leads not to ever more claims of superiority on behalf of man-the-alpha-ape but to a leveling of them.

The promise of Pääbo's work owes much to the continued successes of evolutionary genetics. Neanderthals—as our closest not-quite-human relative—share most of our genetic material, with some significant exceptions, he explains, as he offers his own testable hypothesis as to what future investigations might find this exception to be: "By about forty-five thousand years ago, modern humans had already reached Australia, a journey that, even mid–ice age, meant crossing open water. Archaic humans like *Homo erectus* 'spread like many other mammals in the Old World,' Pääbo told me [Kolbert]. 'They never came to Madagascar, never to Australia. Neither did Neanderthals. It's only fully modern humans who start this thing of venturing out on the ocean where you don't see land." Of course, this adventure requires social collaboration in order to solve the problem of building the boat, Pääbo notes all too briefly. But collaboration may not after all provide that allusive answer to the question of what makes the human unique and superior. Pääbo continues: "'There is also, I like to think or say, some madness there. How many people must have sailed out and vanished. . . . Is it for the glory? for immortality? for curiosity? And now we go to Mars. We never stop.' If the defining characteristic of modern humans is this sort of Faustian restlessness, then, by Pääbo's account, there must be some sort of Faustian gene." In short, for this geneticist, the missing link between the human and nonhuman turns on hubristic madness.

Tragic Overstep and Collaboration across Species

That mythical gene—marking the human defiance of any limit and the definitive demise of rivals for planetary domination—sounds a note of tragic overstep. A nod toward anarchic merrymaking that mocks overreach instead of indulging in it could make for a jollier turn. The tragic tone, however, certainly rings through any range of possible scenarios for our planet's immanent future as one shifts from the perspective of the human to the nonhuman animal upon whom the overstepping human steps. A heartrending hint from the empirical sciences is found in psychologist Gay Bradshaw's research on the changing relationships between humans and elephants in Africa and Asia.[12] Recalling that these species once lived peacefully side by side, Bradshaw and others have begun giving serious study to reports of elephants in the forests of Uganda attacking human villages. These studies portray a species immersed in tight social webs of family and tribal communities that have been frayed by our own species' imperial hubris of cruel hunting and kidnapping elephant tribe members.[13] Orphaned adolescent males stripped of boundary-setting social regulation by missing elders are left to run rogue, and with intentional brutality, they express their trauma and outrage by violating and killing members of their own or other species. Maybe elephants can be Faustian too.

Most of the current work in animal ethics aims to generate sympathy for animal suffering.[14] The variety of approaches in this ethics is diverse, but the most influential stem broadly from the reformist Anglophone literature that has philosophical roots dating back to both Jeremy Bentham's utilitarianism and to the sentimental moral traditions associated with David Hume, Adam Smith, and the Scottish Enlightenment. We will not take these kinds of approaches, although we will borrow from aspects of the latter traditions in our reconfiguration of empathy in chapter 5.

The moral challenge of these modern philosophical traditions to what has been deemed the "heartlessness" of scientific rationalism and the classic unregulated liberal state is illustrated in Susan Pearson's study of the rise of what she calls "sentimental liberalism" in nineteenth-century America.[15] Enlightenment rationalism and classic liberalism, under the influence of thinkers such as Rene Descartes and John Locke, displaced older conceptions of animals together with humans as part of the warp and weft of a common life. For example, in ancient Greek festivals, the sacrifice of a pig would demand the ritual of dripping water on the pig's head to solicit a nod of consent.[16] The induced consent was symbolic, of course, and could hardly save the pig, but it nonetheless exhibits traces of a fading earlier common life that continues even today in indigenous traditions and that lingered in pockets of Europe until the seventeenth century. In medieval Europe, wild and domesticated animals were treated by legal and ecclesiastical authorities as actual members of the parish community. That the rights of animals paralleled those of humans was demonstrated in numerous instances of court trials across every region of Europe. Humans and animals could be tried together for such criminal violations as bestiality, with animals having their own legal representatives at public expense.[17] In one case, a donkey was defended as innocent of illicit sexual acts and hence a victim of rape on the basis of its "honorable character."[18] Even animals that were accused of murder could be successfully defended when they were known to have suffered considerable abuse.[19] Invasive pests were not exterminated but were guaranteed parcels of land in court decisions that were based on a theological argument of original ownership and prior claim.[20] Then, half a century after Montaigne argued against the cruelty of animals and spoke of the joys of shared human and animal friendships despite inevitable failures of communication, Descartes and Locke ushered in their use as resource material in the industrial revolution by pronouncing them machines.[21] As subrational creatures, classical liberalism stripped animals of the rights and fellowship that they once had enjoyed in mixed-species communities.

Pearson's research demonstrates how a milder discourse of sentiment and sympathy won out over a stronger challenge to modernity's abuses: the short-lived radical egalitarian ideals of the U.S. Reconstruction era after Emancipation. In contrast to more radical approaches, the era's sentimental discourse (remember republican motherhood in chapter 1) emerged through an ethics and rhetoric of care and protection for dependents. An appeal to the shared capacities for suffering rather than for agency and communal membership prepared the public to reconcile the perceived dependency of nonrational animals and children with the claim that they were rights-bearing individuals deserving of legal or moral protection from harm despite their subrational status. Previously, the classic liberal doctrine of rights to property and the pursuit of liberty for rational and self-sufficient citizens had deemed children and animals to be nonrational and unworthy of rights of their own. Then, in the nineteenth century, the promulgation of stories documenting the abuse of children and animal cruelty prompted various humane societies in the United States and elsewhere to agitate for the reinvention of the modern state from minimalist to interventionist. From the abolitionist through the Progressive eras, the state in alliance with private agencies was reconceived as a proper vehicle of protection rights for "beasts and babes."[22] These protection rights were granted on the basis of the ability to feel and to suffer, not to reason, and on claims of status of dependency, not on claims for liberty, solidarity, or equality. The reformist movements did not overturn the well-entrenched social hierarchies of the patriarchal family and the human/nonhuman distinction together with its racist legacy; nor did they upset the reason/emotion binary. But they did successfully appeal to public virtue and advocate for social policies that would ameliorate the terrible abuses suffered within hierarchal structures and a doctrine of human exceptionalism.

In contrast to the sentimental movement, the nineteenth-century utilitarian thinkers who likewise came to the fore during this reformist time on behalf of the supposedly nonrational did not appeal directly to feelings as a basis for moral judgments and were not rooted in the eighteenth-century sentimental tradition of Hume and Smith. These earlier modern philosophers of sentiment had challenged philosophical rationalism by arguing that the natural basis for moral judgments and action resided in feelings or sympathy alone. In contrast, utilitarian thinkers including Jeremy Bentham, John Stuart Mill, and in the twentieth century Peter Singer would draw on rational principles to justify human responsibilities to vulnerable and dependent creatures such as animals. These utilitarians, like the Kantians, would lose sight of the centrality of negotiated relationships and turn to a quasimathematical rationalist ground for moral philosophy. One problem with these rationalist approaches is that they would make it exceedingly difficult to understand how nonhumans like humans might be ethical agents too. Nonetheless, for these utilitarians, like the sentimentalists, feelings and desires, not solely the rational capacities of capable human adults, provide at least a solid ground for moral consideration and account for their attention to animal suffering. This wider focus on vulnerability and sentience is central to American social movements of both sentimental liberalism and utilitarianism, and prevails in reformist discourse in the United States today.

The cult of sensibility in Anglo-American culture from the abolitionist to the Progressive eras prepared a context for liberal reformers to shape a public discourse that appeals to our sentiments and common human sympathy in ways that a narrow valorization of Enlightenment reason cannot. Sentimental liberalism arose in response not only to particular acts of cruelty but to the impersonal brutalization and increasingly visible horrors of the industrial revolution. Its relevance has returned with the neoliberal intensification of animals' technological and industrial use, extended to biogenetic engineering as seen in cloning, genetic cross-breeding, accelerated growth through hormones, and the redefinition of the human as the creature able to create the transgenic mouse. After long decades in the twentieth century, when animal rights movements lay dormant and analytic traditions of liberal theory reasserted Enlightenment rationalism as a technical if not academic enterprise, this intensification of abuse on an ever more massive scale has prompted Anglophone philosophical traditions to challenge once again the biopower of the food industry and animal research through an appeal to human sympathy for animal suffering and vulnerability.

The concern for the suffering and vulnerability of dependent creatures provides the moral ground for Martha Nussbaum's massive reworking of modern liberalism in *Frontiers of Justice*.[23] Nussbaum retools liberalism's classic aim of protecting individual liberty by incorporating nineteenth- and twentieth-century ideas of social equality in terms of minimal capabilities (among a list that includes life, emotions, affiliation, and play) that should be guaranteed by the state and that moreover should be extended to include animals, the disabled, and noncitizens.[24] While her proposal does not address the new studies of animal sociality and agency, and it stops short of any consideration for the community life and biosocial networks that exceed individual agency, it does extend liberal rights to the protection of minimal capacities and agencies of animals. Like the abovementioned traditions, her approach ultimately rests on an appeal to sympathy for the suffering of nonrational dependents rather than on classic liberal respect for the dignity of fully autonomous creatures. As she writes, her "solution . . . requires people to have very great sympathy and benevolence, and to sustain these sentiments over time."[25] But note that the paternalism (or maybe maternalism) that Nussbaum explicitly defends as the basis of justice for nonhuman animals neglects intriguing possibilities that other species cultivate ethical norms and various forms of social cooperation, on occasion even in mixed-species communities. The thought that a nonhuman could engage in any sort of shared moral or political citizenship is also dismissed out of hand as "fantastic."[26]

The Scottish Enlightenment themes central to Nussbaum's sentimentalist revision of twentieth-century liberal rationalism have also returned in contemporary scientific research on animal and human cognition. For example, citing David Hume, psychologist Jonathan Haidt argues that there is a sound scientific basis for viewing reason as the "slave of the passions" and that moral feelings (sometimes called intuitions) and empathy play pivotal roles in understanding human morality.[27] We will return to this intuitionist tradition of psychology in chapter 5; however, here we note that its rise can reinforce a sentimental, reformist, and ultimately for our purposes too uncritical an approach to the political interplay of emotions among group-oriented animals within and across species. Our approach draws from both sides of the emotion/reason dichotomy while trying to dig ourselves out from underneath it.

Meanwhile, the field of cognitive ethology has dropped a knowledge bomb that threatens to radically alter the parameters for animal rights discourse as well as for questions of who we are. Research scientists such as Frans de Waal have established capacities for sympathy, and indeed moral feelings of fairness, in nonhuman animals.[28] Various species of animals (without specifically human language or modes of conceptual thought) make demands for social justice and express feelings of compassion, sometimes for the sake of helping out humans.

Our challenge is to take these scientific discoveries a step beyond philosophical modernism's binaries of reason/sentiment or independence/dependence, based as they are on modern models of atomic individualism. If animals have agency, not just vulnerability, and live through networks of interdependence and interconnectedness, not just dependence, and either directly or indirectly through larger ecosystems, then what kind of infrapolitics do their societies reveal? What are the substantial ethical practices, customs, and structures that provide the social glue for their communities and families? Beyond straightforward modernist binaries—the subjective appeal to sentiment and sympathy or an objective appeal to abstract reason—we aim to explore through humor the ethical norms that might emerge for some tentative collaborative efforts at interspecies living. While we support liberal reform measures to expand rights protecting animals against abuse, our starting point is not with vulnerability, dependency, and the compassionate concern for minimal animal capabilities but with animal agency and communities. Animals are not like infants; in surprising ways, they can on occasion be more like us than we might imagine. Our political aim is not ultimately just a reform project for securing animal rights on the basis of their status as needing protection; also, where possible, we advocate for cross-species solidarity with animal coworkers and coinhabitants of interspecies communities. Animals are not merely vulnerable creatures that require protection or recipients of human sympathy but are also sometimes kindred political agents in their own right, with interlocking histories, cultures, and technologies within and across species. Given these aims and concerns, our method draws primarily from critical social theories in the tradition of Audre Lorde and Donna Haraway rather than from liberal theorists. An erotic politics of laughter, to draw kindred motifs from these poet-thinkers, aims for the cultivation of individual feeling as well as for a social infrastructure that substantiates norms and expectations in part on the basis of cross-species codes of reciprocity and solidarity.

Perhaps the strongest nineteenth-century challenge to the sentimental tradition's obscuring of the agency of those who dare to resist oppression is stated by African American abolitionist Frederick Douglass.[29] Douglass explains to his white readership the limits of an ethical appeal to moral sentiments in the context of American slavery; white people could not generate sympathy for an enslaved person unless that person asserted some significant degree of agency and demanded through the assertion of that agency recognition from others. Power yields nothing without a demand. For Douglass, that agency was staged as a call for respect and would eventually take shape as a catalyst for the abolitionist movement. While important, a display of vulnerability and an appeal for sympathy do not always suffice to generate an egalitarian political ethics.

Moreover, Douglass extended the range of his moral concern not only to the emancipation of all slaves everywhere and to nineteenth-century women's movements but also, implicitly, to nonhuman animals. Of course, any appeal to analogies across nonhuman and human species risks reinforcing the worse kind of prejudices against black identity in a white racist culture. This projection of animal qualities on racialized others was a staple of the emerging tradition of blackface humor. Yet Douglass inverted conventional expectations as he proclaimed the agency of the enslaved person in terms of his or her "animal spirits." He envisioned the free spirit of the enslaved person symbolically as an uncaged animal and as a winged bird in flight. Most significantly, Douglass joined his own struggle with those of the beaten-down ox or horse on the plantation, preparing the way toward a truly revolutionary form of worker collaboration. Douglass's prophetic vision stems from risking the charged association of blackness and animality to propose what may well have been this abolitionist's most provocative challenge.

Through the nineteenth and twentieth centuries, abolitionist, feminist, and workers' movements continued to challenge, if not entirely successfully, the classical liberal concept of rights. To varying degrees, new constitutions in Europe would recognize basic rights to social and economic equality. Then, after World War II, the struggle against European colonialism in Africa and elsewhere transformed the meaning and scope of rights yet again to include the recognition of communal bonds (defined in part through those local languages important for a communicative ethics) and environmental rights.[30] More recently, after several generations of rethinking rights, we anticipate yet another radical rethinking that would include rights of animals as not just vulnerable others requiring human protection but also moral agents. Our approach begins with Haraway's invitation to imagine whether nonhuman animals might be our kin (*When Species Meet*). Thus, rather than merely listening for the sad cries of otherwise mute animals, we turn to the playful and sometimes subversive social exchanges within and between species that suggest a missing moral link from which might arise collaborative laughs for social justice.

A Tip of the Hat, a Wag of the Tail: Missing Cues

What if the animal other can speak? Or, given that speaking seems to always involve the use of human language, let's rephrase the question in less speciesist terms: what if the nonhuman subaltern can communicate? After all, what is speech but an address to the other?[31] Recall that Gayatri Chakravorty Spivak's pivotal essay on the communicative capacities of the subaltern suggests that the apparently mute servants of the British empire did not seem to speak in part because the colonialist frequencies were not tuned in to hear them.[32] In a similar vein, ontological gaps between the human and nonhuman animal others have been grossly exaggerated by a human failure to pick up on animal social cues. Just as historian Nancy Hewitt suggests that scholars might tune into neglected women's movements and untold narratives by uncovering a wider band of radio waves heard at different frequencies than those familiar as first-, second-, and third-wave feminism, we too embrace the concept of wave transmissions broadcast beyond the range of human perception in Western cultures.[33] Not all cultures assume the discontinuities and hierarchies between human and nonhuman animals found in the mantra that man is the measure of all things.[34] Borrowing from feminism, we understand the need to make the invisible visible and to reexamine the sources of mixed-species community building. A history that is radically inclusive can reveal a collective ethos outside of any neoliberal master narrative—say of advertising genius, alpha male madness, and lady monkey parts.

Keeping Colbert's spoof of monkeys and advertising in mind, we shift our ethical focus from the vulnerability and infantilization of the animal other to neglected possibilities for cross-species politics enhanced by the communicative vibes of a collective ethos that testifies not only to various species' capacities to care for each other but also to laugh and play across enemy lines. Animals enjoy a communicative agency that enhances the possibilities for coresponsibility through a politics of biosocial eros heard in emancipatory tones. Our erotic politics of laughter makes common cause with what utilitarian Peter Singer calls "animal liberation" in his 1975 manifesto as it has been taken up again in the 2011 Occupy Wall Street and kindred European social movements, but with a subversively comic twist.[35]

The animal subaltern's ability to speak is not a sci-fi moment, like when the human-engineered chimpanzee in *Rise of the Planet of the Apes* challenges his human captors, uttering the word "No." Rather, this ability is documented in animal studies.[36] Chimpanzees, elephants, and any number of species communicate—with varying degrees of intentionality—emotions, beliefs, and social cues that researchers tend to miss, much like those well-documented human cues missed by presumably oblivious chimpanzees. Such outdated experiments claim superior cooperative skills for the human species. But the question of whose cues are being missed seems far from clear.

Consider the experiments featured in the Nova National Geographic documentary *Ape Genius*.[37] While the film provides a fascinating glimpse into some of the new science on animals, the film's interpretative frame for the discoveries is a problem. Research scientist Brian Hare blames a bonobo for his own failed attempts to teach the animal to pick up a cup, without allowing for any larger questions regarding how a human experimenter could be an effective teacher for bonobos, let alone for what we humans might be capable of learning not about but rather from other primates who may be attempting to teach us a thing or two. For example, consider how the experimenter attempts to teach the ape by pointing to the cup, which is a strategy known to be effective for teaching young human children. Human children attend to special features of objects after having those features pointed out with an index finger by a (human) teacher. They also exhibit a natural tendency not shared by other primates to point to objects. This experiment is part of a cluster used unfairly to establish that although other primates can learn through imitation, only humans can learn by being taught. Noting the natural and perhaps unique import of pointing for humans, but without considering other means for communication and teaching for other species, Michael Tomasello all too hastily concludes: "Apes do not, in either gesture or vocalizations, intend to inform another of things helpfully."[38] These approaches to animal studies entirely neglect the significant evidence for alternative means of cooperation and social learning. Sometimes it is important to emphasize similarities across species, other times the differences.

A major problem with these kinds of studies is that they assume that nonhumans are always motivated to learn from someone of a different and disconnected species.[39] In fact, we know that when the teacher is of the same species, animals learn quite well from each other. The elders of an elephant clan pass down crucial ecological and cultural knowledge as well as social ethics to the youth. The loss of an elder through poaching or other disasters is experienced traumatically by the community; it threatens the survival of the entire clan. It also threatens the general peace. The trauma of this loss, and the absence of the educative wisdom of elders, leads to rampages by male adolescents. Orphans who are raised outside of their group by humans may be rejected when reintroduced to established elephant communities when they "commit unwitting trespass because they have not learned social etiquette."[40] The elephant "possesses an extremely large and convoluted hippocampus, the brain structures most responsible for mediating long-term social memory," Gay Bradshaw explains.[41] In an interspecies community, elephants, with their memories and attentiveness to oral cultures, could serve well as social historians.

Hasty claims for human superiority in cooperative capacities are made without any clear evidence that pointing is the most significant way in which social learning occurs for nonhuman animals. From the fact that nonhuman animals do not typically use pointing, it is deduced that they do not engage in genuine social learning. However, as is noted, while apes do not ordinarily use pointing to communicate among themselves, even they can learn to point to make requests of humans. These requests exemplify cross-species social learning, pointing, so to speak, to the potential for an occasionally cooperative ethics crossing species lines—if oblivious human researchers would just tune in.

Tomasello claims that nonhuman apes are not generally helpful to others and thus are not socially cooperative, and thus are unlike humans. He argues that nonhuman primates, along with wolves and lions, lack the capacity to share goals and form a "we" identity.[42] In fact, bonobos demonstrate strongly "altruistic" actions, including rich capacities to console others; indeed, they are called the "most empathetic ape."[43] We shall shortly turn to the role of social play and the capacity for inter- and intraspecies friendships and political alliances among lions, wolves, and other social carnivores. The problem is that too many experiments are designed to contrast human and nonhuman responses with human styles of teaching and human teachers. That's our hubris kicking in again. Don't we all know plenty of uncooperative humans? Indeed, epistemologically stubborn humans are as unlikely to learn from bonobo teachers as these primates are to learn from humans. Yet one conclusion leads to another, and *Ape Genius* ends with the claim that humans are "the most social ape." Given that their competitors for this title include the "make love, not war" bonobos, one has to wonder just what humans might be missing.

Indeed, many of the actual experiments in the film in fact suggest surprising parallels and differences between humans and other primates, not ontological gaps. The capacity for culture and language, for example, is no longer believed to separate humans from the realm of nature. Concerning the question of animal language, Bekoff nicely retorts, "Tails talk to us about what animals are feeling, and so too do various postures, gaits, facial expressions, sounds, and odors. Sometimes I wish I had a tail and mobile ears so I could communicate more effectively with dogs and other animals, whose tails and ears tell us lots about what they're thinking and feeling."[44] Ethologist Joyce Poole's studies of elephants suggest that nonhuman species communicate a range of emotions that humans as a single species may fail to understand because we only share some part.[45] If we listen to nature's rustling, we hear not just the mute animal's silent complaint, not even merely an animal that on occasion says "No" with a nod of a head or an assertion of a tusk, but a creature who can laugh and play.

For many species, playful laughter can be part of a friendly process of social bonding distinct from serious and even life-threatening games of competition, as discussed in our book's introduction.[46] However, as we shall see, nonhuman animals may also mix genres of the serious and the humorous, and use mockery to subvert hierarchies. If so, perhaps human and various nonhuman species are not that different after all—at least not in ways we thought. "Even the most complex mutualistic relationships in nature reflect a tug-of-war between collaboration and exploitation," primate behavioral ecologist Joan Silk writes.[47] Our aim is to find in the mesh of nature/culture those social cues that we oblivious humans have too often missed—cues that allow us to avoid repeating histories of rogue warfare and, at least on occasion, to rejoin with other species in an unexpected, life-affirming bond. History plays out not just as a series of tragedies but sometimes as comedies as well.

Animal Slapstick and Social Bonding

Scientists, notably including Robert Provine, the author of *Laughter: A Scientific Investigation,* have studied chimpanzees and found a link between their laughter-like noises and human laughter, which might point to a common origin for communication. "Laughter is literally the sound of play, with the primal 'pant-pant'—the labored breathing of physical play—becoming the human 'ha-ha,'" Provine observes, establishing an evolutionary continuity between the tickling and the rough-and-tumble play that stimulates chirping in rats and laughter in other species.[48] Jaak Panksepp has published research that reveals "the possibility that our most commonly used animal subjects, laboratory rodents, may have social-joy type experiences during their playful activities and that an important communicative–affective component of that process, which invigorates social engagement, is a primordial form of laughter."[49] Moreover, waves of joy transmit across multiple species, as Panksepp discovered when he found that "inducing laughter in young rats promoted bonding: tickled rats would actively seek out specific human hands that had made them laugh."[50]

Even more astounding, Bekoff notes that "though it's rarely the focus of scientific research we observe animals making jokes or displaying a sense of humor,"[51] providing an example of a scarlet macaw who "roars with laughter; he teases all who come near, . . . and even plays 'magic carpet'—wherein his human slaves race down hallways dragging large towels with the macaw riding aboard."[52] Vicki Hearne observes that when her playful dog finds a dumbbell set on its end instead of its usual position, he "enjoyed the play on form . . . [and would] toss it in the air a few times on his way back with it, to show his appreciation for the joke."[53] Again quoting Provine: "Most candidates for simian humor involve cases of intentional misusing of objects and misnaming of people and things. For example, researcher Roger Fouts observed the signing chimpanzee Washoe using a toothbrush as if it was a hairbrush. Moja, another of Fouts's signing chimpanzees, called a purse a 'shoe,' put the purse on her foot and wore it as a shoe. Francine 'Penny' Patterson observed the signing gorilla Koko treating rocks and other inedible substances as if they were foods, offering them as 'food' to people. . . . The above cases of presumed intentional 'misnaming' and 'misusing' are potential jokes." Provine here proceeds to draw an analogy between adult chimpanzees and human children, but this is a type of analogy that problematically blurs significant differences and overlapping similarities between species, so we set this and related comments aside, and focus instead on actual observations. He continues: "Reports that apes appeared to be in a playful mood, or glanced at the caregiver for evidence of the effect of their errant actions, suggests . . . a joking intent. Another widely noted class of misnaming involves 'name calling.' . . . When upset with her caregiver, gorilla Koko referred to her as 'dirty toilet.' . . . In another possible instance of simian humor, Roger Fouts reported that while riding on his shoulders, the chimpanzee Washoe urinated on him, signing 'funny' (touching her nose) and snorting."[54]

Much laughter stems from play behavior, as Provine establishes. As we have discussed in the introduction, the implications of play behavior for ethics and humor are intriguing. Bekoff's studies of play behavior in social carnivores suggest that play may also provide a training ground for learning egalitarian social norms and expectations for reciprocity—what we humans call the "Golden Rule—do unto others as you would have them do unto you"—among such normally hierarchal species as "wolves, coyotes, red foxes, and domestic dogs."[55] Key features of play provide the ground for an egalitarian ethos, functioning to level the playing field and to build camaraderie. Bekoff explains that "for the time [these carnivores] are playing, they put aside or neutralize any inequalities in physical size and social rank."[56] Their playful exchanges exercise capacities for friendships through the sharing of laughter. If laughter is a great leveler, then the politics of collaboration and cooperation might well develop from skills and experiences acquired during social play. Humor may be one more example of such play.

Mixing species and disciplines, we turn again to de Waal. "Of the three ideals of the French Revolution—liberty, equality, and fraternity—fraternity is probably . . . the easiest to understand from a primate perspective with survival relying so heavily on attachment, bonding, and group cohesion," he observes. "Primates evolved to be community builders."[57] Some species, such as bonobos, exhibit more egalitarian tendencies; others, like chimpanzees, are more hierarchical. Humans, he speculates, lie somewhere in the middle. Malini Suchak, de Waal's collaborator, clarifies that although chimpanzees are more hierarchical than bonobos, on the scale of primates, they are fairly egalitarian. Their hierarchies are not typically linear; they engage in victim support; lower-ranking chimpanzees form coalitions to outcompete with alphas; and they have strong ownership norms (regardless of rank). Animals of higher rank aren't allowed to appropriate food from animals of lesser rank.[58] Recall that social equality is thought to be more prevalent among humans living in the small-scale societies before the Neolithic era; sharp social hierarchies and urban centers began with the rise of agriculture, and further developed with the industrial and now postindustrial revolutions.[59] This ancient egalitarian strain in the human species reemerges from time to time, most recently challenging neoliberalism, as we see, for example, in the Great Recession's anarchist social movements and their subversive delight in play. Above all else, we take our social cues from the primatologist's observation that to laugh together is to "broadcast solidarity and togetherness."[60]

Tricksters, Subversives, and Interspecies Solidarity

To build social bonds, nonhumans may make use of more than just friendly laughter and innocent slapstick routines. De Waal reports the case of a raven playing deceptive tricks on high-ranking males: "The low-ranking male learned to distract his competitor [from food] by enthusiastically opening empty containers and acting as if he were eating from them."[61] Similar evidence suggests that animals can be tricksters and mockers of authority, challenging assumptions that only humans can deceive, protest, or collaborate against oppressive conditions, and establishing elements of an agency that is strategic and even collective. For animals, as for humans, mockery creates a space beyond surveillance, creating a site for self-assertion and a freedom that cannot be controlled by, say, laboratory norms. It can function not only to downgrade the frightening into the risible but also to convert negative emotions into embolding ones, performing a "mini-revolution" aimed against those who may not get that they are the butt of a joke.[62] Of course, laughter may or may not successfully transform an entrenched social system, but it does lift the spirit, generate hope, and assert agency.

It is not surprising that humor might play a part in animal camaraderie and political trickery given what we now know about a sense of fairness in a number of animal species. In fact, even Darwin hypothesizes that ethics is continuous with animal sociality.[63] Bradshaw observes, "In zoos and circuses, elephants are known for what has been called 'retaliatory cunning,' a calculated, directed attack on the someone who has turned on them in the past."[64] These elephants are normally careful to direct outrage against the perpetrators of injustice; they refrain from retaliating against unintentional crimes or innocent bystanders. De Waal reports on a sense of social regularity that is found not only in humans but also in other social animals. He defines this regularity as a minimal sense of fairness, or "a set of expectations about the way in which oneself (or others) should be treated and how resources should be divided. Whenever reality deviates from these expectations to one's (or the other's) disadvantage, a negative reaction ensues, most commonly protest by subordinate individuals and punishment by dominant individuals."[65] Even monkeys, who are considered by some to be less intelligent than apes, display acts of defiance at conditions that they understand as unfair. (But note that the relevance of the word "intelligence" or related notions of reason and understanding for cross-species comparisons has been questioned, given the complexity of cognitive skills across species too easily missed through the use of a single ambiguous and politically fraught term).[66] De Waal describes an experiment performed with his student, Sarah Brosnan, where they found that offering a monkey a lesser reward than his peer (a cucumber instead of a juicy grape) provoked anger in the disadvantaged monkey, who "hurled . . . pebbles out of the test chamber, sometimes even throwing those paltry cucumber slices. A food normally devoured with gusto had become distasteful."[67] Even a simple affect-based response to food can take on a political aftertaste! This experience of injustice requires affect and cognition, but not necessarily an explicit reflection on rules or general concepts. Yet monkeys respond to inequity with Occupy Wall Street–style anarchy and outrage. And while monkey outrage sends a serious message to the experimenter—"no more monkeying around"—protest can take a subversively comic tone as well.

A joke is not always a joke; sometimes it can offer a subtle glimpse into an interspecies political ethics. De Waal again provides rich anecdotes. A wily chimpanzee named Georgia freely engages in teasing and mocking human visitors at the Yerkes Field Station in Atlanta. De Waal reports of occasions when Georgia "hurries to the spigot to collect a mouthful of water before they arrive. She then casually mingles with the rest of the colony behind the mesh fence of their outdoor compound, and not even the best observer will notice anything unusual about her. If necessary, Georgia will wait minutes with closed lips until the visitors come near. Then there will be shrieks, laughs, jumps, and sometimes falls, when she suddenly sprays them."[68] Georgia's "spontaneous ambush tactics" can make a monkey out of any of her would-be human superiors as she turns the research station into a carnival.[69] In this context, political jokes are "the oral equivalent of guerilla warfare," a sign less of resignation than rebellion.[70]

Apes may also use tactics of humor against their own in-group superiors, suggesting that in the animal kingdom, laughing can function as a comic means for defrocking the local tyrants. De Waal reports an incident—what to us humans appears as the equivalent of the slip on the banana peel—at the San Diego zoo, where apes are enclosed in an area surrounded by a dry moat with a chain for access. Apparently when an alpha male bonobo named Vernon would visit the moat, a younger male named Kalind would pull away the chain. "He would then look down at Vernon with an open-mouthed play face while slapping the side of the moat. This expression," de Waal explains, "is the equivalent of human laughter: Kalind was making fun of the boss."[71] Like his monkey cousin, Kalind would seem to express outrage over injustice; but this ape seems to also enjoy an egalitarian sense of what counts as fair that may not be as pronounced in more rigidly hierarchal animal societies. For Kalind, any ape positioning himself as a superior may count as fair game.

Moving out of the lab and onto the farm, it is difficult to be unaware of the range of moods and dispositions of animals within the same species and their modes of making things right. Those who have worked with or lived in close proximity to animals are less likely to be surprised by stories of either species differences or distinct personalities. To be sure, not all animals are particularly savvy or capable of social camaraderie. Barbara Kingsolver, in her agrarian experiment detailed in *Animal, Vegetable, Miracle*, remarks that some animals are stupid, but such animals tend to be man-made—for example, turkeys genetically engineered for food production.[72] At the same time, she tells of one member of the flock chosen for Thanksgiving dinner on the basis of the turkey's unpleasant nature.[73] Her point is that singular personalities permeate animal communities.

Coming of age on a mid-Missouri farm, we too have seen not only animal personalities but also animal politics. Some horses, for example, are much more patient and nurturing, while others have less tolerance for human mistakes. An obstinate pony would frequently sit down on the job, or even roll in the dirt to get rid of an unskilled rider. Horses would rub their unwanted riders against a fence or thorny bush to get the pests off their backs. Other horses would show much more sympathy with any human rider, regardless of skill. Some would even walk gingerly, knowing that their fragile and unbalanced cargo could slip off easily. Like other animals, horses have best friends whom they trust to stand guard as well as swat flies away from their faces, and they too have frenemies that they will never see eye to eye with. There is also a fair share of practical jokers, like an Arabian gelding showing off his ability to unlock not only his stall door but also those of his mates. Collectively, these horses also know when something is awry, running deep into the woods when they hear the unmistakable sound of the veterinarian's clanky truck coming down the gravel driveway. You might say they have a gut instinct—something we all feel and act on. Observing that farmers know to be wary around their donkeys and their tricks, biologist Bekoff does not hesitate to draw the conclusion that creatures that thrive on creating mischief for a laugh can demonstrate real wit as well, posing on occasion as regular "stand-up comedians."[74]

Can history offer us similar kinds of stories—stories that may complicate this renegade science without dismissing it? To be sure, science has often ignored historical context and taken its own slip on the banana peel. A Harvard team reports as straight science the discovery of an amazing horse named Jim Key. This animal wasn't just horsing around when he feigned lameness to prevent his owner from selling him off to a stranger. He even seemed to communicate through spelling out the letters of (English) words to his owner and a team of Harvard scientists. For these scientists, ex–enslaved person and self-taught veterinarian Dr. William Key's horse companion was their sole focus of study, neglecting a complicated history of race and resistance. In *Beautiful Jim Key: The Lost History of a Man and Horse Who Changed the World,* Mim Eichler Rivas tells not only the tale of a remarkable horse but also the turn-of-the-twentieth-century story that shows a black professional negotiating Jim Key—"the world's smartest horse"—with Jim Crow. Stories of this horse continue to reverberate through the contemporary mainstream media. The stories take on a life of their own through the horse's array of unusual feats, and a team of Harvard researchers' verification. We are sure that Harvard scientists are not easy to deceive, yet African American trickster humor also reveals subtle inflections that may make it difficult for those outside the local community to catch on to subplots. Key was no doubt clever at creating the circus drama that would keep him laughing all the way to the bank. Yet we don't want to dismiss his animal collaborator. Instead, we can imagine future reconsidered histories in which the human trickster does not get all of the credit and a privileging of a *longue durée* (the big picture that a historical perspective can give us) that acknowledges animal agency—their tricks, pranks, and infrapolitics—as a means to reveal the workings of authority and power.

Unofficial histories that study challenges to power and authority and paradigm-altering scientific data on animal emotions and behavior afford new understandings and possibilities for collective political change. Jason Hrbal's *Fear of the Animal Planet: The Hidden History of Animal Resistance* presents an agency oriented-theory of animal oppression and presents numerous accounts of animal resistance, solidarity, and revenge against targeted abusers. Jeffrey St. Clair's introduction to the book reports the case of baboons who raid train cars to free captive friends.[75] African lore similarly reports the case of a political alliance between two male lions, who notoriously resisted British colonialism in Tsavo, Kenya. In 1889, the lions worked together to disrupt labor on a railway through their territory. This native uprising was not put down before the rebel lions had killed over a hundred British railway workers.[76] Hribal's argument that these various acts of resistance demonstrate agency turns on evidence that spirited animals willingly undergo acts of rebellion even though they know that if found out, they will be subjected to severe punishment, including death.[77]

Labor historians, among others, should be intrigued by the desire of animal theorists to pull histories from below. Although a call to listen to voices unheard may seem like old-school social history, the problem of human exceptionalism gives it unexpected relevancy. The centrality of social history, and in particular its aim to find agency where official histories were blind, is well understood. Yet histories beyond the traditional archives still uncover tropes that have wrongly deemed groups of historical actors passive. Recall Vicki Ruiz's classic work, first published in 1998, bringing voices and experiences of Mexican American women, *From Out of the Shadows,* and more recently Annelise Orleck's oral histories and subsequent monograph exposing the agency of African American welfare recipients and how they "fought their own war on poverty."[78] Can we push social history to another frontier, one in which animality is no longer the last acceptable figure of mute passivity?

Animal subjectivities challenge narrow assumptions in traditional Marxist histories that assume that only man labors and that only men's labor can be alienating or world making. Feminists argue that child care, service occupations, and emotion work are also skilled and creative labor and can be done under oppressive or world-making conditions.[79] Similarly, histories of animal labor practices should expand beyond accounts of animal suffering to explore the ways in which diverse species give meaning to our overlapping worlds. Animal subjectivities breathe new life into social history by bringing more actors to the stage and by unearthing new energies and visions of collective action.

Tragically, oppressed social groups are not exempt from the general rule that the history of triumph turns on the power of exclusion and not on the ability to hear the subaltern speak. Indeed, great labor historians have found not so much moments of distinct discourses in unison but, in the words of Alexander Saxton, an "indispensable enemy," which, in his study, turns on anti-Chinese sentiment bolstered by subhuman imagery to prop up caste and class unionism.[80] David Roediger has traced the tragic appeal of whiteness in which the racial and gender tropes reemerge in spaces that range from nineteenth-century worker protests and union halls to turn-of-the-millennium sporting events, prisons, and of course presidential elections.[81] And as mentioned in chapter 2, Vijay Prashad has also expressed the problems of seeking simply bread-and-butter multiculturalism that too easily makes its move up the neoliberal ladder in search of bright whiteness.[82] Yet social historians, like social activists searching for an elusive global link or for the intricacies of intimate labor, celebrate when the desire for change engenders, however unexpectedly, a felt connection and a shared consciousness.

Animal tropes that have passed under the radar as second nature in so many histories make us wonder if we should not reconsider these tropes as pointing to some literal basis for human–nonhuman solidarity. Thus far, so-called natural history (including the intersections of human and nonhuman species) has been inextricably bound to studies of indigenous people.[83] For working-class and labor studies, the history of the worker (long assumed to be white and male[84]) finds the only sympathetic animal trope to turn on mute passivity. Popularly imagined in Upton Sinclair's *The Jungle* or in Charlie Chaplin's 1936 mockery of the industrial order, *Modern Times*, capitalism dupes rational workingmen, turning them into nothing more than a mindless herd of cattle or sheep, or a machine.[85] Yet labor historians are also finding emerging patterns of what Donna Haraway understands as worker–companion species camaraderie that defy these animal tropes.[86] In Thomas Andrews's groundbreaking study of human, animal, and natural history—what he defines as a "workscape"—of Colorado's turn-of-the-twentieth-century mines, workers witness the power of collective animal resistance. "Mules," claimed one driver Victor Bazanele, 'had sense like a human.'" Andrews notes, "Drivers even likened the mules' resistance to their own struggles. Victor Bazanele joked that mules 'knew when starting time was and quitting time was.' When 'quitting time came around,' he declared, 'you couldn't make those mules do nothing.' [Alex] Bisculco concurred; the animal workforce, he claimed 'was unionized before some of us.'"[87]

Andrews discusses miners' relationships to mice that go beyond the role of the canary in the coal mine. To be sure, mice hearing and sensitivity to vibrations cause them to scatter when there are underground dangers such as a cracking wall, and like their better-known counterpart, they die from exposure to even small amounts of carbon monoxide. Andrews sees more than practicality as the source of an interspecies sense of common purpose. He notes that miners shared lunchtime food scraps with the mice. The miners, who found the mice amusing, also learned to differentiate among their lunch companions according to markings and behavior; some even began to name the mice. "'Oh yeah,' Dan DeSantis recalled with a smile, 'the little buggers they knew their name, yeah Pete this and that, boy they come out of the crack and they get that close with you.'" Insightfully, Andrews argues, "In the camps above, the act of breaking bread together often cemented communal bonds across deep cultural divides; in the mines below, sharing food across the boundary between species helped colliers turn rodent fellow travelers into friends."[88]

Similar stories of alliances occur between soldiers and dogs on the World War I battlefields in Susan Orlean's *Rin Tin Tin: The Life and the Legend*. Rin Tin Tin's owner and trainer, Lee Duncan, created film scripts for the world-famous canine orphan, which he brought back from Europe, illustrating the dog's heroic actions. Rin Tin Tin's heroism grows out of an empathy that, as Orlean explains, "is broader and deeper and more pure than what an ordinary human would be capable of." The silent films of the 1920s were the perfect medium to shift our human-centered gaze and showcase the virtues of animals who couldn't speak in words but who could express a range of emotions and real personality: "A dog was at no disadvantage to a human in a silent film: both species had the same set of tools for telling a story—action, expression, gesture. In fact, an animal acting without words looked natural and didn't fall into pantomime and exaggeration the way human actors in silent film often did."[89] Here our study of humor and infrapolitics makes visible unacknowledged heroes, raising Haraway's question: "What if not all such Western human workers with animals have refused the risk of an intersecting gaze?"[90]

Conclusions and Implications

We need to move beyond witnessing vulnerable animal others and allow for both the study of and engagement with animal discourse and society. Animals suffer, but they also assert an agency that at times takes a turn toward the comic. Our critique of long-standing Western assumptions of the passivity of animals learns from feminist critiques of traditional, patriarchal histories that have rendered invisible not only the work of caregiving and emotion labor but also the importance of laughter. The idea that women, let alone feminists, could be funny once seemed as far-fetched as a mule that knew the meaning of a fair day's work. Like feminist humor, an animal's work is never done, especially when it comes to invoking signs of visibility that deconstruct the all-too-serious binaries that have left the subaltern animal anything but a laughing matter. Yet it is laughter and joy that render topsy-turvy the very notion of a missing link—now a neoliberal link that purports ontological gaps and other monkey business. Perhaps if we disrupt old-school assumptions that animals can only be funny when they perform human tricks, we will be able to collectively tackle other oppressive norms. The alternative is the reassertion of neoliberal fears and fantasies imagined in sci-fi as the uprising of the planet of the apes. Our own comic version would feature a mischievous Stephen Colbert–ian twist in which instead of enjoying our bread and roses, we must pay monkeys for our Jell-O and porn.

4

A Catharsis of Shame

The Belly Laugh and SlutWalk

> I always celebrate my body, sometimes twice a day.
> —Amber Rose, *Walk of No Shame*

In 2017, the Onion, a parody news site, unleashed a video clip that mocks the academic left's inability to communicate with ordinary people. The clip features a former Trump supporter from a small steel town in Pennsylvania who keeps a straight face as he explains his path to enlightenment: "I voted for Trump because I thought he'd create a better America for everyone. But after I read eight hundred or so pages on queer feminist theory, I realize now just how much I've been duped."[1] Is it really a surprise that a volume-length manifesto is not a call to action? It might be for some. After all, intellectuals have often assumed that revealing life's incongruities through rational thought is all one needs to unlock the masses' false consciousness. At the same time, across the political spectrum, any play on emotions has been deemed not just superficial but also dangerous tools of manipulation. Yet what if belly laughs expose the gut emotions that can act as a powerful impetus for radical awakenings and progressive social movements that challenge gripping forces such as shame? Theorists and organizers caught in a blind "faith in rationality" miss, academic and activist Deborah Gould explains, how "social movements engage in a great deal of what sociologist Arlie Hochschild calls emotion work, which she defines as an attempt to alter one's emotions, to evoke or heighten or suppress a feeling."[2]

In Gould's experience—with the AIDS advocacy group ACT UP, for example—she finds queer camp to be crucial for elevating the mood of the movement and overcoming the turnoff of self-righteousness.[3] Similarly, we turn to emotion work as a means to reveal humor's cathartic power to challenge the stifling patriarchal politics of shame. With acknowledgment to feminist materialism's interest in the gut, not the phallus, as the "second brain,"[4] our holistic approach turns to the deep-down relief of the belly laugh, and its fun and festive affects to spark social change.

First-Brain Approaches to Humor

Before we get to the gut and all that it has to offer, let's look at the prevailing approaches to humor in philosophy and in cognitive psychology, which appreciate wit as a cerebral game but not as a game changer. There are two strands in this cerebral approach. First, incongruity theory focuses on the perception of puzzles occurring when mental patterns and expectations are violated.[5] Second, a new take on an ancient Stoicism views humor as a means to rise above and thus transcend the absurdities of life. We do not deny brainy humor—after all, it takes guts to get to the brain. But we do need to dissect these two prominent first-brain approaches in order to reveal both their strengths and political shortcomings.

Incongruity theory turns on trying to make some sense out of nonsense, as in puzzling over the "the oxymoron 'if pigs could fly.'"[6] This example is central in Noel Carroll's influential philosophical study *Humour*, where it is followed with one of those all-too-infrequent references in philosophies of humor to a female comedian, in this case Sarah Silverman. Carroll's cognitive approach reveals how she "is comically effective because it is so incongruous that such a sweet-looking young woman spouts such obscenities and vitriol."[7] But we find much more is at stake. As Rebecca Krefting explains, the real punch in this shock jock's slutty humor turns on the "nihilistic" thrill of "antipolitical correctness."[8] Here a female comic gets to act like the pig. To be sure, there is an element of incongruity all over in humor, and sometimes a joke is just a joke, but that is not always where the humor does or should stop.[9] Logic-oriented philosophers and cognitive psychologists reduce too much of life to a mental puzzle for the sheer intellectual satisfaction of solving it.

We argue that incongruities in feminist humor abound, but they do not simply pose a sweet-looking yet raunchy young woman for mental delight. These reversals, such as when Silverman puts on a male chauvinist pig face, instead use the roar of laughter to destabilize gender hierarchies and rituals of slut and body shaming. It is this roar from the gut that exposes laughter's high stakes and potential, typically invoking the pivotal social emotions of shame and a sense of who belongs and who doesn't. Belly laughs transform our physical and emotional state, together with our sense of self and social position, via a social atmosphere dense with images and values. These atmospheric changes can in turn precipitate the collective social storms that alter history.

A second cerebral approach is also incapable of accounting for the politics of emotions. Like the cognitive, this second prominent approach emphasizes a mental distance from turmoil and is not a challenge to it. We can characterize the second perspective as fatalistic because laughter draws attention to the absurdities of life while offering only a moment of reprieve before life's inevitabilities. Its cerebral pleasure stems not from pondering cognitive puzzles but from experiencing humor's momentary uplift in the face of the irresolvable absurd.[10] While straight-up incongruity theory draws its support from cognitive psychology, this fatalistic alternative offers an existential twist on the ancient fate-driven philosophies of the Stoics. Simon Critchley cites an example of such an approach in *On Humor*,[11] where he updates the Stoic philosophies of life via a late 1920s essay of Freud's.[12] In this essay, Freud moves away from his earlier and now all too readily dismissed relief-based theory of the joke. Freud's early theory features an interpretation of catharsis as a venting and release of pent-up affects through verbal acts of transgression against social taboos.[13] Freud's updated theory turns to a detached and controlled mode of humor where a visceral relief might be felt but is largely left unexamined. Critchley cites a passage from the essay where "Freud speaks of a criminal who, on the morning of his execution, is being led out to a gallows to be hanged, and who remarks, looking up at the sky . . . 'Well, the week's beginning nicely.'"[14] As the British might say, with a stiff upper lip, this kind of humor invites us to do little more than "keep calm and carry on." For such a head–brain approach, humor emanates from the mind, where it produces, as Critchley explains, the "modesty of the chuckle or the humble smirk," or even just the simple "smile."[15]

Fumerists, however, never just lie back and take it. Wanda Sykes and her audience understand the laughter over a detachable pussy often conjures more than modest chuckles and humble smirks. The feeling of relief is real. Turning cerebral humor on its head, the raucous roar of the belly laugh can offer something other than a Stoic reprieve. Laughter that comes from deep down can threaten the normal rules of social control with verve but also with aim and social purpose. Above all else, laughter's physiology prepares us to understand how belly laughs catalyze anger and transform negative affects and emotions toward liberation. As a punch back from the fomenting nether regions of society, a contagious guffaw from the bottom up exerts undeniable biosocial force. Humor can offer a cathartic conversion of a harmful shame to a promiscuous pride—the kind of pride that is central to norm-changing social movements like SlutWalk, a now global movement that first began as a 2001 protest after a Toronto police officer chastised women by suggesting that they should "avoid dressing like sluts in order not to be victimized."[16] Resisting derogatory identities and social positions that colonize the self, risqué humor promulgates practices of self-care while altering the norms of belonging. These cathartic practices do not occur in the cerebral exclusivity of mental space alone but also transform emotional processes and a volatile social climate by throwing a wrench in "the old slut-shaming machine."[17]

Comic Relief and the Affects and Physiology of the Belly Laugh

While the affective and physiological benefits of a good belly laugh have been downplayed in cerebral approaches to humor, common folklore that laughter is the best medicine suggests that we might revisit older theories of comic relief. John Morreall explains that humor has been thought to function on our nerves like a pressure relief valve in a hydraulic system such as a steam boiler.[18] We are also reminded of the laughing barrel designed to capture the threat of the out-of-control laughter of enslaved people in the American South, thereby maintaining the status quo.[19] Clearly there's something more to relief theories than first meets the eye. But if relief theories have until quite recently been largely neglected and even mocked (as are Freud's early writings on humor), aspects of them are strikingly salvageable for a feminist perspective on gut-based humor.

Morreall begins by looking at Lord Shaftsbury's *Sensus Communis*, which in 1709 first proposed a version of comic relief theory that could be experienced as mentally liberating for those suffering from oppression or tyranny.[20] This freethinker, who was tutored when he was young by John Locke, believed that the pressure transmitted by the nerves from the muscles and sense organs to the brain carried a fluid and gaseous substance called animal spirits, which naturally sought release: "The natural free spirits of ingenious men, if imprisoned or controlled, will find out other ways of motion to relieve themselves in their constraint; and whether it be in burlesque, mimicry, or buffoonery, they will be glad at any rate to vent themselves, and be revenged upon their constrainers."[21] Such humor offers an important expression of frustration, a source of resilience, and the experience that in one's own mind one is free, even if it is not, as this disciple of the Stoics observes, socially or politically transformative.[22]

Lord Shaftsbury's theory was picked up by social Darwinist Herbert Spencer in his 1875 essay "On the Physiology of Laughter," in which humor does nothing more than deflate emotions and rid the body of excess energy.[23] Spencer translates emotions into levels of nervous energy that are released when transmitted to the muscles and then, ordinarily, expressed as action. The discharge of nervous energy, however, can also happen through laughter, where it offers relief but does not prompt action. For example, rather than expressing any direct anger at an unfair boss, one simply laughs it off. In humor, the basis for an emotion such as anger disappears; having lost its purpose, the energy dissipates through the shallow throat muscles in a chuckle. If still more energy needs to be relieved, it spills over to the muscles connected with diaphragmatic breathing, and if the movements of those muscles do not release all the energy, the remainder moves the arms, legs, and other muscle groups.

Freud's scandalous take on comic relief is much better known. In his 1905 *Jokes and Their Relation to the Unconscious*, Spencer's animal spirits become Freud's repressed sexual and aggressive urges—for example, the kind we might find in the taboo rape joke.[24] Freud argues that laughter comes not directly from the expression of the prohibited emotions but rather from the energy used to repress those emotions—admittedly a byzantine move. Yet if "today almost no scholar in philosophy or psychology explains laughter or humor as a process of releasing pent-up nervous energy,"[25] this wholesale dismissal of relief theory stems from data demonstrating that those who let off steam become angrier, not calmer.

Despite these negative results regarding simple venting, well-known social psychologist James Pennebaker finds a significant correlation between writing about an upsetting or traumatic experience and lasting health benefits.[26] After curiously failing to find the same correlation with music or dance, he argues that the benefits of writing must stem from two factors: the expression of pent-up emotions, which offers temporary benefits, and which might occur even in nonverbal arts; and the use of words to create meaning and understanding out of our raw experiences, which would generate longer-term effects. He concludes that solitary journal writing exemplifies true benefits of cathartic healing.[27]

This psychologist's research, however, is compatible with a larger story of multiple dimensions of relief and catharsis, some of which are exemplified in laughter and humor. As social animals, our affective entwinement with others and our felt status are key to our health, suggesting greater benefits when cathartic processes go beyond solitary sense making. Drawing on recent research on comic relief as well as ancient communal rituals, we examine how a collective catharsis might heal as it empowers by transforming the very field of value that we inhabit.

We begin to explore this transformative process through comic relief's impact on what psychologist Daniel Stern describes as the feel of being alive, and terms vitality affect.[28] Vitality along with other affects are typically considered felt aspects of emotion, while full-fledged emotions also contain prominent belief components and can be more easily verbalized.[29] The feel of being alive, more than just sensations of pleasure or pain, appears through tonal qualities, timbres, and a sheer force expressed through intensities and rhythms of movement.[30] Stern traces his understanding of vitality affect to Freud's theory of psychic energy, which is also significant to our own foray into the comic. An expression of psychic energy plays a pivotal role in Freud's interpretation of comic relief as release, which in turn recalls Lord Shaftsbury's explanation of laughter as the release of animal spirits.

Other philosophers and theorists have suggested the further relevance of vitality affect for aspects of humor. Around the time of Freud, philosopher Henri Bergson explained laughter as a reawakening of an élan vital deadened in man becoming machine, seemingly predicting Chaplin's *Modern Times*.[31] This association of laughter with revitalizing affects appears again in American philosopher Susanne Langer's 1953 *Feeling and Form*.[32] Most importantly, Audre Lorde invokes a life force, which she terms eros, and traces the joy expressed through creative activities such as poetry and dance as well as laughter.[33] Although Lorde doesn't explore humor, just a generation earlier, literary scholar Northrop Frye had declared the mythic Greek figure of Eros to be the presiding spirit and driving force of theatric and film comedy.[34] In contrast to the Stoic use of humor for a turtle-like defense and turn of the self inward, the laughter of a Lordian eros presses animal spirits outward, but now less as release than a force for connecting mind to body and self to other.

If for Lorde this élan vital can be fostered and communicated in dance, nonverbal arts too might have some dimension of cathartic power that begins in the physiology of the healthy belly laugh. Infectious laughter can spread its revitalizing force across audiences, offering some semblance of relief even when those laughing don't get the verbal content of the joke. That feeling of being alive was something glimpsed but not grasped by Kant, who observed that the physical cause of laughter is found in the relaxation of the gut through the expulsion of air, which may be in part true; but he misses the significance of this gut reaction when he then dismisses humor as about "nothing" at all.[35] This nothing seems to have been the only way that a top-heavy theorist could locate laughter's visceral force. Feelings of aliveness travel through our bodies and even from body to body through rhythms of movement. When we experience tension, breathing shifts to the upper chest and becomes shallow and rapid. When we are relaxed, breathing occurs more fully and deeply from the abdomen. Deeper breathing carries more oxygen to the organs, stimulating the parasympathetic nervous system. While tension and anxiety keep you up in your head, the parasympathetic system promotes a state of calmness together with enhanced feelings of connectedness of mind and body.[36]

This physiology challenges the Stoic's mental amusement, which is supposed to distance the mind from the body. Even the Stoic's controlled chuckle and smile might lend themselves to a greater degree of connection with the body than has been thought. Accounts of chakra in laugh-based yoga underscore such connectivity. First, there is the chortle laugh, which is centered in the head and throat; second is the chuckle, which is situated in the heart; and third the guffaw, or belly laugh. Each is said to benefit a distinct energy center, with the throat-based chortle improving capacities for communication, the chuckle lending itself to feelings of inner calm, and the belly laugh releasing one from fear and generating a sense of empowerment.[37] Laughter does not just release tension as predicted by the standard model of relief. It is not just venting. It gathers and circulates positive energy, what the Chinese term qi, for a model of relief as flow and regeneration.

The physiological benefits of laughter take us to one meaning of what Aristotle called catharsis. In ancient Greek, this term refers both to religious rituals of purification and to medicinal purges of bodily toxins. We return to this complex notion in our discussion of emotions later in this chapter, but here we note that simple purging or perhaps even purification can be experienced in the raw physicality of comic relief. Deeper and more powerful breaths may lead to the "more efficient excretion of bodily toxins" through the lungs.[38] The belly laugh may also enhance a near-spiritual sense of well-being through the release of endorphins, which act like opiates by reducing emotional and physical pain and inducing a sense of calm or even euphoria.[39]

Whereas comic relief is typically thought to offer a momentary reprieve from pain and sorrow, in fact laughter bolsters the long-term functioning of the cardiovascular and immune systems. It affects regions of the brain that regulate emotion (by suppressing stress hormones), and it activates the brain's memory center, the hippocampus, thus explaining why memorable moments may involve laughter. The memory of past events reconstructed through humor or ridicule may function to drive out noxious forces that colonize our psyches, further enhancing basic feelings of vitality. Moreover, such moments of laughter may strengthen our sense of connection with others. Recall that when rats are tickled by lab researchers, they emit a chirping sound that is believed to correspond to the human laugh.[40] Tickling these rats increased their oxytocin levels, leading to enhanced bonding between the rats and their lab partners—a new kind of rat pack.

Other things can also increase oxytocin levels. Critchley, while dismissing it as vulgar, notes that as "a bodily phenomenon, laughter invites comparison with similar convulsive phenomena like orgasm."[41] This comparison raises the question, to what degree is the science of laughter all that different from the science of the orgasm? Psychologist Julie Holland suggests that very little is different. Much like the conclusions we have drawn about the belly laugh, she observes that "orgasms are good for you." That's another no-brainer; for example, they too help you live longer by improving your cardiovascular system. But it is the mental benefits that most intrigue Holland. Even in the early stages of sexual pleasure, neurotransmitters turn on the brain's pleasure center. Endorphins that reduce pain are coupled with the release of the love hormone oxytocin. As Holland puts it, "Climax itself owes its mind-bending effects to the triple threat of oxy, endorphins, and PEA, the hallucinogen-like brain chemical, which just might make you feel like you are really 'way out there' when climaxed." This "trippy, out-of-body experience" may include a combination of crying and laughing; it may also "engender tremendous feelings of openness, trust, and bonding."[42]

But feminists have long known that orgasms are good for you, in much the same way our research reveals the importance of comic relief. Scientific discourse, in contrast, has not always been so willing to embrace the benefits, especially of the female orgasm. Instead, much like laughter, it was supposed to have its place. In the late nineteenth century, even male adolescents troubled with acne were admonished for what was then seen as the cause—"'sexual derangement' such as masturbation or promiscuity" as well as simply "impure or lascivious thoughts." As Joan Jacobs Brumberg suggests, "Each agonizing new blemish was read as a sign of moral failure, a situation that created deep anxiety in respectable middle-class homes with adolescent sons and daughters." Thus, "many people in this era believed that marriage—the only acceptable outlet for sexual expression—cured acne."[43] Even worse, for women, the problem was linked with hysteria. As in the case of those unruly outbursts constricted to the laughing barrel, dirty thoughts, like the dirty body, were not welcome in plain sight and instead were muffled in favor of the "modesty of the chuckle or the humble smirk" that cerebral humorists are willing to recognize.

What do you do with the cynic who doesn't get it? Perhaps you show them how it's done. In Rob Reiner's 1989 romantic comedy, *When Harry Met Sally,* Meg Ryan plays the optimistic Sally Albright, who for most of the film appears as the sunny girl next door. This is why her over-the-top and very public rendition of a fake orgasm comes as such a surprise to movie audiences. Yet a comic reversal becomes the most effective way to teach her protagonist a thing or two about female capabilities and give moviegoers some belly laughs of their own. Billy Crystal plays the carefree cynic Harry Burns, who reads the last page of every book first just in case he dies so at least he knows how it ends. His postdivorce self has led him into a downward spiral and a habit of love 'em and leave 'em one-night stands. Eventually Sally confronts what she considers to be Harry's annoying sexual nonchalance: "So what do you do with these women? Just get out of bed and leave?" she complains. A confused Harry can't figure out why she is getting so upset. "This is not about you." Yet Sally snaps back: "You are a human affront to all women and I am a woman." With confidence, he boasts, "I don't hear anyone complaining." And that's when Sally realizes Harry's inability to tell real female sexual pleasure from surface theatrics. Sitting in a crowded Lower East Side delicatessen, Sally precedes to prove her point with deeper and deeper erotic breaths, and rhythmic moaning. Tossing her hair back and forth, she acts out her pretend moment of ecstasy, banging on the table, screaming in orgasmic joy, "Yes, yes, yes." The climax and real comic relief does not stop with Sally's performance but when a nearby middle-aged woman turns her gaze to the waiter and says, "I'll have what she's having." Humor may on occasion be just a cerebral moment, but the belly laugh, like a table-pounding orgasm, offers relief that's hard to ignore.[44]

Two Prominent Conceptions of Catharsis: Allopathic and Homeopathic

Humor may not only enhance our immediate feelings of being alive and of connection with others; it can also strengthen our sense of agency and enable us to challenge abusive forms of social power. To be sure, we have seen humor used as a weapon against the vulnerable, giving rise to a pyramid of oppression. Insensitive jokes prepare the ground for further forms of degradation and cruelty. But that kind of power flows in more than one direction. As a means for shaming or humiliating others, ridicule raises questions with regard to the distribution of shame in society.[45] The emotional work of humor can also be used to counter the impact of wrongful shaming. Indeed, a full cathartic processing of emotions through humor might heal us together with the body politic.

Aristotle offers the classic defense of the serious arts through their general function as cathartic. Plato's *Republic* had argued that tragic and comic arts are a danger to society and should be banned. Comic techniques of malicious ridicule as well as simple clowning are said to harm citizens by lowering their status and value. Against political threats of censorship, Aristotle argues that some kinds of comic and tragic are valuable. Good art, he notes, empties the rational mind of inappropriate and/or irrational emotions while stabilizing society, and in this sense, it is cathartic. As suggestive as Aristotle's account of art is, there are problems with his version of catharsis. If we are visceral and indeed social creatures down to our ethical core, as many psychologists currently argue, catharsis would seem to require more than the purging of problematic emotions if it is to counter toxic environments.[46]

Feminist humor invites a reexamination of the politics of catharsis. Raucous laughs can stir up the social atmosphere, altering the very air we breathe. In contrast to a mental catharsis, subversive humor may reorient an affective and emotional comportment with others and instigate real change in the biosocial climate. Such a transformation demands a seismic conversion of the kind that comes when women called sluts take on the heavy weight of shame. When we feel shame, we often feel dirty, but feminist humor is not about just escaping such toxins or simply cleaning them up. Rather, it is about transforming, deep down, negative energy into a political tour de force. The #MeToo campaign stirs up collective feelings of disgust and outrage. Feminist comedians demonstrate that they know how to add fire to the fury, not denying or moderating anger but instead steering it away from toxic self-righteousness and toward a powerful social movement. Consider how a British group of Muslim comedians and actors use the alchemy of humor mixed with a fumerism detox to address period shaming. In a video clip, women are relentlessly confronted with the question "why aren't you fasting?" during Ramadan, when those menstruating are excluded. After having enough, a woman unleashes her frustration—and a rush of primal forces—by daring to utter the forbidden "p" word, then throwing an Always pad at an accuser, who collapses against a background of booming Germanic music, Karl Orff's "O Fortuna." The Orff cantata is known for its fierce conjuring of primal forces, along with its aim for sexual and holistic balance—forces we appropriate for our own analysis of catharsis.[47]

Let's take a look in more detail at the belly laugh's visceral force in action as we uncover more layers of catharsis. In 2008, *Saturday Night Live*'s comedic duo, Tina Fey and Amy Poehler, along with Casey Wilson and Kristen Wiig, took aim at drug companies with their own satirical advertisement for the made-up Annuale, a miracle pill for the girl on the go who simply doesn't have time for her period every month. By consuming a mere "forty-four weeks of active pills [that] keep you on a constant stream of hormones" and reduce periods to a once-a-year event, you too will get a grip on your body and emotions. Smirks turn into belly laughs as Fey, in a mockingly rational tone, announces the Frankensteinian list of side effects that will "make you want to hold onto your fucking hat." The skit erupts with images of out-of-control menstruating women as the once natural cycles of the female body unleash a monstrous purge of toxins thanks to big pharma's attempt to subject them to rational control. Like big philosophy's emphasis on regaining control of the rational self, big pharma makes the emotional messiness and the dirty taboos of the female menstrual cycle a subversive vehicle for feminist humor.[48]

As feminist humor breaks up taboos that have shamed and silenced women for centuries, it raises a challenge for the intellectual take on catharsis. Recall that for the misogynist ancient Greeks, what is really dirty are women's bodies and their emotions, which are what are presumably in need of purging or purification as well as cerebral control. In fact, as it turns out, the ancient Greek term *catharsis* hints at a central role for women's cycles in its root meaning, suggesting yet another meaning for our model of relief as flow. Even Aristotle's brief mention of catharsis in the *Poetics*'s discussion of tragedy (his work on comedy has been lost) refers back to his earlier uses of the term for menstruation. This connection was uncovered in 1988 by philosopher John McCumber, who suggests that in ancient piggish drama, the tragic fear is about becoming *miaros*, "literally covered with blood," as were women during their monthly cycles.[49] McCumber speculates on the meaning of this so-called state of disgrace for that culture. He argues that in ancient male-dominated culture, to be disgraced "is to be 'defined' by something ignoble, and unworthy of a life of the city and its higher arts, and the political freeborn men of rank, to be worthy only of a life in the villages, where comedy, in contrast to great tragic drama, is said to have developed and belong."[50] McCumber then states his key claim: "The psychological catharsis effected by tragedy thus mirrors, in the male, the biological process undergone monthly by the female."[51] Tragic drama, he suggests, is a process of "social menstruation or catharsis. In it, something in itself good but present to excess is driven out of the social organism."[52] For the ancient cultural elites, this excess is readily associated with the second sex and comic buffoons. When it comes to women and laughs, a little goes a long way.

McCumber's attention to women and buffoons offers an important corrective to the traditional oversight of the root meaning of the word *catharsis*, as glimpsed in Martha Nussbaum's neo-Aristotelian account of the emotions.[53] Nussbaum, following other scholars, traces the etymology of *catharsis* to a Greek word for cleaning up what is dirty or muddy, and remarks that by the time of Aristotle's *Poetics*, the word's meaning extended to a clarifying mental process. She argues that Aristotle brings in the notion of catharsis to understand how emotions might be useful for rational cognition and perception if properly trained. In this tradition, only well-behaved emotions are intrinsic elements of well-being and happiness. As Nussbaum explains, "We know . . . that for Aristotle appropriate responses are intrinsically valuable parts of good character and can, like good intellectual response, help to constitute the refined 'perception' which is the best sort of human judgement."[54] Even seemingly irrational emotions like fear, if properly trained, can be significant constituents of how we perceive and judge the world. Nussbaum's commentary on Aristotle shares a widespread feminist interest in the role of emotions for human life. However, her emphasis on the achievement of clear perception favors cerebral processes in this account of catharsis at the expense of its biosocial force. To be sure, cathartic practices can offer a clear perception, even a moral vision. But from the perspective of the unwashed, much more is at stake.

The inferior female body remains as a constant theme in the ancient tradition. While overlooking McCumber's original research, Elizabeth Belfiore's 1992 study of catharsis in classical tragedy reinforces the same central tenet: "Aristotle most frequently uses 'katharsis' for the ejaculation of the menstrual fluid . . . , which is also a removal of a harmful material."[55] She notes that for Aristotle "the female is a deformed male, and that her reproductive discharge has closer connections with disease than does the male's" too often revered ejaculation.[56] One has to wonder what the cathartic process might look like without the misogynist distortion.

Belfiore pursues the analogy between the use of catharsis in medicine and in the dramatic arts. She introduces two notions of the cathartic process, homeopathic and allopathic, both of which are distinct from the hydraulic model of release found in later theories of comic relief. Before investigating the two kinds of medicine, she explains that for the Greeks, the body's cathartic riddance of menstrual fluid accompanies a sense of shame that is necessary for the stability of the prevailing social order. By analogy, she suggests, ancient drama would cultivate that proper degree of shame by ridding the social body of toxic excesses. But for Aristotle, she adds, the therapeutic process of drama does not function homeopathically, as mistakenly assumed; it functions allopathically.

In homeopathic medicine, inoculation reduces the risk of pathology by injecting a small amount of a disease in order to build up immunity. We can find an example of homeopathic catharsis in Ralph Ellison's 1985 essay, "An Extravagance of Laughter." Ellison illustrates how the targets of Jim Crow racism would use homeopathic humor to produce a tougher skin.[57] Slinging ridiculing racial epithets at each other served as a means of surviving antiblack rituals of racialized humiliation. This humor takes that self-irony—typically understood as a form of humility or as rolling with the punches—in another direction: toward self-strengthening. This self-strengthening also may explain the reappropriation of insults, as in the use of the N-word in hip-hop culture and among black stand-ups. Analogously, the prominent use of the word "slut," together with the flagrant display of "tits and ass" accompanying protest in the SlutWalk movement, seems to function to inoculate against misogynist objectification and humiliation. This is humor as homeopathic medicine.

Allopathic catharsis functions differently. A vice—out-of-control arrogance, unchecked privilege—is not likely to be cured by small doses of the same sense of entitlement. In contrast to homeopathy, an allopathic catharsis would directly oppose the vice of hubris with fear or shame. Comic ridicule might call the target back to common social ideals.

The problem for feminists is that this all assumes that there are such common ideals—a problematic assumption in a misogynistic culture. To be sure, both these medicinal notions of catharsis are useful for understanding salutary aspects of the tragic or comic arts. Both offer practices for self-care and social stability. Anyone who has experienced a flash of shame or embarrassment through ridicule knows that the threat of laughter can curb an overblown sense of entitlement, potentially warding off hubristic acts. Similarly, homeopathic humor, as in the trading of insults in a subculture, may shield one against the blows of oppression from dominant cultures. But our question has been how to bring down warped social ideals, not live with them. Let us step outside the legacy of a misogynist culture and the two prominent definitions of catharsis to consider a third—one that lends nasty women the power to tap into their flow and overturn oppressive norms. We call this third type collective catharsis, and we understand it to contain both homeopathic elements (reclaiming the word "slut") and allopathic elements (ridicule), but also something more.

"Dirty Woman" and a Collective Catharsis

Some decades ago, anthropologist Mary Douglas ago defined dirt as that which is out of place.[58] What if the dirt that was out of place did not turn into shame, something that should be cleaned up or hidden from view, but rather was celebrated with a female body and attitude that didn't know when to quit when it came to raucous comic reversals. Neofeminist mixed-race social media sensation Amber Rose takes on the double standard that has long celebrated men's sexual conquests but blamed and shamed women for rape while condemning any female embrace of sexual expression and pleasure as dirty. Rose's *Walk of No Shame* video features the model/actress walking home the morning after a one-night stand "in a little black dress and stilettos with her head held high," greeted with surprising shouts of approval against the backdrop of a pristine suburban neighborhood, complete with white picket fence and nosy neighbors. As she steps out of the house and tugs on her short skirt, she first encounters the milkman, who snappily observes, "Say, it looks to me like you had sex last night!" After hearing her equally proud affirmation, he adds, "Sounds like you are living your best life." Various neighbors who look as though they'd be the judgmental type tell her "congratulations," and an elderly lady suggests that sex with no strings attached ain't "nothing I haven't done before." A father shouts out his car window, "You're an inspiration to my daughter." Even a construction worker applauds her behavior, telling her, "I respect that you enjoyed yourself last night. I think we can all agree—having sex is fun." Finally, in this topsy-turvy world, the mayor gives this morning-after girl the key to the city while exclaiming that they celebrate "your confidence and the choices you make and your ability to celebrate your body." Not missing a beat, Rose accepts the mayor's accolades and reassures her audience that "I always celebrate my body, sometimes twice a day."[59]

In the fall of 2015, as her comedy sketch went viral, Amber Rose became the face of the feminist SlutWalk movement. The initial demonstration encouraged women to dress however they wanted. "Soon the walks spread across the globe, as women in Colombia, India, and South Korea staged their own protests" to create a better world, or a feminist revision of what Mikhail Bakhtin's describes as "a second world and a second life outside officialdom." Recently at what is now an annual SlutWalk festival in Los Angeles, Rose donned a pink "Captain Save a Hoe" superhero cape in a movement that takes on a range of issues, including sexual violence and victim blaming.[60] Heather Jarvis, who helped originate SlutWalk, has embraced Rose's celebrity status and carnival humor—comic strategies featured also in the gay pride movement—as a means to "create some amazing conversations." Jarvis notes that this radical flip in how a woman should behave in public is often criticized. More provocatively, the movement also brings in sex workers, who as a class are often dismissed for their presumably dirty deeds. The movement's original intent "'was about recognizing sex workers as part our community.' At the same time, it 'was very trans-inclusive,'" continues Jarvis. "It was about being gender-inclusive and feminist and intersectional," something often lost in the media, yet "Rose is making sure those complexities are front and center."[61] Looking forward to the second annual SlutWalk in Los Angeles in fall 2016, Rose imagined it to "be a safe place for women to come twerk, go topless or wear pasties, get to know each other as women and understand we're sexual beings." Acknowledging hers is not by any means a movement of perfect angels, she adds: "We all have skeletons in our closets, and we're all allowed to do whatever a man does because *he* doesn't get judged for it."[62] In 2015, the walk "spread to 250 cities across the globe," altering social space so that "now when you google the word 'slut,' SlutWalk comes up!'" revealing the comic makeover of a word that has haunted women for centuries.[63]

When Amber Rose's *Walk of No Shame* went viral, it not only brought about a cosmetic makeover for a word but also released a social movement that allows women to feel good about their bodies while taking back control of their sexuality. The SlutWalk movement uses humor for more than homeopathic self-strengthening. It does something different from an allopathic shaming that appeals to dominant ideals. SlutWalk humor challenges the powers that be by marking as contemptible the social norms themselves. This challenge begins with dissolving the shame targeted at victims in a process that is, in yet a third way, cathartic.

Silvan Tomkins poignantly describes "shame as an inner torment, a sickness of the soul. It does not matter whether the humiliated is shamed by derisive laughter or whether he mocks himself. In any event he feels himself naked, defeated, alienated, lacking in dignity or worth."[64] Ridicule and other forms of shaming wound the self where it is most vulnerable and exposed to others, constituting the most invasive aspect of physical acts of violation, such as rape and sexual abuse.[65] Comic catharsis as found in SlutWalk humor deflects derisive shame away from the self and back toward patriarchal norms and values and acts of misogynistic hubris. Against prevailing social norms, a belly-deep laugh shared with others regenerates pride in the self and the body. It channels via movement politics a sense of communion analogous in some ways to that found in ancient communal rituals of catharsis. A collective catharsis is not just a psychological process but also a biosocial one. SlutWalk's catharsis converts the sickly feeling of isolation and shame into head-held-high pride and a fervent sense of belonging on altered terms. Its humor transforms negative attitudes by recharging the social atmosphere. Here too laughter is medicine.

As medicine, SlutWalk's humor draws from alternative cathartic traditions—not merely classical allopathic or homeopathic but also holistic traditions that reconnect the medicinal with the collective spirit. SlutWalk humor offers a radical version when it destabilizes an intrinsically flawed social order that fosters cultures of rape and slut and body shaming. Understanding this process requires a feminist revamping of the root meaning of catharsis in menstruation. Shaking off taboos that associate the menstrual cycle with bouts of female irrationality, menstruation can be viewed alternatively as a productive process that does not require management by an all too often oppressive social order and capital-R Reason. From the perspective of the women whose social shaming has all too often been sanctioned, cathartic processes would bring not purges or purification of the diseased female but a communal sloughing off of old norms for a renewal and revitalization of the mind, body, and collective animal spirits.

Consider the situation in which women who express themselves as freely as men are often condemned as out-of-control sluts while society turns a blind eye toward male sexual license, boys-will-be-boys antics, and humor as a release for the rational man. This has fostered a rape culture embedded in the foundations of civilization, where men are given permission to violate and ridicule the vulnerable while condemnation turns on the victim, who is blamed and shamed by society. Deeply felt shame in the victim—understood as "debilitating shame"[66] or "contempt"[67]—drains her of energy and verve, diminishes self-esteem along with social position, and paralyzes her as a social agent while leaving her isolated. The "self lives where it exposes itself and where it receives similar exposures from others,"[68] as Silvan Tomkins writes. Alone, these shamed victims can have difficulty countering the physical and mental struggle that they must endure. Shame can leave them feeling as though, ever out of place, they should be hidden from view. Even the fact that one experiences shame can itself feel shameful, inducing a downward spiral of negative emotion.[69] Moreover, there are physical repercussions. One study found that female undergraduate students who reported feelings of body shame also reported more infections and worse health.[70] Other studies link the experience of shame with increased proinflammatory cytokine activity and cortisol.[71] Even the mere intellectual discussion of rape can trigger shame and anxiety, contributing to gastrointestinal illness, and thus disturbances to the gut and in turn the second brain.[72]

As college campuses, social media, and global society engage in serious discourse to dismantle a weighty history of misogyny, we, with due caution, suggest that a new wave of feminist humor that takes aim at rape culture may shake off shame's entrenched mental and physical embodiment. This is not by any means to say that the victims of rape culture just need to simply lighten up and laugh it off. Just laughing it off as though it doesn't matter can lead to an unhealthy dissociation and disconnect. The kind of belly laugh we investigate connects the body and mind, working through biosocial desires and energy levels as even a therapist like Freud might recommend. This laughter, however, is more than a simple relaxing of psychic tension. Cathartic processes' impact on gut-wrenching emotions like shame requires a more holistic approach; it requires an exchange of the "rational" for the "relational" self.[73] As it reconnects us with ourselves, it reconnects us with others. No connection, no catharsis. As a loosely holistic phenomenon, humor realigns the forces in the social field, creating new agents and sites of energy and power. It does not release tension without regenerating life force. Augmented through social media propagation, these changes loop back around to renew, recharge, and revitalize social emotions and thus networked relational lives.

When it comes to new agents and power, there is a plethora of stand-up comedians across social media who are far from perfect, yet whose network of energy has challenged rape culture with those belly laughs that can clear an atmosphere of cruel shaming. Samantha Bee, Wanda Sykes, Adrienne Truscott, Amy Schumer, and Sana Khan, for example, have all turned the old misogynist formula on its head. Performing at New York City Comedy Strip Club in 2017 as part of the Muslim Funny Fest, Khan challenges the idea that Muslim women can't be funny, let alone mock their own culture along with misogyny: "I found out the holy month of Ramadan was happening, for example, because it was trending on Twitter. I did wait until sunset to go down on my boyfriend. You guys, I felt really bad that he was fasting and I wasn't—you know, but not bad enough to swallow."[74]

Schumer's widely viewed *Football Nights* (2015) reveals how a rape joke can be reappropriated to take on a hegemonic culture. It is set in a small Texas town where football is everything; Schumer plays the wife of the high school's new coach, who plans on doing things differently. When he insists his players commit to a strategy that includes "No Raping!!!" a confused high schooler reminds the coach, "We play football?" Other disillusioned high school boys ask if they could at least "rape at away games? What if it's Halloween and she's dressed like a sexy cat? . . . What if she thinks it's rape but I don't. What if my Mom is the DA and won't prosecute, can I rape? What if she is drunk and has a slight reputation and no one will believe her?" Or what if "the girl said yes to me the other day about something else?" It is not just the boys but the entire town that is outraged. Even two elderly women march by the coach's house and spit on his lawn. "How are our boys supposed to celebrate a win? Or blow off steam if they lose?" After all, it is not just men who think that boys need hydraulic relief. As the coach's jaded wife, Schumer offers her husband nonsensical advice: "You can't take a wet mule to a hot corn oven." With each folksy lie she pretends to believe, her wineglass, like Pinocchio's nose, grows to a ridiculous size. The last ironic slap comes as the frustrated coach tries to figure out why his team isn't getting the message about rape as he motivates them for the big game: "Football is about violently dominating anyone that stands between you and what you want." Above all else, "you gotta get yourself into the mind-set that you are gods, and that you are entitled to this. The other team isn't going to just lay down and give it to you. You've got to go out there and take it!"

The brilliance of this sketch is that it does not just turn the tables to laugh at the naivete of a handful of high school boys who have never been taught any different and who lack even a trace of shame. Such humor exposes the deeper hypocrisy and points out where the real shame should reside when the well-intentioned coach simultaneously chastises his players on rape while defining football in its terms. It targets an atmosphere deeply saturated in toxic misogyny, with everyone in the community complicit for the sake of a winning team (and the rational man). In making rape culture—not its victim—as the butt of the joke, belly laughs can rock the foundations of a misogynistic civilization while liberating women from slut shame.

Humor offers not a cure-all but a chance for a change. Amber Rose's viral video for the SlutWalk movement propagates waves of humor targeting rape culture and a toxic climate of shame. Its discordant humor promotes a catharsis of negative emotions like despair, fear, and shame, to draw on an ancient Stoic motif, but it does so in very different terms. The Stoic seeks to rise above these emotions and cultivate an elevated sense of tranquility. Stoicism has developed genuinely useful therapeutic techniques of positive mental visualization and interior dialogue with the aim of achieving that tranquility. But such therapy has no use for pride or even hope. Their fatalistic wit detaches the rational mind from the murky politics of biosocial life, leaving everything pretty much as it is. Rather than retreat to a solitary realm of tranquility and control, feminist belly laughs risk it all to unsettle a biosocial field loaded with distorted values and perceptions, generating not just private images and interior dialogue but media-propelled images and amazing conversations. In the end, these raucous laughs perform a sense of renewal, as does a good social orgasm, so that we might "have what she's having" and, like Amber Rose, celebrate our bodies "sometimes twice a day."

5

Solidaric Empathy and a Prison Roast with Jeff Ross

I think the reason I can get away with roasting my way
through life is because it comes from a place of love.
—Jeff Ross, *Jeff Ross Roasts Criminals*

The lack of empathetic connection with prisoners obscures the tragedy of mass incarceration. Empathy plays a key role in our interactions with others, determining who is met with warm compassion
instead of cold indifference. It shapes public opinion and policy. Yet
ordinarily we find it difficult to connect with those who are dissimilar
to ourselves. Further, differences in social status, as well as conflict and the stereotypes that perpetuate conflict and social stratification, block empathy, and restrict the scope of moral and political
concern. Prisoners are especially dismissed through stereotypes as
violent thugs, making it difficult for many people to establish any
emotional connection with and concern for even the most basic prisoner rights, let alone more radical reforms. Humor, however, offers an
unexpected clue as to how we might break down walls of indifference
or even hostility. Humor can be used as a radical vehicle for establishing seemingly impossible connections.

Comedy Central's "Roastmaster General," Jeff Ross, chose
Texas's Brazos county jail and the Boston police department to
bring some serious laughs and unexpected changes of heart to captive audiences both inside and outside prison walls. As the two
performances—*Jeff Ross Roasts Criminals* (2015) and *Jeff Ross*

Roasts Cops (2016)—continue to circulate via Comedy Central and YouTube, they illustrate the potential for media events to channel empathy across indifferent or even antagonistic audiences.[1] To be sure, this white male comic is in many ways an imperfect vehicle for establishing an emotional bond between privileged media audiences and the incarcerated. Ross risks perpetuating the very stereotypes that need to be dismantled and yet he also puts them out there to keep it real. Through his authenticity, together with his advowedly privileged social identity and celebrity status, he is able to reach a large demographic, including those who are unlikely victims of mass incarceration and who may lack any sense of shared humanity with prisoners. The opening frame of his 2015 performance powerfully points out that there is something wrong with a system that contains more unfree black Americans than the institution of slavery did in 1850, but this history lesson is just where the comic's work begins. The humor of someone we laugh with can bring life to simple facts and statistics. While not romanticizing the inmates at the Brazos jail, Ross's humor performs more than a temporary break from the stric-tures of prison life that he claims to offer. The comic's empathetic humor takes the form of an entertaining roast that toys with stereo-types to break through them and reach his viewing audiences.

Roasts are typically inclusive and have a celebratory tone; to roast prisoners is thus already to elevate their stature to someone you laugh with, not simply at. By seeing prisoners as worthy of a roast, Ross honors those too often viewed by his audiences as exiles, anointing them as members of the larger community. The roast is a major device for creating community through the comedic use of a type of play-fighting that carefully balances ridicule with empathy. Like bouts of play-fighting among siblings, teasing and taunting can be a form of flirtation and fun, generating camaraderie. But more than sibling teases, the empathetic humor we explore in the prisoner roast exemplifies the radical potential to cross class, race, and political boundaries. Its derisive laughter breaks down bars of separation often seen as impenetrable and resistant to ordinary forms of empathy; it creates surprising moments of intimacy even in zones of intense con-flict. Unlike the ordinary use of empathy, this mix of empathy with soft ridicule offers a potential for solidarity while avoiding claims to understand those whose experiences and social position are in tension with one's own. A willingness to play or to throw the ball with someone too often demonized and dismissed makes the roastmaster's open-ended dialogue techniques politically worth playing with.

Setting the Stage

"Armed with nothing but [his comedic] insults," Jeff Ross entered Cell Block 3B Maximum Security with no intent to proselytize or bring salvation, but simply to find connections wherever he could. In his gut, he must have known that he was messing with a conflict zone, tampering with multiple structures of power and animosity. When a petite prison guard named Courtney Waller reassures Ross, "You don't have to worry—I will protect you," he wonders how, especially given that she has no gun, or indeed a weapon of any kind. Signaling an awareness of his own privileged position, Ross, in a mock-nervous tone, jokes, "So do you just *ask* people politely to stop beating me?" then teasing, "If I die, it's on you." Waller declares, without hesitation, "We will die together," and as Ross announces they are "blood brothers and sisters," they pound their fists together in solidarity.

Inside the cell block, Ross finds conflicting groups of blood brothers with attitudes toward him that range from amusement to indifference. As Ross makes the rounds, shaking hands, asking "What's up?" he crosses boundaries that seem impermeable. First, he chats with black inmates, where his nice-to-meet-you's are followed with a sincere and yet to-the-point inquiry: "What are you in for?" One inmate explains, "I assaulted a police officer" because "they tried to take me to jail for something I didn't do." Ross, with a touch of warmth, adds, "You didn't want to go," yet the comedian cannot resist a playful tone of mockery when he rhetorically asks, "Who won that argument?"

Moments later, this self-identified Jew finds himself face to face with the "Dirty White Boys," "a prison gang with close ties to the Aryan Brotherhood and the Nazi Low Riders." Undeterred, Ross poignantly asks, "Who's the baddest motherfucker?" as he approaches a bare-chested prisoner covered in muscles, swastikas, and the words "Texas Made." "Does anyone ever get offended by your tattoos?"

Ross inquires. After getting a sheepish nod, Ross wonders, "How long are you in for?" When the inmate admits he will be serving ninety-nine years, Ross, with absolute seriousness, jokes, "It should fucking be six million for every Jew that died in the Holocaust." The inmate looks momentarily shocked and displeased, but he is quickly swept up with the raucous laughter of his prison mates, causing this baddest motherfucker with ties to the Aryan Brotherhood to humbly smile and acquiesce. A playful antagonism with his audience proliferates as Ross begins his onstage performance, taunting some volunteers waiting to be roasted by pronouncing them "the ugliest police lineup I've ever seen." With a little warm-up, he singles out the infamous prison gang, inquiring, "Is this where the white dudes hang out?" As the prisoners let loose deep belly laughs, he goads "the fucking whites-only section" by wishing them a "Happy Hanukkah." They too burst out in the kind of laughter that shakes the prison's walls.

Humor serves as an exemplary vehicle of what we might call a solidaric mode of empathy—an empathy that can travel across conflicting social groups, as different as guards and their prisoners, or as jailed neo-Nazi gangs and Jews, to embrace viewing audiences. In laughing with others who are laughing at themselves, we find ourselves unexpectedly unlocking streams of amity for those whom we may or may not be able to identify with. While straight satire and ridicule can subvert or reinforce lines of power, empathetic humor laced with playful mockery that forces all to expose their vulnerabilities may offer more than just a momentary escape from prison life. This humor has the potential to de-escalate tensions and reveal the humanity of mortal enemies, thus opening up across social divisions a horizontal field of fellow feeling. In this volatile field, comedy and raunchy roasts may begin to redress heavy histories of social tensions. Such effervescent moments of deterred hostility transformed into shared laughter should not be dismissed as politically vacuous. The Roastmaster General reveals how laughing it up and taking one's turn as the butt of the joke offers a compelling glimpse of fellowship, and can do so without recreating indispensable enemies. This empathetic laughter that embraces real talk offers the chance of attitudinal change right down to the viscera of the second brain. All the more in this age of mass media, when social platforms can hold anyone hostage, laughter can burst through prison walls and insulating bubbles. In much the way that an earlier era of social justice flowered with the soulful music of the 1960s and 1970s, the emotional engine of social change over the last couple of decades has grown much out of the truth tellers in stand-up comedy.[2] Indeed, since the 1990s, and with ever greater intensity after 9/11, U.S. culture has entered an age of satire and irony, but one mixed on occasion with empathy too.

The Sympathy Revolution and Humor

Modern humor's association with sympathy provides a backdrop for the more recent rise of empathy in stand-up comedy. The history of modern humor's dominant strains, American intellectual and cultural historian Daniel Wickberg tells us, begins with the eighteenth century's sympathy revolution and then changes with the rise of corporate liberalism.[3] During the eighteenth century's cultural revolution, an egalitarian wave of political change altered laughter's predominant tone from ridicule and wit to a sympathetic amusement at the oddities of other people. Then in the later nineteenth century, the ground for mainstream humor shifts again with the rise of corporate culture. Corporate liberalism encouraged adaptability to the social order through the development of what has colloquially since been referred to as "having a sense of humor."[4] To have a sense of humor required an attitude of self-transcendence that one finds in the refusal to take oneself too seriously. The use of a corporate-friendly and politically liberal capacity for humor was thought to result in not only a more efficient workplace but also a tolerant political community by offering a sense of proportion and perspective. Thus, a good sense of humor guides the worker and citizen to transcend bothersome annoyances and avoid conflict. Wickberg further insists that the advantages of learning to work well with others applied not only to white men in professional or working-class jobs but also to ethnic minorities who, when facing prejudicial stereotypes and belittling ridicule, learn to roll with the punches and avoid conflict. No doubt, under these circumstances those who confront difficult situations rather than avoiding them could readily earn a reputation for lacking humor, and as the buzzkill or killjoy are set up for a fall.[5]

The sympathy revolution of the bourgeois class may be traced to Adam Smith's 1759 *Theory of Moral Sentiments*, but its association with laughter, albeit in a rational and orderly form, was gradual.[6] Historians contrast bourgeois humor with an older European politics of ridicule aimed at social inferiors. Ridicule was a primary tool for the preceding age of satire from 1660 to more or less 1800.[7] Cultural studies scholar Linda Hutcheon suggests that at that time, satire generally (though not always) functioned on the side of authority, ridiculing nonnormative behavior and reinforcing aristocratic cultures.[8] As the story goes, these forms of ridicule gave way during the breakdown of feudalism as European elites engaged in refined games of cleverness that they called wit. In contrast to ridicule, the exercise of wit did not aim to attack or abuse others, and for this reason, its general cultivation struck many as an advance of modern egalitarian culture. Wit operates through juxtaposed ideas and images, such as wordplay based on the principle of incongruity and intellectual surprise. Nonetheless, Wickberg discerns that in exhibiting the successful practitioner's verbal dexterity and mental superiority over their rivals, the display of dry wit declared one's membership and status among the postfeudal intellectual elite in high society.[9] Gradually, the egalitarian leveling of the revolutionary era weakened the presumed high status of the "useless post-feudal" class of intellects, with its air of a bygone aristocracy. The aristocratic cultures gave way to the sympathy revolution, ushering in a bourgeoisie with an alternative sensibility of cultivating not ridicule or dry wit but rather sympathetic feelings—although only those deemed appropriately rational.[10]

Wickberg explains that by the early nineteenth century, the rising white middle class believed that the cultivation of humor deepened feelings of sympathy by perceiving other's foibles or laughable features through their "concrete particularity."[11] At least in theory, it was difficult to ridicule another as inferior when one came to know them not as an abstraction or stereotype but as a "whole person," someone with experiences and flaws much like one's own.[12]

In reality, there's an undercurrent of unaddressed tensions in

dominant modes of nineteenth-century humor, signaling deep problems with its alleged egalitarianism. The sympathy that may have
fostered delight in the eccentricities of others among the white bourgeoisie nonetheless threatened to reduce those others to stereotypes.
Think of the sympathy cultivated by Harriet Beecher Stowe toward
"Uncle Tom," the properly subservient black man in *Uncle Tom's
Cabin*, the novel said to have launched the Civil War. The use of
such figures, even if meant to be sympathetic, perpetuates minstrel
humor. Minstrel humor was not just sideshow. It was the vicious core
of American humor from slavery through our new Jim Crow era, as
film director Spike Lee exposes in his didactic satire, *Bamboozled*
(2000).[13] The dogma nonetheless prevailed that while laughter had
taken delight in unexpected incongruities, now humor developed as
a valued capacity for the sympathetic and yet distanced perception
of oddities in other people. When we laugh at others, we see their
incoherencies without resorting to demeaning ridicule.

Then, in a new twist on the modern theme, the spotlight of
humor focused not on other people but on the self. Or as Wickberg
elaborates, from the 1870s to the 1930s, corporate and managerial
capitalism gave birth to a new type of self with the capacity to not
take itself too seriously.[14] A sense of humor came to require the sympathetic capacity to see oneself from an external point of view, and
thus as an object from the perspective of others. The light of humor
now shines warmly on one's own incongruities.

Wickberg traces the development of this capacity for self-
distancing to the changing world of the marketplace, where men had
to learn to see themselves from the viewpoint of others and to understand the motives of an "ever-shifting terrain of strangers."[15] In this
"constant navigating back and forth between the self as object and as
subject," laughter shifts between sympathetic humor aimed toward
tolerating the other to an elevated sense of self.[16] Of course, the modern workplace demanded the ability to adapt to a range of personalities and problems with a degree of distanced sympathy. Yet having
a sense of humor primarily enhanced the ability to separate oneself
from overly emotional reactions to workplace pettiness and conflict
in the name of efficiency and getting along. Like an industrial work
ethic, having a sense of humor, and thus a degree of detachment,

would come to define the modern man. Indeed, self-transcending humor would come to serve a modern and postmodern culture "in which estrangement, standing outside of oneself, is the preferred stance," Wickberg comments.[17] The epitome of a refined sense of humor lies not in the hearty laugh at or even with others, but in the capacity to smile at oneself.[18]

To be sure, transcendent humor as a type of escape and elevation could prove to be a healthy response when one is required to accept an unalterable situation. This quasi-Stoic humor of self-transcendence may well have been the quintessentially twentieth-century approach to the horrors of world wars and economic collapse, which were viewed through dark comedy as inevitable absurdities of civilization. It certainly offers a much-needed elevated stance in the face of the absurd. Yet what Freud by the 1920s had located as the reemergence of a Stoic strain of humor and Wickberg characterizes in one of its modern guises as bourgeois self-irony has its political limitations. The distancing mechanism of corporate-friendly humor, which functioned to maintain the status quo, diminishes the significant yet problematic role of sympathy for others that was prominent in humor during the earlier bourgeois era.

Although the earlier kind of sympathy may have generated a degree of social understanding and bonds of connection across society, it failed to disrupt underlying patterns of hierarchy and oppression that infected the status quo. Not only did that sympathy serve as a ready vehicle for racial or class stereotypes ("Uncle Tom"), and thus a cover for the minstrel nightmare of America; it was also gendered exclusively masculine. This gendering of sympathy not only limited its scope but also restricted its range of meaning. As Wickberg explains, true sympathy was said to demand the high-level mental capacity to take the perspective of others as well as to view how others perceive oneself in contrast to an emotion-based empathy linked with the intellectually weak. That allegedly lower type of sympathy, presumed by the Victorians to be a female virtue, was not the type of sympathy to be cultivated in the public sphere; nor was it viewed as necessitating a sense of humor. (Incidentally, the higher type is consistent with current efforts to engineer an "artificial sympathy" as part of the artificial intelligence of companion robots.[19])

While men were said to possess the mental capacity for perceiving the perspective of the other with objectivity and thereby transcend the affects and social identities of the self, women were thought to be limited by their emotions. As Wickberg explains the alleged difference, "The sympathetic imagination allowed for intellectual breadth, an understanding of complexity, a guide to the motives of others," not mere emotional reaction. "Sympathy allows for at least the affectation of detachment from the narrow concerns of the circumscribed self. It was this idea of sympathy, as tied to humor, that was invoked when women were said to lack a sense of humor. . . . Emotional identification that was characteristic of women's nature, then, was not the sympathy of intellectual and perceptual self-transcendence necessary for male negotiation of the public sphere."[20] Wickberg also observes that as Victorian gender ideology diminished in the early twentieth century, one is less likely to hear that women lack a sense of humor. This claim does not completely fade, even if now it is more likely to have been replaced with the charge that feminists lack a sense of humor.[21]

Yet as we know, feminists, along with other subversives, not only laugh but laugh differently. Ross's humor joins with that of Wanda Sykes, Ali Wong, and Hannah Gadsby, stand-ups who have altered the comic stance to mix laughter with modes of empathy and a didactic intent. The trait of humor that lends a flexible sociability pacifying corporate culture can also serve a critical vibe, but only if it undergoes a bit of a transformation. Old-school renditions of this trait are rooted in a gendered legacy. Cast as a mental quality, having a sense of humor was believed to be beyond the capacities of women and other weaker minds, whose emotions and passions would blind them from taking rational aim. A detached reflection mixed with proper modes of sympathy and self-irony went along with dismissing those seemingly so caught up in their emotions they couldn't see straight. In other words, the type of detached humor prominently hailed as important for the American democratic ethos, with its healthy business climate, can hold thoughts and actions captive, especially when it comes to those perceived as humorless social underlings, or worse yet, enemies. We understand that emotions can run too hot and can undermine human connections and conversations. At the same time, a warm sense of empathy may intimate a welcomed recognition of a distant other. Operating beyond the reason/emotion binary and its jaded gender history, Jeff Ross's roasts, with their open-ended dialogue, serve as a fairly successful vehicle for a distinctly radical mode of empathy, one that has the potential to generate a sense of a common ground across hardened differences. Being so detached that you feel next to nothing or so emotional that you are trapped by your own biases and projections undermines the real talk and real connection that Ross pulls off in his stand-up comedy.

Yet a rational distance from the heated passions of conflict and struggle continues to appeal to philosophers and psychologists. Too often, empathy seems hopelessly saturated with emotionally based prejudices, in-group preferences, and an underbelly of hostile affects. While psychologist Paul Bloom does not examine humor, a detached stance is relevant for his defense of "rational compassion" in his popular 2016 polemic *Against Empathy.*[22] "Compassion" is the term that Bloom uses to stand in for the older term, "sympathy," in order to avoid the predominantly sad connotation that the latter's contemporary use carries. Rational compassion strips away the emotionality that philosophers and psychologists find untrustworthy in affect-laden empathy. As we will see in the next section, philosophers have recently attempted to similarly salvage empathy by redefining it as primarily a type of perception. Yet all too often such an appeal to reason or correct perception has little political or social force, at least as a solo act.

As we know from the harrowing cries recorded in 2018 of children from inside a U.S. detention center at the Mexican border after forced separation from their migrant families, compassion for the plight of a foreigner is moved less by an abstract appeal to rights or a clear perception of harm, let alone countless pages of theory and numbing statistics, than a moment of heartfelt empathy. Despite our innate human tribalism, or rather because of the embodied social creatures that we are, feeling-oriented empathy, in contrast to modes of empathy that are primarily a form of cognition or perception, solicits the binding emotion that, together with symbolic images, energizes and inspires the commitment and action that can alter social norms. As gut-driven tribal creatures, our best hope is to break open the circle of moral concern rather than depend on some elite civilization's ideal of reason, with its own abject underbelly, to transcend our animal nature. Humor in turn provides a vehicle for that sense of felt connection that calls on empathy as a primarily emotional rather than cognitive intelligence and a tool for social change.

Empathy via Affects and Emotions

For feminists and others viewed as incapable of self-transcendence or rational modes of sympathy, the presumed benefits of having a good sense of humor are sorely limited. Such humor does little to tamper with the structures of power. Women and oppressed groups are expected to face prejudicial stereotypes and belittling ridicule by rolling with the punches to avoid conflict.

Feminist and activist humor operates differently. As feminists along with other social critics increasingly laid claim to the public sphere through comedic interventions, empathy as a sense of felt connection with a fully engaged emotional component has worked alongside ridicule with liberatory aims. Ross's work in the context of the anti–mass incarceration movement serves as an example of how humor can channel an engaged connection with those ordinarily outside the bounds of empathy for a potentially transformative effect. Ross stands side by side with white supremacists. He holds the hands of prisoners who have dozens of priors and who have committed violent crimes. He does not identify with neo-Nazis or murderers; nor does he stop judging them. Yet in this era of mass incarceration, there is a palpable connection with the inmates without any presumption of knowing their pain.

"Empathy is always perched precariously between gift and invasion," writes the essayist Leslie Jamison in *The Empathy Exams*.[23] There are several modes of feeling-oriented empathy. Without ever being able to explain it, we feel that the humor Ross brings to the Brazos jail is not an invasion. The question is what kind of empathy is appropriate in extreme circumstances. "I feel your pain" is a colloquial expression of an ordinary kind of emotional empathy and can serve as a fitting instance of what is called the matching theory of empathy. A matching theory, as philosopher Amy Coplan explains, defines empathy as "a complex imaginative process in which an observer simulates another person's situated psychological states while maintaining clear self–other differentiation."[24] There are times when a good-willed effort to experience via the imagination another's suffering is a fully appropriate response. Ross, however, is aware that he is free to walk out of prison while the inmates are not. He knows the privileges of his social position. Under these tense circumstances, the claim to match their pain risks theft and appropriation.

There is a second limit with the matching approach. The matching of another's pain doesn't work well when even the other person has little understanding of it. Consider how trauma fragments experience. Or as Jamison writes, a painful event "bleeds . . . out of wounds and across boundaries," presenting less a buried secret to be uncovered than a murky "rhizome" of incoherent meanings.[25] Jamison suggests that this fragmentation of experience calls for a "superlative kind of empathy."[26] It "requires knowing you know nothing" and "asking questions that have to be listened to"; it requires a "kind of porousness in response."[27] Only then can an empathetic other "deliver my feelings back to me in a form that [would be] legible."[28] For "feeling something was never simply a state of submission but always, also, a process of *construction.*"[29] Clearly, this need to actively respond and participate in the meaning of another's experience is more than listening alone. The other's experience is "something actual and constructed" by both parties at once.[30]

Yet in a situation lacking in mutual trust—where a traumatic history of race and a neoliberal calculus of winners and losers builds walls between us—even superlative empathy has trouble traveling across barriers. From a privileged position in a stratified society, the aim of delivering another's feelings back to them (like the claim to know their pain) risks appropriating the experience of those whose suffering one may even be tacitly complicit in producing. Under regimes of racial supremacy, too many whites have found themselves unable to identify with, or even match emotions with, persons of color except through fantasies and projections.[31] These kinds of concerns lead some feminists and critical theorists to reject empathy as a moral or political tool, leaving them struggling to find any path for the solidarity that a sense of connection can bring.[32] A third kind of emotionally engaged empathy, or empathy as a sense of felt connection—

resonating with others rather than matching or constructing their emotions—has the radical potential for generating solidarity across social divisions.[33] We explore radical empathy as a capacity to bond where one would not expect to find it through a form of humor.

Empathy as Felt Connection

As signaled in some uses of the hip-hop lingo "I feel ya," it may be possible to establish a tentative sense of solidarity across zones of social conflict and disconnect without invasive claims. Among urban definitions, the use we have in mind is closer to the "I hear ya" or "I'm here with you" than "I feel your pain," but it involves from the empath a more self-aware and vulnerable stance than suggested by attentiveness alone. Consider how the laughter of the roast spreads in waves from prisoners to viewing audiences through a playful needling that turns freely on itself. A radical mode of empathy, one that moves beyond tribal loyalties, requires weakening defenses that sustain social tensions and hierarchies. This is a major function of humor. Humor breaks down defenses and serves as a catalyst for a mode of affective empathy by drawing on capacities for self-depreciation, unexpected role reversals, and a mockery that, as the Roastmaster avows in his opening remarks, comes from a place of love.[34] Indeed, in this respect, the joker takes on the role of the mischievous eros figure from the tradition of romantic comedy. In this tradition, the eros figure is typically an enslaved person or servant concocting a plot to overcome patriarchal and other blocking forces, performing the work of intimacy and ushering in emancipatory social norms. In this case, as the empathetic humor flows beyond the prison walls, the viewing audience becomes a participant in the laughter too.

We can think of this radically empathetic humor in terms of what Bekoff describes as an egalitarian mode of social play that generates a mutual sense of connection and reciprocity. Recall our introduction's discussion of how play can suspend social hierarchies as well as predatory instincts among carnivores and their prey to build friendships within and across species. Humor too is a form of social play with radical potential. It too can build unexpected alliances across lines of indifference or conflict. Aspects of social play that are central for humor include (1) the exposure of vulnerability and sore spots, as in self-deprecatory remarks, together with the ability to take a hit through ridicule, which is especially important for those occupying privileged positions; (2) self-handicapping or soft biting, as in the carefully gaged use of one's wit in the soft ridicule of another, which is again important for those in privileged positions; (3) a role reversal between those of higher and lower status for mutual teasing, as who mock-attacks whom constantly changes; and (4) the right motivation fueled by the joy of camaraderie to establish the grounds for mutual trust and a level playing field. In a politically charged atmosphere, self-handicapping and exposing vulnerability allow social capital to be yielded to those occupying a weaker social position. The positive emotions of play and humor—excitement together with waves of joy in communion and mutual validation—can crack open this unlikely possibility. In short, radical empathy demands laying down privilege, and this is what humor's promise of jovial camaraderie can achieve. The twists and turns of humor can assist a solidaric empathy by generating an unlikely zone for intimacy and emotion-laden communication without assuming that the participants are coming from the same place. The result is a tentative leveling of social divisions for felt moments that offer unexplored possibilities.

Key to this kind of humor is the willingness to take one's turn as the butt of the joke, and thus to display vulnerability in a playful exchange of mutual teasing. Contrast empathetic humor with the scenario of joke telling that Freud proposes in his *Jokes and Their Relation to the Unconscious* (1905). Freud explains the pleasure of a joke through the release of energy otherwise used to repress sexual and aggressive drives. This type of joke telling turns on a fixed target of the joke and too often on gender hierarchies, thus inadvertently providing a formula for toxic masculinity: "In Freud's account, the joke in its basic form requires three parties—two men and a woman. The first man initiates the joke to release an aggressive impulse, originally sexual, toward the woman. He forces her to participate in the joke through her embarrassment, her acknowledgment that she understands its content. . . . Through its cleverness, the joke veils and makes socially acceptable its underlying aggression. The joke does not exist until the laughter of the second man confirms it; the woman, as the joke's passive butt, thus enables the bond between the two men."[35] Empathetic humor of the kind we have in mind avoids targeting an innocent object for the sake of a joke and cheap bonding. When successful, such humor has the potential for generating a vital sense of connection without relying on appropriating the feelings of others but instead resonating with them.

The capacity of a noninvasive empathy to generate a sense of felt connection is made palpable in Ross's gestures of touch during his performance. With one hand on the shoulder of an older man, Ross explains his own identity when asked: "I'm Jewish, but don't tell those fucking Nazis up there." Amid a roar of laughter from the prisoners and guards, he calls out the neo-Nazi with whom he spoke earlier, urging him to take off his shirt and bare all: "Let me see those tats. Don't be shy! Oh my god, dude. Let me tell you something. The war is over, but tattoos are permanent."

But it is when Ross enters the women's jail that we see how empathetic humor mixed with a poignant moment of cathartic touch offers radical play. The exchange begins when Ross finds that he is not the only comedian in the house. As he starts to warm up the crowd by setting himself up as the object of a cheesy porn, Big Mama Jo, the prison matriarch, creates ripples of laughter as she asserts her own claim to the comic stage when she shouts out, "It's raining men, hallelujah!" Her dynamic presence encourages Ross into an open dialogue. Instinctively pushing back the invasive cameras at this crucial moment, he walks closer to Big Mama Jo as she holds out her hands in a tender moment of connection. This is not an instance where the stand-up puts a heckler back in his place to reclaim dominance of the comic stage. We sense instead a connection that is not downward-looking sympathy. It is not rational compassion and it is not matched emotion. It is an unlikely solidarity that viewers might not only feel but also share.

The connection grows with the banter between them. Big Mama Jo is surrounded by several younger women, whom Ross playfully casts as "her three illegitimate daughters." Every bit the celebrity's equal for laughs, this quick-witted humorist insists that what she needs is child support. To be sure, playing the dozens has a long and too easily neglected history in both black and Yiddish cultures.[36]

Trying to keep up with his rival, Ross resorts to an old schoolboy taunt about her middle-aged figure, suggesting, "You don't need child support—how about some boob support?" Unphased by his body-shaming jives, she gives him credit for staging a comeback in this comic duel and reaches out to shake his hand to screams of laughter. When the Roastmaster starts up again—"You aren't my mama, are you?"—without a moment's hesitation, she snaps back, "I might be." The threat of inmates—perceived by the viewing audience as sympathetic objects perhaps, but minstrel characters nonetheless—is real and ongoing. At times the performance falters under the weight of this threat. Yet through an unexpected exchange of wit with a prisoner able to hold her own, the audience witnesses moments when differences between two comics are leveled. Transforming mockery into flirtatious banter, we sense in them an appreciation of each other as equals.

This striking moment of unexpected chemistry between a Jewish comic, a black female prisoner, and the audience watching them makes us rethink how cognition and emotion are mixed in empathic humor. In the cultivation of empathy, both emotions and thoughts are relevant. In order to twist out of the reason/emotion and associated binaries, it is helpful to recall studies of brain dysfunction from neurologist Antonio Damasio. When parts of the orbitofrontal cortex are damaged, people lose most of their emotional capacities. In situations where ordinarily people would feel emotions, they feel nothing. One would think that these hyperrational folks would have the advantage of making decisions without subjective biases and blinding emotions. In fact, they find themselves incapable of making any significant decision whatsoever. This is because, as psychologist Jonathan Haidt explains, the decision-making capacity is not primarily a rational one but is rather visceral.[37] Without feelings of what they like and dislike, it is difficult to make any kind of choice at all. Because empathetic humor's connection with others is felt, not just seen or heard, it carries the spark of a socially and politically transformative eros.

Increasingly, philosophers, like psychologists, are critical of any sharp distinction between reason and emotion. Indeed, as Silvan Tomkins writes, "There is a real question whether anyone may fully grasp the nature of any object when that object has not been perceived, wished for, missed and thought about in love and hate, in excitement and in apathy, in distress and in joy."[38] Yet philosophical analyses of empathy reproduce tendencies from the old binary. On the one hand, analyses that rely exclusively on matching affects risk overemphasizing the capacity for sharing the same feeling—a problematic assumption in circumstances where social hierarchy persists and conflict is rife—and a more critical stance is required. On the other hand, efforts to correct this bias by treating empathy as a mode of rational thought or accurate perception of the particular other risk duplicating the problematic tendencies of nineteenth-century approaches.

Among these latter efforts, some argue that empathy relies on mental capacities to think abstractly and infer qualities present in other minds, while others focus on our capacities for the perception of others' emotions.[39] The former approach rests on what psychologists term theory of mind—that is, the claim that in order to understand another's feelings, one must be able to represent them abstractly in one's own mind. The second phenomenological approach, developed by Husserl, Edith Stein, Merleau-Ponty, and Dan Zahavi, insists that we perceive emotions directly and without inference: we see shame in a blush, joy in the tail-wag of a dog or in human laughter. Both theory of mind and phenomenological traditions emphasize a cognitive or perceptual take on empathy in contrast to an emotionally engaged and feeling-centered approach. Both traditions capture different aspects of empathy in noncontentious situations. But they do not weigh in affects and desires that constitute the core of who we are, that give texture and meaning to our reflections and perceptions, and that carry ever more significance when we occupy unequal positions and degrees of complicity in a fraught social climate. It's these messy visceral aspects of feeling that humor productively engages for a radical mode of empathy.

The problems with the contemporary emphasis on accuracies of perceptual attentiveness or cerebral cognition (in contrast to murkier scenes of affective engagement) are easiest to see in contexts plagued by histories of trauma and social conflict. In these contexts, the demand for accurate perception or careful reflection, however valuable, risks obscuring unknowable histories of suffering beyond our ability to imagine or understand. "Empathy means acknowledging a horizon of context that extends perpetually beyond what you can see," Jamison writes in her essay on superlative empathy.[40] Moreover, horizons that carry histories of violence aggravated by entrenched group tensions locate us with defenses that are as difficult to bring down as they are to see through. A careful attentiveness or a cognitive-based empathy sidesteps messy affects, only to risk falling into a morass of implicit biases and intellectual blind spots. Again, the specter arises of an invasive empathy, one that inadvertently violates, instead of opening itself up to, the other.

Yet the empathy that uses humor as a soft tool of power offers a real, if humble, chance. After all, who is going to really believe an "I feel ya" from the straight man who is unwilling to reveal his own underbelly, yielding aspects of privilege and control as he lowers his defenses to laugh at himself along with unlikely others. The visceral force that Ross channels in his roasts illustrates the potential of empathy to give access to aspects of the perspectives of others as well as to poke holes in makeshift borders and unsettle set identities. Indeed, his comic routine does not end with an all-knowing smirk and shrug but with failed attempts and unexpected moments as he occasionally takes his turn as the butt of the joke. Fueled by these topsy-turvy belly laughs, empathetic humor delivers hope.

Humor enhances empathy's transformational capacity to "feel ya," including those whom we might otherwise easily dismiss, as it tampers with the status quo. Rather than transcending an underbelly of affects, empathy combined with humor renders us more porous and relational. Through empathetic humor, bodily openness to affects and emotions streaming from others enhances the fluidity of identity, shifting lived social positions along with the cultural landscape. Instead of fostering an attitude of adaptation that rises above a fraught situation, such humor serves as a catalyst. If self-transcendent humor culminates in, as mid-twentieth-century sociologist C. Wright Mills warns, the "cheerful robot,"[41] empathetic humor breaks open the social circle of belonging, altering and widening the sphere of amity, and offering the potential for political realignments along with social and psychic change.

Empathetic Humor as a Social Catalyst

Humor has not been the only cultural force to invoke felt connections across the social landscape. Music has also been inextricably bound to a long history of struggle and liberation. Thus, against the backdrop of powerful social movements that include Black Lives Matter, Ross's prison roast unsurprisingly pays tribute to Johnny Cash's iconic 1968 performance in Folsom Prison. The late 1960s and early 1970s were a time when musicians and their songs captured the soul and vision of street politics. For Cash, country music was an expression of love, and his performance a mix of raw cynicism and soulful empathy. His music was such a powerful force that one former inmate recalls Cash could have set off a riot the day he played at Folsom. Cash was welcomed with open arms from a relatively homogeneous white working-class prison population whose life struggles seemed similar to each other as well as to the Man in Black. A half century later, Ross can also hear the train a comin' as he relies on a classic Cash guitar riff and a somber glimpse of Texas train tracks to set the mood. The audiences, both free and unfree, know what side of the tracks they are on, just as they did when Cash strummed his guitar. But it is empathy tinged with biting humor, not the pathos of country music, that mediates divisive social identities, antagonistic ideologies, and territorial boundaries. To be sure, Cash did a bit of stand-up back in the day, pretending to choke on prison drinking water and purposely using foul language to mock jailhouse rules, while pointing out the injustice of doing time for petty crimes like stealing eggs. If Cash's performances tapped into comedy, it was the music that defined much of the era. In 2015, Ross borrowed much from Cash, and now comedy has found the political spotlight.[42]

In the counterculture of the 1960s generation, Cash was not the only example of how the power of music gives shape and momentum to our passions. Songs as diverse as the civil right's soulful refrain "We Shall Overcome" and antiwar protestors' bitter recognition of just who was and was not, as Creedence Clearwater Revival put it, a "Fortunate Son" recall the expansive musical range of 1960s and early 1970s social movements. We are not suggesting that music does not continue to reflect and move political thought. Hip-hop rose up in the late 1970s and for decades has provided the soundtrack to the new Jim Crow of mass criminalization and incarceration.[43] Ava DuVarnay's 2016 documentary *13TH* narrates the roots of mass incarceration and the prison–industrial complex in slavery with rap lyrics from Public Enemy's "Don't Believe the Hype." Yet in 1968 it was Cash who entertained prisoners in Folsom, and in 2015 it is a stand-up comedian who captures social media through his performances at Brazos county jail. The spotlight on prisons in 1968 was part of larger cultural revolutions across the globe, but when the Nixon administration initiated a war on drugs, something new happened. This law-and-order president targeted his internal political enemies, smearing blacks along with draft-dodging hippies as drug users. The right-wing backlash against the earlier civil rights and antiwar movements recoded his shifty politics and cynical manipulation of the race card as an attack on criminals.[44] Demands for an end to mass incarceration, marijuana legalization campaigns, Black Lives Matter, prison-abolition movements—all provide inspiration for Ross's prison roasts, pointing to the centrality of comedians in contemporary political thought and culture.

Such media-savvy figures as Dave Chappelle, Tina Fey, Jon Stewart, Stephen Colbert, Trevor Noah, John Oliver, Wanda Sykes, and Samantha Bee reveal that we are living in the age of the comedian. Perhaps this is why in the spring of 2016 singer-songwriter Bono insisted that the U.S. Senate "send in Amy Schumer, Chris Rock and Sacha Baron Cohen" to fight violent extremism. The laughter of stand-ups, jokesters, and satirists infuses our movements with the ripples of social challenge. These decentered currents of critique operate outside the mold of past centuries' social movements driven by leaders and ideologies. The movements of the 1960s and 1970s, playing against the backdrop of the Cold War, were often troubled by ideological splits easily perceived through moral dichotomies—something that social media and news bubbles also engender. Yet today there are profound differences. In a decentralized social media–saturated world filled with both promise and nightmares, the comedian has found a niche, especially at a time when social change flips and flops with a notorious meme or middle-of-the-night tweet. Comic memes and tweets spreading through social media remind us of how the Internet energizes and sometimes replaces street politics. The layout of this new social media landscape seems particularly unwieldy, making elections hard to predict and social unrest hard to map out. The unpredictable shifts and restlessness of public mood reflect more than technological change. Leftist elites in the past have all too readily pinned the label of false consciousness on the "ignorant masses."[45] We argue that the variability in attitudes and values exposes not a false but rather a mixed consciousness.[46] Individuals and groups have fluid identities and contradictory views. The variable flow of a mixed consciousness is too easily dismissed as a display of irrational behavior and beliefs. Yet comedy has the potential to reveal how such behavior and beliefs, no less than ideologies, are far from fixed and thus offer the possibility of felt moments of good humor between otherwise sworn enemies.

We are not necessarily looking for comedians to lead a social movement. Instead, the absence of iconic top-down leaders, foundational political ideologies, and a grand narrative style set the comic stage to address social conflict differently. Alongside such serious decentered movements as Occupy Wall Street, Black Lives Matter, and #MeToo, the comics work from experiences of pain and trauma. They expose the hypocrisy and lies of the powerful, the undeserved suffering of the oppressed, and the inequities that mark the 99 percent. And like other decentered and increasingly digitally propelled movements, the energy and power of those who can laugh forge an altered basis for solidarity from the top-down, ideologically driven movements. But if serious movements, decentered or not, mine the collective pain of victims, then solidarity for the audiences of comedy grows less from vicariously sharing the collective pain of the victims than fellow feeling among those who can laugh at themselves and with others. This laughter ensues as they confront the diversity of unjust suffering with the pleasures of an unexpected sociability. Laughter lowers defenses and crosses enemy lines because it does not rely on a common identity or collective pain to generate that wave of sociability. The suffering of Jews or black Americans may place them far afield from a neo-Nazi's rogue life, yet in their shared humor, there is an incipient political demand.

Doing mischief in the age of misinformation, the comedian

riddles mockery with the empathic humor that taps into the mix of gut emotions of post-9/11 anxiety-ridden America. The aim is not to give in to fear or to give anxiety free rein, but to redirect them to the facts. Against media bubbles and the echo chambers of friends liking friends, truth-teller comedians strip away the facade of *Fox and Friends* while turning fake news into real news. Increasingly, the millennials and the iGeneration find trusted sources less among the diminishing ranks of journalists than among professional jokesters. After all, Ross produces comedy as a documentary, performing the work of the investigative reporter. Like the child who exposes the emperor as having no clothes, these comedians offer what the ancient Greeks from the days of some of the first stand-ups, the Cynics, called parrhesia—the naked truth.

These comedians do more than preach to the choir. To be sure, the sharp ridicule of the Samantha Bees aims less to convince their political opponents than to energize their core. Such energizing moments can whip up enthusiastic audiences in a way that reasoned argument does not. The power to charge up an audience's fury and disrespect against the powerful points to why authoritarian regimes for centuries have censored comedy more than tragedy. This censorship underscores the social force of comedy in that laughter may well bring down the tyrant. But if the agents of ridicule energize the base with an "us versus them" strategy, then comics who use empathy have the means to nudge us out of our respective bubbles.

Ross, for example, roasts not only prisoners but also the police, and in so doing exposes his Comedy Central audiences and YouTube fans to the hypocrisy of the criminal justice system and the humanity of those touched by it. What makes Ross's documentary roasts such a success is more than his quick wit. The definition of who and what makes good comedy is doubtless contested terrain. Ross understands this as he reveals an assortment of comedic devices as well as other tools of the trade. However, it is his empathy that offers the kind of belly laughs that get to the guts of the matter and allows him to bridge differences and alter the collective mood. Empathy may well be why he considers himself lucky to be a comedian. In his words, "I have the best job in the world. I make fun of people for a living. And I think the reason I can get away with roasting my way through life is because it comes from a place of love." In good humor, he adds, "I love everybody—even cops!"[47]

Proving his love for cops, however, was not so easy. After pictures circulated of Ross at a 2016 antipolice violence rally in his New York City neighborhood, he was quickly branded as a cop hater. Only one police department in the United States would even consider letting him roast their men and women in blue. Boston police commissioner William Evans believes he runs a "compassionate department" with a clean record, and thus he wanted to "break the stereotype that we are the bad guys." He felt that a good police roast was just what his community needed. In fact, Evans fully embraced the spotlight. "We don't mind you making fun of us because I want the public to know that we are real people." Nevertheless, on the morning Ross arrived in Boston, tensions were running high—not only because a police officer had been shot but also because the local police union had urged all officers to stay away from Ross. Unlike the prisoners at Brazos county jail, where they felt appreciated, even elevated, by the comedian's attention, the Boston police felt threatened. In such a cynical milieu, roasting pigs seemed like a recipe for disaster. After all, how could you make someone laugh when they felt like a victim? Such a strong sentiment of audience mistrust and discontent was far removed from loyal customers' frequenting their favorite comedy club.

While Ross understood that going to a prison or a precinct would not be like his previous comedy tours, he did not consider himself to be anticop. With both compassion and a determination to not let anyone off the hook, Ross struggled with a charged political atmosphere that makes even questions and inquiry seem suspect. At an antipolice rally, Ross was visibly moved by the protesters who took to the streets in an attempt to bring an end to the growing list of unarmed black Americans that had been shot by police or died while in custody—so many names, Ross tragically pointed out, that reading them all would take all day. One protester after another tells Ross about a lost loved one gunned down by police. A grieving mother of a slain eight-year-old girl confesses to the camera, "My anger keeps me going." Another woman, Madge Morgan, is haunted by the past and present. "I was nine years old during the 1967 riots and [sic] white national guard pointed bayonet rifles at me and my baby brother and sister's head . . . and told us 'you little nappy-headed niggers get your asses back in that house before I blow your heads off.'" Upset and yelling, she passionately admits, "I want people hurt." This is where Ross's empathic touch comes into play amid a roller-coaster ride of emotions. Not wanting violence ever, Ross asks Morgan, "Can I have a hug?" as he jokes about how he "cops a feel." This skillful move instantaneously turns Morgan's anger and Ross's ambivalence into laughter. Feeling reassured, Morgan asks Ross if he thinks blacks and whites are equal. He replies with affirmation as he mischievously adds a reminder of another contemporary out-group: "Of course, Mexicans are better than all of us." Taking down pieces of a wall rather than building one, the rejoinder causes both of them to laugh more as they hug each other tighter.

For Ross, empathy is not simply a performance but a gut instinct that makes it impossible to separate the terrifying violence suffered in black communities through police action from unfair blanket hatred and targeted attacks on the police. In New York, at the anti-police violence rally, surrounded by the "families of the victims . . . it's like a funeral. A big angry funeral," insists Ross, who is almost at a loss for words when he meets armed protesters ready to shoot. Violence begets violence. As angry protesters shout threats in the face of police positioned to protect their lives and keep the peace, Ross becomes overwhelmed: "This is intense, weird and disturbing." It is an all too familiar political conflict; everyone wants to know "what side you are on," assuming that if you are not for one cause, you are against it. Meanwhile, Ross concludes, "People are dying on both sides and nobody is talking to one another."

Just as the names and statistics of black victims haunt Ross and his performance, so too do the occupational stresses, strains, and violence faced by police. The often poorly paid job of the cops, we learn from Ross, leaves them with a 70 percent greater chance of heart attacks than other Americans. On a ride-along, Ross brings his audience out of their social bubble as he documents what it feels like to put on a bulletproof vest as part of a daily routine. Recall, a cop had just been shot when Ross arrived in Boston; luckily, not only did he survive, but the assailant was restrained without gunfire. There is little sympathy for the police, and they know it. The police joke about being hated except for that brief moment after the 2013 Boston Marathon bombing, when "everybody else runs away, you run in."

For Ross, wondering just how he can build up trust across what feels like an impenetrable blue line is not easy. As he was told by one of the officers, "Part of a cop's nature is to be cynical . . . it takes a while to feel you out," which is why this same man in blue suggested to Ross if you want them to trust you, start by "buy[ing] them lunch!" After all, "the way to a cop's heart is through his stomach." Getting to the guts of felt mistrust demanded not only that Ross bring pizza to the officers but also a round of belly laughs. Along with handshakes, fist bumps, and humorous jibes, a once chilling if not hostile reception transformed into a comedy club atmosphere. After some warm-up acts and ride-alongs, Ross gains the trust he needs to address the issues at hand. Without hesitation, Ross tells his police audience, "I have a theory why cops love donuts so much—because they look like they've been shot." Continuing on his comedic course, he treats the crowd to more raunch, joking, "I beat my penis so much I call it Rodney King. And just like the LAPD, I always get off." Like Ross, his audience understands that there is a kind of natural propensity to laugh deep to handle hard times. After all, as one cop told Ross after listening to a desperate man who needed help from nonexistent social services, "You got to laugh at this shit or you cry." Yet Ross is not providing laughs simply for their immediate relief. He is creating moments that humanize those who are demonized without losing a critical stance toward police-based terror and the new Jim Crow. While highlighting the problems of police brutality, he nonetheless is able to transform anger and mistrust into a laughter that ripples across divisions that were once thought to be impenetrable.

Bottom-up Humorists Steal the Scene on the Streets of Boston

Out of the precinct and on the streets, empathetic humor opens ever more doors for rehumanizing the other, and with them, ourselves. With Bobby and Brian, two of Boston's finest, Ross finds himself in an impromptu exchange of jokes and real talk between the white cops and a group of black friends nonchalantly hanging out in front of a storefront sign that warns: "No Loitering, Police Enforced." As Ross and the police officers approach the group armed with jokes, not threats, the camera captures how the affect of the comic stage takes a life of its own. Laughing with not against the white cops, the black men loitering on the sidewalk are happy to be on camera as long as they don't have to "stop smoking [their] weed." Amid the joviality, a young man toys with the irony of his ankle monitor, and thus a previous far-from-pleasurable encounter with the law. Unwittingly, the ankle monitor nicely sets up Ross, who scores another round of laughs when he all too innocently asks, "Does this mean you can't go near a schoolyard?" Ross then jokes with someone whom he dubs Spike Lee, a young black man with a San Antonio Spurs cap and vintage glasses who insists that "this is real talk—cops killing black people," yet who also implies something more nuanced: "It's not [always] like that. They're doing their job. You feel me." But, he adds, "Fuck the fake ones. The real ones they don't come out here for violence." As real talk slips back into jokes and jibes, Ross's open-ended technique reveals he is not the only roastmaster on the streets that night; his newfound friends mock him for humor they consider so old school that he must be "Jerry Lewis." With a grin, he takes his turn as the butt of the joke, yielding for series of moments to their scene-stealing wit, showing us viewers how it's done.

There are occasions when this street comedy and camaraderie tragically threaten to turn on out-groups. Ross, for example, is taunted for wearing a winter coat with fur that looks like "Chinese pubic hair," and as everyone laughs, we are reminded once again of the long-standing need for an indispensable enemy. Ross and his street friends seem to find nothing off limits, yet this take-no-prisoners approach to a roast is deeply entrenched in an empathy that challenges the solidification of the other as enemy. "Hating all cops for what some cops have done, that is also prejudice," insists Ross. He gestures toward another layer of racial anxiety when he explains, "It's like hating all Mexican people because you got diarrhea from a chimichanga." As Ross feigns a meal gone wrong, he groans, "Fuck the Mexicans . . . I'm voting for Trump," reminding us just how easy it is to find an outsider to blame, and how easy it is to build walls rather than breaking them down.

Who would have thought that a roast in situations as raw as the line that divides cops and blacks on the street would provide the way open toward a more generous and truthful life? Yet in the wake of the war on drugs and other backlashes against the freedoms that defined the 1960s and 1970s, laughter offers a chance to connect with others in a world rent by struggle and strife. Music has long been a means to find that bond with others, mixing strong empathic impulses with symbols of unity and a desire for social and political change. Since 9/11, these impulses and symbols of longing for change have found their way through comic truth tellers as real talk elsewhere has become hard to find. The cathartic propensity to laugh from the gut to handle hard times takes out chunks of a wall rather than building one when empathy transforms the anger and mistrust that fester across histories of crimes not easy to forget or forgive on both sides of the line.[48] Ridicule turns into a free-for-all and defenses weaken as a bottom-up roast offers a chance for each side, if only they can open themselves enough to take their turn as the butt of the joke. Recall that empathy together with reciprocity ground our animal sense of fair play—and so too our golden rules for both ethics and comedy. With no one fixed as the permanent enemy, each side exposes its vulnerability to the biting humor of the other in a gesture of friendship and camaraderie as old and as common as the play among carnivores and those who would have been their prey. "Can you feel me?" does not demand that either side relinquish its judgment of the other or fail to acknowledge the real crime of white supremacy in America. On the contrary, the roastmaster mixes with his humor lessons in history. Yet comic play introduces into ridicule a solidaric empathy that can penetrate impenetrable boundaries, rehabilitating not only the criminal but also humanity itself.

Conclusion
Humor Can't Wait

In the Tragic with Tig Notaro and Hannah Gadsby

> It's weird because with humor, the equation is tragedy plus
> time equals comedy. I am just at tragedy right now.
> —Tig Notaro, *Live*

"Good evening, hello. I have cancer, how are you?" stand-up Tig
Notaro told her 2012 audience. In just a few short months before
that appearance, she had been faced with a breakup, the loss of her
mother, and the life-threatening diagnosis of breast cancer. Yet for
Notaro, "this is when everything started to seem funny." On stage, not
knowing whether she would live much longer, she ponders a standard
comedic formula: "tragedy plus time equals comedy." "I am just at
tragedy right now." Not sure if time was on her side, Notaro emphat-
ically embraces comedy in the here and now. As she begins a comic
routine in the midst of the tragic, she teasingly asks her audience
for dating advice: "Should I go online and make a profile?" But what
would it say? "Profile: 'I have cancer. Serious inquiries only.'"[1]

The standard equation that tragedy plus time is comedy may
trace back to the era of Mark Twain, the nineteenth-century Missouri
satirist who signaled major changes in American cultural takes on
the comic. At that time, the dominant culture in the United States
wavered between a minstrel show turning on humiliation and the
humor of self-transcendence. While the aphorism encapsulated well
the modern humor of detachment, Notaro's sketch points toward the
rise of a humor of connection. In response to an interview inquiring

whether it's "weird that so many strangers . . . know . . . her stuff," she responds, "I'm just so completely used to it. And I'm fine with it. It's part of the strength of sharing and vulnerability and honesty and comedy, all mixed in. You can't go wrong when you're that wide open." Confronted by the tragic, the comedic soul chooses to share and engage, to work through, not detach, as we live in the moment to change the moment. This is why we embrace Notaro's philosophy that humor can't wait.

When thinking back to the first chapters of this book, we look to humor to throw out the old formulas and replay comedy from the bottom up; now we turn to another stand-up who comes from the margins to take on the tragic. Hannah Gadsby tells us in her 2018 performance, *Nanette*, that she came of age in what she describes as the Bible belt of Tasmania, when being a lesbian was a still a crime—and also the butt of the joke. Trained in art history, she found in her routine a means to reject the legacy of a discipline and a culture that celebrated without question the reputations of "dead men" who "were dead then" and "are just deader now." A middle-aged Pablo Picasso justified having an affair with a seventeen-year-old girl because they both, in his troubling words, were in their prime. Gadsby sees a legacy that celebrates the brilliance of Cubism with its perspectivism, yet masks a history of misogynist crime in the name of reputation. "Well, tell me, any of those perspectives a woman's?" she asks. No—otherwise he would not have referred to an underage girl as someone in her prime. Reputation seems to be all that matters. "I'm gonna call it: High art—bullshit!" Of course, she knows "I will probably now never get a job in a gallery," which is why she defiantly proclaims "Comedy? Lowbrow! . . . nobody here is leaving this room a better person. We're just rolling around in our own shit here, people."[2]

As we roll around in the carnivalesque, we see that there is more in her roller-coaster performance than first meets the eye. Gadsby presses us to rethink yet another standard formula in comedy that rests on minstrel punch lines: "What sort of comedian can't even make the lesbians laugh—every comedian!—classic," she says sarcastically as she reminds her audience that there are people such as herself who are injured and do not find such jokes funny. "But we have got to laugh, because if we don't, it proves the point." Gatsby quips that this joke "was written before women were funny. Back then, a lesbian was just any woman not laughing at a man." Hence the all-too familiar taunts: "Why aren't you laughing? What are you, some kind of lesbian? You need to lighten up—you need a good dicking." Such misogyny, which has long dominated the comic stage, demands that we, like Gadsby, pivot and look at humor from the margins to reject the old patriarchal formulas for laughs. Stunning her audience, Gadsby suddenly declares, "I need to quit comedy. I built a career on self-deprecating humor, and I don't want to do that anymore, because do you understand what self-deprecation means when it comes from someone who already exists in the margins? It's not humility. It's humiliation." In this serious break from her comedic routine, she explains how for too long, "I put myself down in order to speak in order to seek permission to speak. And I simply won't do that anymore, to myself or anyone who identifies with me."[3]

Yet, Gadsby doesn't actually quit comedy. Instead, she powerfully rejects that standard good old boy formula that only allows her a voice if she engages in a ritual of self-humiliation. In so doing, she changes the rules of the game, first through an anger that uses fumerism to punch up and tear down the misogynist, as would a drill sergeant. Taking command of her male audience, Gadsby uses scathing ridicule to raze the old social identities: "I don't think it's an easy time for you fellas. . . . Because, for the first time ever, you're suddenly a subcategory of human. Right?" Imitating a male response, she declares: "No, we invented the categories. We're not supposed to play! We're human-neutral." Sorry, "not anymore." I know, she reassures them, "You hear 'straight white man,'" and "you're like, 'No. No, that's reverse sexism.'" But recall: "You wrote the rules. Read them." By calling men out for any sign of their weakness or an inability to roll with the punches, she insists that they lighten up; after all, these are "Just jokes! Banter. Don't feel intimidated. It's just locker room talk." Gadsby then lays it out: "A joke is simply two things . . . a setup and a punch line. . . . But in this context," she says with a gendered flip, "I have artificially inseminated tension" to create "an abusive relationship." And why not? Angry men who do the same on the comic stage have been celebrated as "heroes of free speech."[4]

Gadsby, taking her "freedom of speech as a responsibility,"

however, does not leave her "story [or her audience] defined by anger" because it is "toxic" and "infectious." Anger, Gadsby insists, "knows no other purpose than to spread blind hatred." Thus, instead of quitting the emotion work of humor, she conjures laughter's power to convert shame to anger as she treats her audience to a cathartic sloughing off of debilitating identities and norms, and a collective space for creating new ones. Along the way, she completes her heart-wrenching story of assault and rape, even sharing her own vulnerability in a final "appeal to the humanity of people we disagree with." Empowered by her anger, she is now free to sprinkle an element of self-depreciation in her final joke in an effort to establish a "tether, a connection to the world." Returning to the art of stand-up, "I speak to you now, particularly the white men, especially the straight white men. Pull your fucking socks up! How humiliating!" she mischievously opines. "Fashion advice from a lesbian." In the face of tragedy, amid waves of laughter, we find a new formula in which anger plus catharsis plus empathy defines the kind of comedy that speaks truth.[5]

Gadsby's transformative stand-up reminds us that by privileging the serious laughter of subversion, we can ditch those flawed philosophies of humor that assume mind/body splits and patriarchal reason. In our effort to reconceptualize humor, we have explored comics who eroticize unexpected sources of power and joy. Such mockery alters comedy's aim and direction in order to dissolve stereotypes and turn the tables on slut shaming, ethnophobia, and other waves of toxic affect. Those who have been ridiculed as a subcategory of the human—those down with the animals—punch up to challenge established hierarchies and make egalitarian claims.

Indeed, the humor of transcendence as found in the old aphorism turns on the supposed ontological gap between the human and the animal. For the human, the animal has been the ultimate trope of ridicule. But humor, far from elevating the human above other animals, is shared by these nonhuman animals. At the same time, like other social creatures, humans are, deep down, tribal creatures with gut feelings. As social animals, we find suspect solutions to the limits of our animal nature that turn on superhuman powers and ideal theories of reason or transcendence. Much like that rebel primate,

Georgia, who is assumed to do little more than roll around in her own carnivalesque world yet strategically spits on human tourists, we find more chances for hope in shared laughter with the rest of our tribe against a common oppressor.

Along with Gadsby, we also see how a body politics of humor needs to do more than mock superiors and solidify tribal alliances. Our final two chapters revisit catharsis and empathy—functions of comedy and art generally. Too often, when comic catharsis is mentioned, it is assumed that laughter is just a momentary release and a distraction from real problems, when in fact the notion of catharsis has a more complicated history. The ancient Greek philosophers searched for some redeeming quality of comedy, which was then viewed as the ridicule by elites of social inferiors, or as the out-of-control laugher of the buffoon. Aristotle points to the mystery of a catharsis that is never fully explained—something that moderns, with their use of mechanistic formulas, have flattened to simple venting and temporary relief. Instead, we find in holistic ancient rituals and healing medicines hints of how a communal catharsis might offer not a distraction but a transformation of a once-shamed soul and an oppressive society.

For a full transformation, a solidaric mode of empathy is required, one where souls are bared and truths are told, as Notaro so well understands. Empathy typically affords emotional connection—but only within communal boundaries. It thus seems limited. As empathy serves to reinforce borders, it all too often fails to cross enemy lines. If each side would lower defensive walls and consent to a playful vulnerability, empathy mixed with humor might offer a chance of opening, even crossing, what were once perceived to be impenetrable lines. Shared felt moments make a tragedy faced by one a tragedy faced by all. Deep down in the belly laugh, tragedy finds comedy without distance. In so doing, it envisions unpredictable alternatives to disavowed boundaries of exclusion and otherness. This is why humor can't wait.

Acknowledgments

We are grateful to the many scholars, colleagues, and friends who helped to shape the development of our project, whether they know it or not: Ellie Anderson, Amber Batura, Emanuela Bianchi, Stephanie Borst, Susan Bredlau, Jeremy Brown, Shouta Brown, Regina Burch, Kim Calvert, Edward Casey, Sharyn Clough, Erin Collopy, Darian Condarco, Dean Conrad, Amy Coplan, Sharon Crasnow, Ann Cudd, Sean Cunningham, Ben Davis, Duane Davis, Sarah Fayad, Taina Figueroa, Frank Garro, Ann Garry, Mercer Gary, Mani Gil-more, Erinn Gilson, Tiffany Gonzalez, Elizabeth Goodstein, Lauren Guilmette, Barbara Hahn, Pam Hall, Heidi Higgins, Sabrina Hom, Katie Howard, Dustin Howes, Krystal Humphreys, Marta Jimenez, David Joannides, Tamsin Kimoto, Lisa Knisely, Stephanie Koziej, Samantha Lack, Melissa Lambert, Kyoo Lee, Sarah Lee, Kirsten Leng, Liliana Levy-Hermecz, Anne Libera, Sheila Lintott, Jorge Lizarzaburu, Kym Maclaren, Jackie Manz, Noelle McAfee, Ian McDowell, Sean Meighoo, Ron Millam, Albert G. Mosely, Makina Moses, Sarah Myers, Chloe Nathan, Emalee Nelson, Jacques Ntonme, Kelly Oliver, Susan Ottzen, Alonso Padron, David M. Peña-Guzmán, Julie Piering, John Protevi, Elizabeth Stordeur Pryor, Reda Rafei, Michael Rangel, Mary Rawlinson, Rebecca Ring, Dave Roediger, Monique Roelofs, Whitney Ronshagen, Sheryl Tuttle Ross, Deboleena Roy, Ingra Schellenberg, Kim Schreck, Gretchen Schulz, Caroline Schwenz, Yael Sherman, Eric Shouse, Alan Singer, Coleen Sisneros, John Sitter,

Lissa Skitolsky, Courtney Slavin, Elizabeth V. Spelman, Victoria Stambaugh, Tracy Stewart, Malini Suchak, Ronald Sundstrom, Sitar Terrass-Shah, Sam Timme, Giang Trinh, Heather Turveville, Joanne Waugh, Alison Weir, Alice Weiss, James Winchester, and George Yancy.

We thank our editors at University of Minnesota Press, Danielle Kasprzak, Mike Stoffel, Ana Bichanich, and Anne Carter for their expert and enthusiastic guidance. We are grateful to Emory University's Sarah E. McKee for her guidance with the online-access edition and to Rebekah Spera for her excellent assistance with the index.

Finally, we thank our families for the laughter and love that helped so much along the way: Chloe Willett, Liza Willett, Grant Beecher, Dylan McBee, Joe Boettcher, Vickie Fridge, Gabriella Villalobos, Leslie Chiang, Matt Aharonov, our parents Joe and Ellen Willett, and especially Stefan Boettcher and Randy McBee.

Notes

Introduction

1 Larry Nichols, "All Is Well: The Wanda Sykes Interview, Part 1," *Philadelphia Gay News,* September 20, 2018, http://www.epgn.com/.

2 Jennifer Earl, "Wanda Sykes Flips Off Booing Crowd after Anti–Donald Trump Joke Bombs," *CBS News,* November 14, 2016, https://www.cbsnews.com/.

3 Nichols, "All Is Well."

4 For larger statements on our age of political satire, see Amber Day, *Satire and Dissent: Interventions in Contemporary Debate* (Bloomington: Indiana University Press, 2011); and Cynthia Willett, *Irony in the Age of Empire: Comic Perspectives on Democracy and Freedom* (Bloomington: Indiana University Press, 2008). See also Lauren Berlant and Sianne Ngai, eds., "Comedy Has Issues," *Critical Inquiry* 43, no. 2 (2017); Sophia A. McClennen, *Colbert's America: Satire and Democracy* (New York: Palgrave Macmillan, 2012); Arpad Szakolczai, *Comedy and the Public Sphere: The Re-birth of Theatre as Comedy and the Genealogy of the Modern Public Arena* (London: Routledge, 2013); and Jeffrey Gottfried and Monica Anderson, "For Some, the Satiric *Colbert Report* Is a Trusted Source of Political News," Pew Research Center, December 2014, http://www.pewresearch.org/.

5 Hannah Gadsby "Three Ideas. Three Contradictions. Or Not," TED Talk 14.32, April 2019, https://www.ted.com/. See also Clarissa Sebag-Montefiore, "Hannah Gadsby on Autism and the Risk of Failing after *Nanette*: She's Back Exploring the Nature of Comedy," *New York Times,* April 1, 2019, https://www.nytimes.com/.

6   For a historically nuanced account, see Sheila Lintott, "Superiority in Humor Theory," *Journal of Aesthetics and Art Criticism* 74, no. 4 (2016).

7   Christopher Hitchens, "Why Women Aren't Funny," *Vanity Fair*, January 2007, https://www.vanityfair.com/. See Linda Mizejewski, *Pretty/Funny: Women Comedians and Body Politics* (Austin: University of Texas Press, 2014), 1–29, for a discussion of how Hitchens's essay exemplifies the "pretty versus funny" cultural bias of women's history in comedy and for the rise of comics such as Tina Fey.

8   On intersectionality, see Kimberlé Crenshaw, "Mapping the Margins: Intersectionality, Identity Politics, and Violence against Women of Color," *Stanford Law Review* 43, no. 6 (1991): 1241–99; Patricia Hill Collins, *Black Feminist Thought* (Minneapolis: University of Minnesota Press, 1998); and Collins and Sirma Bilge, *Intersectionality* (Cambridge: Polity, 2016). Work in the field of comic studies sensitive to aspects of intersectional approaches include Viveca Greene and Ted Gournelos, eds., *A Decade of Dark Humor: How Comedy, Irony, and Satire Shaped Post-9/11 America* (Jackson: University Press of Mississippi, 2011); Yael Kohen, *We Killed: The Rise of Women in American Comedy* (London: Picador, 2013); Rebecca Krefting, *All Joking Aside: American Humor and Its Discontents* (Baltimore, Md.: Johns Hopkins University Press, 2014); Mizejewski, *Pretty/Funny*; Matthew R. Meier and Casey R. Schmitt, *Standing Up, Speaking Out: Stand-up Comedy and the Rhetoric of Social Change* (New York: Routledge, 2016).

9   Collins and Bilge, *Intersectionality*, 2.

10 Collins and Bilge, *Intersectionality*, 27.

11 Tina Fey, "String of Pride," *30 Rock*, October 18, 2012.

12 Hitchens, "Why Women Aren't Funny."

13 John Morreall, "Philosophy of Humor," *Stanford Encyclopedia of Philosophy*, 2016, https://plato.stanford.edu/.

14 Lintott, "Superiority"; Morreall, "Philosophy of Humor"; Daniel Wickberg, *The Senses of Humor: Self and Laughter in Modern America* (Ithaca, N.Y.: Cornell University Press, 1998).

15 Morreall, "Philosophy of Humor."

16 Mikhail Bakhtin, *Rabelais and His World*, trans. Hélène Iswolsky (Bloomington: Indiana University Press, 2009).

17 Sara Ahmed, *The Cultural Politics of Emotion* (Edinburgh: Edinburgh University Press, 2004); Andy Clark and David Chalmers, "The Extended Mind," *Analysis* 58, no. 1 (1998): 7–19; Carol Gilligan, "In a Different Voice: Women's Conceptions of Self and of Morality," in

The Gender and Psychology Reader, ed. Blythe Clinchy and Julie K. Norem (New York: New York University Press, 1998); Eva Feder Kittay, *Love's Labor* (New York: Routledge, 1999); Daniel J. Siegel, *Mind: A Journey to the Heart of Being Human* (New York: Norton, 2016); and Cynthia Willett and Ellie Anderson, "Feminist Perspectives on the Self," *Stanford Encyclopedia of Philosophy,* 2016, https://plato.stanford.edu/.

18 For the model of this affect-laden, layered self, see Cynthia Willett, "Reflections: A Model and a Vision of Ethical Life," in *Interspecies Ethics* (New York: Columbia University Press, 2014), 131–46. On the gut brain, see Michael D. Gershon, *The Second Brain* (New York: Harper Perennial, 1999). For a nice summary of the functions of the brain and empathy, see Efrat Ginot, "The Empathic Power of Enactments," *Psychoanalytic Psychology* 26, no. 3 (2009): 290–309. On affect generally, see Margaret Wetherall, *Affect and Emotion: A New Social Science Understanding* (London: Sage, 2012), 4. Following Wetherall and many others, but in contrast to some scholars working through Deleuze and/or Spinoza, we do not reduce affect to sheer intensity, although this is definitely one dimension of affects and emotions generally. Such a rhetorical extreme blurs the distinction between animate creatures and inanimate things. For evidence that emotions are constructed via concepts in a process involving the whole brain and that no affect is necessary or sufficient for any emotion, see Lisa Feldman Barrett, *How Emotions Are Made* (New York: Houghton Mifflin Harcourt, 2017). The research consistently challenges the reason-versus-emotion paradigm dominant in much of Western culture.

19 Scott Weems, *Ha! The Science of When We Laugh and Why* (New York: Basic Books, 2014).

20 Wickberg, *Senses of Humor.*

21 Krefting, *All Joking Aside,* 1. Along with comic and American studies scholar Krefting, our shared "jumping off point . . . [is with the] Kondabolu[s] and other comic performers who intentionally produce humor challenging social inequality and cultural exclusion" (2). Krefting defines this mode of humor as charged humor, which aims to assert cultural citizenship and build community. More generally, our theory-based approach complements her economic analysis of charged humor while broadening the focus to include not just the aim of building cultural citizenships but also the ridiculing of stereotypes and mocking of authority. We also examine community and solidarity across lines of class, race, and other social divisions. On cultural

citizenship, see William Flores and Rena Benmajor, *Latino Cultural Citizenship: Claiming Identity, Space and Rights* (Boston: Beacon, 1998).

22 Plato, *Philebus*, trans. Dorothea Frede (Indianapolis, Ind.: Hackett, 1993), 48–50.

23 Thomas Hobbes, *Leviathan* (Indianapolis, Ind.: Hackett, 1982), 32.

24 Morreall, "Philosophy of Humor"; C. John Sommerville, "Puritan Humor, or Entertainment, for Children," *Albion* 21, no. 2 (1989): 227–47.

25 For the debate on the cartoons, see Albena Azmanova, "Are We Charlie?," Berkeley Blog, January 16, 2015, http://blogs.berkeley.edu/; and Justin Smith, "Why Satire Matters," in *Chronicle of Higher Education*, February 23, 2015, https://www.chronicle.com/. While Smith's essay was written as a defense of the French satiric rag, his conception of humor maps onto conceptions of humor as transcendence. Azmanova explains the function of free speech in terms of its role in protecting against oppression. For freedom in relation to the comedic, see Willett, *Irony*, chap. 5.

26 "Who Is Charlie Hebdo," Charlie Hebdo, 2018, https://charliehebdo.fr/en/.

27 Cynthia Willett, "The Sting of Shame: Ridicule, Rape, and Social Bonds," in *Oxford Handbook on Philosophy and Race*, ed. Naomi Zack (Oxford: Oxford University Press, 2017).

28 Thomas Flynn, "Foucault as Parrhesiast: His Last Lecture Course at the College de France (1984)," in *The Final Foucault*, ed. James Bernauer and David Rasmussen (Cambridge, Mass.: MIT Press, 1991), 102–18. On power as a dynamic relationship, not a static thing to be possessed, see Collins and Bilge, *Intersectionality*, 26.

29 Lindy West, "How to Make a Rape Joke," Jezebel, July 12, 2012, http://jezebel.com/.

30 Collins and Bilge, *Intersectionality*, 25.

31 Henri Bergson, *Laughter: An Essay on the Meaning of the Comic*, trans. Cloudesley Brereton and Fred Rothwell (1911; reprint, Mineola, N.Y.: Dover, 2005).

32 Northrop Frye explores this motif through the figure of the imposter rather than the hubristic, obscuring aspects of the political stakes relevant for feminist and related forms of humor; see *Anatomy of Criticism: Four Essays* (Princeton, N.J.: Princeton University Press, 1957), 39.

33 For a philosophical analysis of the asshole, see Aaron James, *Assholes: A Theory* (New York: Doubleday, 2012), 5. For the dick as tar-

get, see Lori Marso, "Feminist Cringe Comedy: Dear Dick, the Joke Is on You," *Politics and Gender* 15, no. 1 (2018).

34 Nichols, "All Is Well."

35 Rob LeDonne, "Bono's Plan to Combat ISIS with Comedians Suggests He's Lost the Plot," *Guardian*, April 13, 2016, https://www.the guardian.com/.

36 Bakhtin, *Rabelais*, 426.

37 *National Lampoon's Animal House*, dir. John Landis (Universal Pictures, 1978).

38 Lord Shaftsbury (Anthony Ashley Cooper), *Sensus Communis: An Essay on the Freedom of Wit and Humour, 1709, Characteristicks of Men, Manners, Opinions, Times*, foreword by Douglass Den Uyl (Indianapolis, Ind.: Liberty Fund, 2001), 1:37–94, http://oll.libertyfund .org/.

39 Herbert Spencer, "The Physiology of Laughter," in *Essays on Education, Etc.* (London: Dent, 1911), 298–309.

40 Sigmund Freud, *Jokes and Their Relation to the Unconscious*, trans. James Strachey (New York: Norton, 1963).

41 For a somewhat helpful discussion, see James W. Pennebaker, *Opening Up: The Healing Power of Expressing Emotions* (New York: Guilford Press, 1997). See also Jacqueline Garrick, "The Humor of Trauma Survivors: Its Application in a Therapeutic Milieu," *Journal of Aggression, Maltreatment, and Trauma* 12, no. 1 (2006): 169–82.

42 Carimah Townes, "The Feminist 'Slutwalk' Movement Just Landed the Perfect Celebrity Spokesperson," Think Progress, October 3, 2015, https://thinkprogress.org/; Alanna Vagianos, "Amber Rose Owns Her Sexuality with Hilarious 'Walk of No Shame,'" Huffington Post, September 15, 2015, https://www.huffingtonpost.com/.

43 Ahmed Ahmed, Maz Jobrani, Aron Kader, and Dean Obeidallah, "The Axis of Evil Comedy Tour," Comedy Central, 2007.

44 Nicholas A. Cristakis and James H. Fowler, *Connected: The Surprising Power of Our Social Networks and How They Shape Our Lives* (New York: Hackett Book Group, 2009).

45 Morreall, "Philosophy of Humor."

46 Noel Carroll, *Humour: A Very Short Introduction* (Oxford: Oxford University Press, 2014); Robert Hurley, Daniel Dennett, and Reginald Adams Jr., *Inside Jokes* (Cambridge, Mass.: MIT Press, 2013). Ted Cohen draws on Kant to sever the question of the offensive from the funny in *Jokes: Philosophical Thoughts on Joking Matters* (Chicago: University of Chicago, 1999), 84. We suspect rape jokes wouldn't be experienced as funny if they trigger retraumatization.

47 Simon Critchley, *On Humor* (New York: Routledge, 2002); Sigmund Freud, "Humour," in *Art and Literature* (1927; reprint, London: Penguin, 1976). Throughout our book, we contrast our view with a Stoic conception of life and humor. We do not deny the power of Stoic techniques to navigate our fate, but the Stoics make too sharp a dichotomy between what we can and can't control, then anchor that dichotomy in a mind–body binary. Our reflections on humor operate in the nebulous zone of what is partly but incompletely under our control, and thus from the vantage point of our vulnerability to harm together with our ability to challenge harmful norms and identities that would otherwise seem to be our fate.

48 Hitchens, "Why Women Aren't Funny."

49 Elizabeth Wilson, *Gut Feminism* (Durham, N.C.: Duke University Press, 2015).

50 Lindy West, "Comedy Helps Us Love Our Bodies," interview by Lily Percy, *Creating Our Own Lives*, NPR, June 8, 2017, https://onbeing .org/programs/humor-as-a-tool-for-survival/. Note that Day differentiates the irony of detachment, and implicitly its stoicism, from the irony of earnest political engagement in *Satire and Dissent*, 29–30. Her study of earnest humor in U.S. culture in effect calls into question the play/serious binary that has been used to define all humor.

51 Dan Zeleski, "Guy Performs Magic Trick for Orangutan," YouTube, December 7, 2015, https://www.youtube.com/watch?v=FIxYCDbRGJc.

52 Frans de Waal, *Primates and Philosophers: How Morality Evolved* (Princeton, N.J.: Princeton University Press, 2006), 59.

53 Merrit Kennedy, "This Parrot Has an 'Infectious Laugh,' Scientists Say," NPR, March 21, 2017, http://www.npr.org/.

54 Morreall, "Philosophy of Humor"; Jaak Panksepp, "Rough and Tumble Play: A Fundamental Brain Process," in *Parent–Child Play*, ed. Kevin MacDonald (Albany: State University of New York Press); and Max Eastman, *Enjoyment of Laughter* (New York: Halcyon House, 1936).

55 Morreall, "Philosophy of Humor."

56 Eastman, *Enjoyment*, 15; also cited in Morreall, "Philosophy of Humor." Eastman bases humor on the distinction between the playful and the serious, a binary that does not account for much of recent U.S. comedy.

57 Morreall, "Philosophy of Humor."

58 Bakhtin, *Rabelais*.

59 Marc Bekoff, *The Emotional Lives of Animals* (Novato: New World Press, 2007), 89.

60 Bekoff, *Emotional Lives of Animals*, 87.

1. Fumerism

1   Philip Auslander, "'Brought to You by Fem-Rage': Stand-up Comedy and the Politics of Gender," in *Acting Out: Feminist Performances,* ed. Lynda Hart and Peggy Phelan (Ann Arbor: University of Michigan Press, 1993), 316; Gail Finney, "Introduction: Unity in Difference?," in *Look Who's Laughing: Gender and Comedy,* ed. Gail Finney (Langhorne, Pa.: Gordon and Breach, 1994), 11; Danielle Russell, "Self-Deprecatory Humour and the Female Comic: Self-Destruction or Comedic Construction?," *thirdspace* 2, no. 1 (2002), http://www.thirdspace.ca/.

2   Susan J. Douglas, *Where the Girls Are: Growing Up Female with the Mass Media* (New York: Times Books/Random House, 1995), 165; see also Susan J. Douglas, *Enlightened Sexism: The Seductive Message that Feminism's Work Is Done* (New York: Times Books/Henry Holt, 2010).

3   Sally Haslanger, "Changing the Ideology and Culture of Philosophy: Not by Reason (Alone)," *Hypatia* 23, no. 2 (2008): 210–23.

4   Michel Foucault, *Discipline and Punish: The Birth of the Prison,* trans. Alan Sheridan (New York: Vintage Books, 1995), 30.

5   Audre Lorde, *Sister Outsider: Essays and Speeches by Audre Lorde* (New York: Crossing Press, 2007), 53.

6   Janet Halley, *Split Decisions: How and Why to Take a Break from Feminism* (Princeton, N.J.: Princeton University Press, 2006).

7   Halley, *Split Decisions,* 13.

8   Halley, *Split Decisions,* 7. For an account of an erotic politics that traces back to Audre Lorde, see Willett, *Irony,* 38.

9   Lorde, *Sister Outsider,* 53.

10   This exchange was replayed as a "Meet the Press Minute" in Take Two, *Meet the Press,* October 18, 2009, http://www.msnbc.msn.com.

11   Kathleen Rowe, "Roseanne: Unruly Woman as Domestic Goddess," in *Feminist Television Criticism: A Reader,* ed. Charlotte Brundson, Julie D'Acci, and Lynn Spigel (Oxford: Clarendon Press, 1997), 82.

12   *Roseanne,* "Life and Stuff," October 18, 1988. For the interview, see Joel Samuel, "Roseanne Barr: First Television Interview 1984," YouTube, September 21, 2006, http://www.youtube.com/watch?v=s8AlNnYQwOk.

13   On blues singers, see Angela Davis, *Blues Legacies and Black Feminism: Gertrude "Ma" Rainey, Bessie Smith, and Billie Holiday* (New York: Vintage, 1999). On the further use of humor in feminist movements, see Kirsten Leng, "When Politics Were Fun: Recovering a

History of Humor in U.S. Feminism," *Synoptique* 5, no. 1 (2016), special issue on "Humorous Disruptions," http://synoptique.ca/. Leng characterizes our current era as the "golden age of feminist comedy." Leng further clarified the significance of Kennedy in an October 23, 2018, e-mail conversation with the authors.

14   Gloria Steinem, "I Was a Playboy Bunny," in *Outrageous Acts and Everyday Rebellions,* 2nd ed. (New York: Holt, 1995), 367.

15   Ali Wong, *Baby Cobra* (Netflix, 2016).

16   Clinton as quoted in Regina Barreca, *They Used to Call Me Snow White . . . But I Drifted: Women's Strategic Use of Humor* (New York: Penguin Books, 1992), 178.

17   Donald Critchlow, *Phyllis Schlafly and Grassroots Conservatism: A Woman's Crusade* (Princeton, N.J.: Princeton University Press, 2005); Nan Enstad, *Ladies of Labor, Girls of Adventure* (New York: Columbia University Press, 1999); Estelle B. Freedman, *No Turning Back: The History of Feminism and the Future of Women* (New York: Random House, 2002); Lori Ginzberg, *Women and the Work of Benevolence: Morality, Politics, and Class in the 19th Century United States* (New Haven, Conn.: Yale University Press, 1990); Linda Kerber, *Women of the Republic: Intellect and Ideology in Revolutionary America* (New York: Norton, 1986); Mary Beth Norton, *Liberty's Daughters: The Revolutionary Experience of American Women, 1750–1800* (Ithaca, N.Y.: Cornell University Press, 1980); and Christine Stansell, *City of Women: Sex and Class in New York, 1789–1860* (Urbana: University of Illinois Press, 1987).

18   Douglas, *Where the Girls Are,* 284

19   Barr as quoted in Douglas, *Where the Girls Are,* 284.

20   CHO Revolution 2004.

21   Quotation from Saul Alinsky, *Rules for Radicals* (New York: Vintage, 1971). This quotation has been cited by alt-right troll and propagandist Andrew Aglin; see Luke O'Brien, "The Making of an American Nazi," *Atlantic,* December 2017, 63. For a discussion of the antifeminist politics of ridicule among the alt-rights in response to a perceived puritanical and self-righteous stance among feminists, see Angela Nagle, "The Evolution of the Alt-Right," *Atlantic,* December 2017, 69.

22   Halley, *Split Decisions* 28; Catherine MacKinnon, "Feminism, Marxism, Method and the State: An Agenda for Theory," *Signs* 7, no. 3 (1982): 515.

23   Zahra Noorbakhsh, "It's Not This Muslim Comedian's Job to Open Your Mind," *New York Times,* May 6, 2017, https://www.nytimes.com/.

24   First quote is from "Rape Victim Abortion Funding," *Daily Show,* February 7, 2011, http://www.thedailyshow.com/; second from Wanda Sykes, *Sick and Tired* (HBO, 2006); and third from Tina Fey, *Bossypants* (New York: Little, Brown, 2011), 141.

25   Fey, *Bossypants,* 11–12.

26   Fey, *Bossypants,* 14.

27   Fey, *Bossypants,* 136.

28   Fey, *Bossypants,* 141.

29   "Kotex Classic," *Saturday Night Live,* season 27, 2002, https://www.nbc.com/.

30   Fey, *Bossypants,* 14–15.

31   "Rape Victim Abortion Funding."

32   Sykes, *Sick and Tired,* part 7, 3:33. For a larger history of black female satirists, see Jessyka Finley, "Black Women's Satire as (Black) Postmodern Performance," *Studies in American Humor* 2, no. 2 (2016): 236–65.

33   Finley, "Black Women's Satire."

34   Finley, "Black Women's Satire."

35   Gilbert Gottfried, "If You Don't Want to Hear an Edgy Joke, Don't Listen," CNN, July 16, 2012, http://www.cnn.com/.

36   *Daily Show with Jon Stewart,* "Louis C.K.," clip, http://www.cc.com/video-clips/4per11/the-daily-show-with-jon-stewart-louis-c-k-.

37   Jennifer L. Pozner, "Louis C.K. on Daniel Tosh's Rape Joke: Are Comedy and Feminism Enemies?," Daily Beast, July 18, 2012, http://www.thedailybeast.com/. Louis C.K.'s pattern of this kind of humor undergirds not just the sexist climate in comedy and the entertainment business but also the multiple counts of sexual misconduct and abuse that he has admitted to.

38   "Violence Pyramid," CCASA Your World, http://ccasayourworld.com/.

39   West, "How to Make a Rape Joke."

40   Cameron Esposito, *Rape Jokes,* 2018, https://www.cameronesposito.com/.

41   Lorde, *Sister Outsider.*

42   Lorde, *Sister Outsider,* 55. Lorde's use of the ancient Greek word *eros,* which signifies passion and a strong sense of connection, is useful as an alternative to the ancient Stoics and their practices of detachment (as in the humor of transcendence).

43   Humor is not a cure-all for our social ills. On the contrary, as cultural theorists, historians, and philosophers warn, comedy all too often reproduces narrow forms of community and identity in ways that can

pose serious challenges to the egalitarian emphasis of our fumerism. The reactionary function or aims of many jokes coheres with broader claims about comedy from historian Gail Finney. It is her observation that "comedy is based on shared experience, attitudes, and values; it creates in-groups and out-groups by mocking aberrations from the norm or the norm itself." See her introduction to *Look Who's Laughing*, 6–7. This mocking of aberrations from the norm produces pleasure in the audience through feelings of superiority that come from punishing or excluding so-called inferiors. Lawrence E. Mintz similarly warns that a potentially narrow identity is central to a community that is held together through ridicule or in-jokes: "The comedian must establish for the audience that the group is homogenous, a community, if the laughter is to come easily." See his "Standup Comedy as Social and Cultural Mediation," *American Quarterly* 37, no. 1 (1985): 78. Philip Auslander highlights the specifically gendered nature of some of these groups. He notes that when, for example, the female comedian addresses female audience members, she "creates a community with other women based on common experience (frequently of men) . . . [and even] a shared subjectivity that excludes men." Of course, as Auslander notes, this kind of comedy can be empowering for women by offering forms of identification or recognition. It may operate in the same way that separatism does in a social movement, thereby enabling an oppressed minority to claim an identity, a shared history, and a voice. The subversion of comedy can thus operate through cementing forms of identity and by inverting assumed superiority and inferiority, and this dynamic of exclusion might not always be bad, or for that matter even avoidable. See Auslander, "Brought to You by Fem-Rage," 320–21. As Joanne R. Gilbert argues, "Hierarchy is essential to most humor." Gilbert, *Performing Marginality: Humor, Gender, and Cultural Critique* (Detroit, Mich.: Wayne State University Press, 2004), 324. This research should leave us wary that despite its understandable appeal for marginalized groups, comedy may reinvoke insider/outsider and hierarchical social structures. The humor of marginalized communities may invert but not fundamentally alter the system of oppression, and for this reason it may sow the seeds of resentment and backlash rather than progressive social change. In chapter 5, we turn to the use of solidaric empathy in humor to address some of these concerns.

44   Mary Douglas, "Jokes," in *Implicit Meanings: Essays in Anthropology* (London: Routledge and Kegan Paul, 1985), 95.

45 On resentment, see Wendy Brown, *States of Injury: Power and Freedom in Late Modernity* (Princeton, N.J.: Princeton University Press, 1995), xi.

46 Lisa Henderson finds that "humor both reveals and produces . . . a cultural mortar or strain of recognition and alliance among even the most tenuously related persons." See "Simple Pleasures: Lesbian Community and Go Fish," in *Chick Flicks: Contemporary Women at the Movies,* ed. Suzanne Ferriss and Mallory Young (London: Routledge, 2007), 135–36.

47 Regina Barreca, introduction to *Last Laughs: Perspectives on Women and Comedy* (New York: Gordon and Breach, 1988), 15. See also Judy Little's classic study of feminists using humor to critique social norms, *Comedy and the Woman Writer* (Lincoln: University of Nebraska Press, 1983).

48 Mintz, "Standup Comedy," 77.

49 For the classic conservative view of satire's social function, see Bergson, *Laughter.*

50 See Charlotte Bunch, "Not by Degrees: Feminist Theory and Education," in *Passionate Politics: Feminist Theory in Action* (New York: St. Martin's Press, 1987), 244, in which she argues that feminism needs a utopian vision.

51 A utopic vision aimed toward a new, more inclusive, and egalitarian society is a common feature of comic drama; see Frye, *Anatomy of Criticism,* 182–83.

52 Ladelle McWhorter, *Racism and Sexual Oppression in Anglo-America: A Genealogy* (Bloomington: Indiana University Press, 2009), 34.

53 McWhorter, *Racism and Sexual Oppression,* 30.

54 McWhorter, *Racism and Sexual Oppression,* 31.

55 Iris Marion Young, *Justice and the Politics of Difference* (Princeton, N.J.: Princeton University Press, 1990), 100.

56 Halley, *Split Decisions,* 200.

57 Michel Foucault, *The Order of Things: An Archeology of the Human Sciences* (New York: Vintage Books, 1994), xv.

58 Lynne Huffer, *Mad for Foucault* (New York: Columbia University Press, 2009), 210.

59 Todd May, "Approaching Neoliberalism Genealogically: Methodological Considerations," paper presented at the American Philosophical Association, Eastern Division, New York City, December 27–30, 2009.

60 Susan Bordo, *The Male Body: A New Look at Men in Public and in*

Private (New York: Farrar, Straus and Giroux, 1999), 120; Barbara Ehrenreich, *The Hearts of Men: American Dreams and the Flight from Commitment* (New York: Anchor Press/Doubleday, 1983), 41.

61   Steinem, "I Was a Playboy Bunny."

62   Flynn, "Foucault as Parrhesiast," 102–18.

63   Huffer, *Mad for Foucault*, 242.

64   Philip Hearst, *Wimmin, Wimps, and Wallflowers: An Encyclopedic Dictionary of Gender and Sexual Orientation in the United States* (Boston: Intercultural Press, 2001); G. Louis Heath, *Off the Pigs! The History and Literature of the Black Panther Party* (Lanham, Md.: Rowman and Littlefield, 1976); Peniel E. Joseph, *Waiting 'Til the Midnight Hour: A Narrative History of Black Power in America* (New York: Holt Paperbacks, 2007); Manning Marrable, *Race, Reform, and Rebellion: The Second Reconstruction and Beyond in Black America, 1945–2006*, 3rd ed. (Jackson: University Press of Mississippi, 2007).

65   Mel Watkins, ed., *African American Humor: The Best Black Comedy from Slavery to Today* (Chicago: Lawrence Hill, 2002).

66   Crenshaw, "Mapping the Margins," 1241–99; Collins, *Black Feminist Thought*, 201–38; and Lorde, "The Master's Tools Will Never Dismantle the Master's House," in *Sister Outsider*, 110–14. However, many others have also contributed to intersectionality theory, including *This Bridge Called My Back*, an anthology of writing by radical women of color edited by Chicana feminists Gloria Anzaldúa and Cherríe Moraga (Watertown, Mass.: Persephone Press, 1981), and Elizabeth V. Spelman's *Inessential Woman* (Boston: Beacon Press, 1988). For an important account of the term's history, see Collins and Bilge, *Intersectionality*, esp. 63–87.

67   Collins and Bilge, *Intersectionality*, 22.

68   Wanda Sykes, *I'ma Be Me* (HBO, 2009).

69   Wanda Sykes, *I'ma Be Me*.

70   Wanda Sykes, *I'ma Be Me*.

71   Recall that for Friedrich Nietzsche, grammar is the last refuge of piety: "I am afraid that we cannot get rid of God because we still have faith in grammar." Nietzsche, "Twilight of the Idols" (1889), in *The Portable Nietzsche*, trans. Walter Kaufmann (New York: Viking, 1968), 483.

72   Margaret Cho quoted in Allison Fraiberg, "Between the Laughter: Bridging Feminist Studies through Women's Stand-up Comedy," in *Look Who's Laughing*, 324.

73   Januaryfairy, "Margaret Cho Discusses Lots of Things in Cincinnati," YouTube, December 1, 2008, http://www.youtube.com/watch?v=iY9G52IKsyc.

74 Margaret Cho, *I'm The One That I Want* (2002).

75 C-SPAN, "Wanda Sykes at the 2009 White House Correspondents Dinner," YouTube, May 9, 2009, https://www.youtube.com/watch?v=zmyRog2w4DI.

76 Russell, "Self-Deprecatory Humour."

77 Mintz, "Standup Comedy," 74.

78 Jefferson Cowie and Lauren Boehm, "Dead Man's Town: *Born in the USA*, Social History, and Working-Class Identity," *American Quarterly* 58, no, 2 (2006): 361.

79 Lauren McGaughy, "Texas Board Votes to Eliminate Hillary Clinton, Helen Keller from History Curriculum," *Dallas News*, September 14, 2018, https://www.dallasnews.com/.

80 Sykes, *I'ma Be Me.*

81 Sykes, *I'ma Be Me.*

82 Sykes, *I'ma Be Me.*

83 Sykes, *I'ma Be Me.*

84 Claude M. Steele, "A Threat in the Air: How Stereotypes Shape Intellectual Identity and Performance," *American Psychologist* 52, no. 6 (1997): 613–29.

2. Fighting Back against Islamophobia and Post-9/11 Nationalism

1 Ahmed et al., "Axis of Evil Comedy Tour."

2 Stephen Sheehi, *Islamophobia: The Ideological Campaign against Muslims* (Atlanta, Ga.: Clarity, 2013).

3 Toni Morrison, tweeted from @MsToniMorrison, April 3, 2013.

4 Nadine Nabor writes countering not only with "decolonizing methodologies" that deconstruct Orientalism, as well as the essentializing and objectifying narratives of Arab life and their occlusion as agents used for imperialism, but also that they "[replace] Orientalism with new forms of knowledge." Nabor, *Arab America: Gender, Cultural Politics, and Activism* (New York: New York University Press, 2012), 15.

5 Toni Morrison may have claimed Bill Clinton as the first Black U.S. president, but like political thinkers such as W. E. B. Du Bois, she also understands that to be American implies some strong degree of whiteness. See Du Bois, *The Souls of Black Folk* (1903; reprint, New York: Pocket Books, 2005); and Toni Morrison, "Clinton as the First Black President," *New Yorker,* October 1998.

6 We draw from many theorists, including Melissa Gregg and Gregory Seigworth, eds., *The Affect Theory Reader* (Durham, N.C.: Duke

University Press, 2010); Melissa Gregg and Gregory Seigworth, "An Inventory of Shimmers," in Gregg and Seigworth, *Affect Theory Reader,* esp. 1–28; Ahmed, *Cultural Politics*; Sara Ahmed, *The Promise of Happiness* (Durham, N.C.: Duke University Press, 2010); John Protevi, *Political Affect* (Minneapolis: University of Minnesota Press, 2009); Daniel N. Stern, *The Interpersonal World of the Infant* (New York: Basic Books, 1985); Cynthia Willett, *Maternal Ethics and Other Slave Moralities* (New York: Routledge, 1995); and Willett, *Interspecies Ethics,* on resonance, affect clouds, and network theory.

7   Teresa Brennan, *The Transmission of Affect* (Ithaca, N.Y.: Cornell University Press, 2004), 1.

8   Daniel N. Stern, *Forms of Vitality* (Oxford: Oxford University Press, 2010), 4–5, 46.

9   Ahmed, *Cultural Politics,* 1.

10   For more on this history, see Brennan, *Transmission of Affect,* 18.

11   Cristakis and Fowler, *Connected.*

12   Willett, *Irony,* 37–40.

13   Jamil Abu-Wardeh, "The Axis of Evil Middle East Comedy Tour," TEDBlog, July 2010, http://www.ted.com/.

14   Bassem Youssef, "Egyptian Political Satirist Bassem Youssef on Media and the Arab Spring," NPR, March 19, 2017, http://www.npr.org/.

15   Youssef, "Egyptian Political Satirist."

16   Ahmed et al., "Axis of Evil."

17   *Real Time with Bill Maher,* season 9, episode 212, May 6, 2011.

18   Malcolm X and Alex Haley, *The Autobiography of Malcolm X* (New York: Ballantine, 1999), 327.

19   Caitlin Flanagan, "Is Late Night TV Helping Democracy or Debasing It?," *Atlantic,* May 2017, 58–61.

20   Slate, "Muslims Can't Take a Joke about Islam? Don't Tell That to These Muslim Comedians," YouTube, August 16, 2017, https://www.youtube.com/watch?v=NsyeZUjHJ9w.

21   *Late Show with Stephen Colbert,* "Ramy Youssef Is Expecting a Hogwarts Letter from ISIS," YouTube, May 12, 2017, https://www.youtube.com/watch?v=I9R6vtcD09I.

22   Frans de Waal, *The Age of Empathy* (New York: Random House, 2009), 19.

23   Stephen Colbert, "Fear for All, Part One," *Colbert Report,* October 28, 2010, and "Fear for All, Part Two," *Colbert Report,* October 28, 2010, http://www.colbertnation.com/.

24   Colbert, "Fear for All, Part One."

25   Colbert, "Fear for All, Part One."

26 Colbert, "Fear for All, Part Two."

27 Abu-Wardeh, "Axis of Evil."

28 *Tickling Giants,* dir. Sara Taksler (Gravitas Ventures, 2016).

29 Cristakis and Fowler, *Connected.*

30 Cristakis and Fowler, *Connected,* 108.

31 Cristakis and Fowler, *Connected,* 108.

32 Youssef, "Egyptian Political Satirist."

33 Cristakis and Fowler, *Connected,* 116.

34 Cristakis and Fowler, *Connected,* 120.

35 Hari Kondabolu, *Warn Your Relatives* (Netflix, April 27, 2018).

36 Cristakis and Fowler, *Connected,* 133.

37 Ujala Fehgal, "Katie Couric: Maybe We Need a Muslim *Cosby Show,*" *Business Insider,* December 31, 2010, https://www.businessinsider.com/.

38 Jon Stewart, "Allah in the Family," *Daily Show,* February 17, 2011, http://www.thedailyshow.com/.

39 On neoliberalism's tragic underside, see Michelle Alexander, *The New Jim Crow: Mass Incarceration in the Age of Colorblindness* (New York: New Press, 2012); and Cynthia Willett and Julie Willett, "Trayvon Martin and the Tragedy of the New Jim Crow," in *Pursuing Trayvon Martin: Historical Contexts and Contemporary Manifestations of Racial Dynamics,* ed. George Yancy and Janine Jones (Lanham, Md.: Lexington Books, 2012), 215–24.

40 Ahmed et al., "Axis of Evil."

41 Joseph Boskin and Joseph Dorinson, "Ethnic Humor: Subversion and Survival," *American Quarterly* 37, no. 1 (1985): 86.

42 X and Haley, *Autobiography,* 347.

43 Kondabolu, *Warn Your Relatives.*

44 "Kumail Nanjiani Standup Monologue," *Saturday Night Live,* YouTube, October 14, 2017, https://www.youtube.com/watch?v=z2X0TaXknVE.

45 Lawrence E. Mintz, "The 'New Wave' of Standup Comedians: An Introduction," *America Humor* 4, no. 1 (1977): 1.

46 Nancy Fraser and Linda Nicholson, "Social Criticism without Philosophy," *Theory, Culture, and Society* 5 (1988): 373–94.

47 Samuel P. Huntington, *Who Are We? The Challenges to America's National Identity* (New York: Simon and Schuster, 2004).

48 Aasif Mandvi, "Amnesty Unintentional," *Daily Show,* May 23, 2007, http://www.thedailyshow.com/.

49 Stephen Colbert, "Citizenship Down—Akhil Amar," *Colbert Report,* August 10, 2010, http://www.colbertnation.com/.

50   Vijay Prashad, *Everybody Was Kung Fu Fighting: Afro-Asian Connections and the Myth of Cultural Purity* (Boston: Beacon Press, 2002), 69.
51   Prashad, *Everybody Was Kung Fu Fighting*, x.
52   Prashad, *Everybody Was Kung Fu Fighting*, x.
53   Prashad, *Everybody Was Kung Fu Fighting*, x.
54   Watkins, *African American Humor*.
55   Manning Marable, *Malcolm X: A Life of Reinvention* (New York: Viking), 11.
56   Steve Estes, *I Am a Man! Race, Manhood, and the Civil Rights Movement* (Chapel Hill: University of North Carolina Press, 2005), 156.
57   Todd Boyd, *The H.N.I.C.: The Death of Civil Rights and the Reign of Hip Hop* (New York: New York University Press, 2003), 28.
58   Laura Pulido, "A Day without Immigrants: The Racial and Class Politics of Immigrant Exclusion," *Antipode* 39, no. 1 (2007): 3; Kevin R. Johnson and Bill Ong Hing, "The Immigrant Rights Marches of 2006 and the Prospects for a New Civil Rights Movement," *Harvard Civil Rights–Civil Liberties Law Review* 42 (2007).
59   Michelle Chen, "The Day without Immigrant Workers Has Begun," *Nation*, May 1, 2017, https://www.thenation.com/.
60   Arturo Rodriguez, "Take Our Jobs," *Colbert Report*, July 7, 2010.
61   Rodriguez, "Take Our Jobs"; United Farm Workers, June 24, 2010, http://takeourjobs.org/.
62   Lin-Manuel Miranda, *The Hamilton Mixtape* (Atlantic Records, 2016).
63   Lalo Alcaraz, "Cartoon: Mexico Built the Wall for Free," Daily Kos, March 8, 2016, https://www.dailykos.com/.
64   Ahmed et al., "Axis of Evil."

3. Can the Animal Subaltern Laugh?

1   For a discussion of the continuities and parallelism, see de Waal, "Appendix A: Anthropomorphism and Anthropodienial," in *Primates and Philosophers*, 59–68. See also Bekoff, *Emotional Lives of Animals*. For a rich discussion of culture and communication in birds, see Eugene Morton, "Culture Shapes Bird Communication, Too," Duke Research Blog, June 19, 2012, https://researchblog.duke.edu/.
2   "Advertising to Monkeys," *Colbert Report*, June 28, 2011, http://www.colbertnation.com/.
3   Rowan Hooper, "The First Advertising Campaign for Non-human Primates," *New Scientist*, June 27, 2011, https://www.newscientist.com/.

4   De Waal, *Primates and Philosophers*; de Waal, *Age of Empathy*; Donna
    J. Haraway, *When Species Meet* (Minneapolis: University of Minne-
    sota Press, 2008); Kelly Oliver, *Animal Lessons: How they Teach Us to
    Be Human* (New York: Columbia University Press, 2009); and Cary
    Wolfe, *Animal Rites: American Culture, the Discourse of the Species,
    and Posthumanist Theory* (Chicago: University of Chicago Press,
    2003). For use of animal imagery in literature and media, see Susan
    McHugh, *Animal Stories: Narrating across Species Lines* (Minneapo-
    lis: University of Minnesota Press, 2011).

5   See Helmuth Plessner, *Lachen und Weinen, Gesammelte Schriften*,
    vol. 7 (Frankfurt a.M.: Suhrkamp, 1984); and Critchley, *On Humor*,
    28.

6   Primatologist Malini Suchak confirms that she has on many occasions
    had chimpanzees laugh at her; e-mail conversation with authors,
    April 20, 2013.

7   See Ranajit Guta, *Elementary Aspects of Peasant Insurgency in Co-
    lonial India* (Durham, N.C.: Duke University Press, 1999), for an
    intriguing list of criteria for subalternality that includes alternative
    channels of communication. Among these channels, she mainly fo-
    cuses on rumor, but her analysis might be extended to include laugh-
    ter and mockery.

8   De Waal, *Age of Empathy*, 47. For a study of laughter primarily among
    humans and primates, see Robert R. Provine, *Laughter: A Scientific
    Investigation* (New York: Penguin, 2000).

9   On infrapolitics, see James C. Stott, *Weapons of the Weak: Everyday
    Forms of Peasant Resistance* (New Haven, Conn.: Yale University
    Press, 1987).

10 *Rise of the Planet of the Apes*, dir. Rupert Wyatt (20th Century Fox,
    2011). On biopower, see Roberto Esposito, *Bíos: Biopolitics and Phi-
    losophy*, trans. Timothy C. Campbell (Minneapolis: University of Min-
    nesota Press, 2008).

11 Elizabeth Kolbert, "Annals of Evolution: Sleeping with the Enemy—
    What Happened between the Neanderthals and Us?," *New Yorker*,
    August 15, 2011.

12 Charles Siebert, "An Elephant Crackup?," *New York Times Magazine*,
    October 8, 2006; G. A. Bradshaw and Allan N. Schore, "How Ele-
    phants Are Opening Doors: Developmental Neuroethology, Attach-
    ment and Social Context," *Ethology* 113 (2007): 426–36.

13 For a study of that characterizes communal ties as clusters among
    elephants as nodes of social networks, see Patrick I. Chiyo, Cyn-
    thia J. Moss, and Susan C. Alberts, "The Influence of Life History

Milestones and Association Networks on Crop-Raiding Behavior in Male African Elephants," *PLoS One* 7 (2012), https://doi.org/10.1371/journal.pone.0031382.

14 J. M. Coetzee, *The Lives of Animals* (Princeton, N.J.: Princeton University Press, 1999); Jacques Derrida, "The Animal That Therefore I Am (More to Follow)," trans. David Wills, *Critical Inquiry* 28, no. 2 (2002): 369–418; Oliver, *Animal Lessons*; Chloe Taylor, "The Precarious Lives of Animals," *Philosophy Today* 52, no. 1 (2008): 60–73.

15 Susan J. Pearson, *The Rights of the Defenseless: Protecting Animals and Children in Gilded Age America* (Chicago: University of Chicago Press, 2011), 9.

16 Euripides, *Women on the Edge: Four Plays,* ed. Ruby Blondell, Mary-Kay Gamel, Nancy Sorkin Rabinowitz, and Bella Zweig (New York: Routledge, 1999), 12.

17 E. P. Evans, *The Criminal Prosecution and Capital Punishment of Animals* (1906), cited in Jeffry St. Clair's introduction to Jason Hribal, *Fear of the Animal Planet: The Hidden History of Animal Resistance* (Petrolia, California: CounterPunch, 2010), 2.

18 St. Clair in Hribal, *Fear of the Animal Planet,* 7.

19 St. Clair in Hribal, *Fear of the Animal Planet,* 8.

20 St. Clair in Hribal, *Fear of the Animal Planet,* 4.

21 Michel de Montaigne, "On Cruelty," in *The Complete Essays of Montaigne* (Palo Alto: Stanford University Press, 1958).

22 Pearson, *Rights of the Defenseless,* 16.

23 For an alternative approach to rights that emphasizes sentience and agency and is thus more congruent with our own emphasis on affect, emotions, and agency, see Sue Donaldson and Will Kymlicka, *Zoopolis: A Political Theory of Animal Rights* (Oxford: Oxford University Press, 2011). They argue for various sorts of citizenship and autonomy as well as rights for nonhumans.

24 On the importance of sympathy, see Martha Nussbaum, *Frontiers of Justice: Disability, Nationality, Species Membership* (Cambridge, Mass.: Harvard University Press, 2007), 35.

25 Nussbaum, *Frontiers of Justice,* 409.

26 See Martha Nussbaum's "Beyond 'Compassion and Humanity,'" in *Animal Rights: Current Debates and New Directions,* ed. Cass R. Sunstein and Martha C. Nussbaum (Oxford: Oxford University Press, 2004), 299–320. Her aim is to move the compassionate consideration of other creatures from the private, moral realm into the realm of justice. Her approach remains, as she explains, paternalistic.

27 David Hume, *A Treatise of Human Nature* (Oxford: Clarendon Press,

1960); Jonathan Haidt, *The Happiness Hypothesis: Finding Modern Truth in Ancient Wisdom* (New York: Basic Books, 2005), 17.

28   De Waal, *Primates and Philosophers*, 65.

29   This section borrows from Willett, *Maternal Ethics*, 129–56. For the key texts of Frederick Douglass, see *Narrative of the Life of Frederick Douglass, an American Slave*, ed. Houston A. Baker Jr. (New York: Viking Penguin, 1982); and "The Heroic Slave," in *Three Classic African-American Novels*, ed. William L. Andrews (New York: Mentor, 1990), 27–28.

30   See Willett, *Irony*, chap. 5, for the three generations of rights and freedoms beyond their liberal conceptions.

31   Much attention has been given as well to technical dimensions of language as a recursive phenomenon. Those who claim that only human language is recursive overlook its role in music, which, as Steven Mithen explains, provides an evolutionary origin for human and nonhuman language; see *The Singing Neanderthals: The Origins of Music, Language, Mind, and Body* (Cambridge, Mass.: Harvard University Press, 2006), 17.

32   Gayatri Chakravorty Spivak, "Can the Subaltern Speak?," in *Marxism and the Interpretation of Culture*, ed. Cary Nelson and Lawrence Grossberg (Basingstoke: Macmillan Education, 1988). See also Spivak's response to interpretations and revision of the essay in Rosalyn Morris, *Can the Subaltern Speak? Reflections on the History of an Idea* (New York: Columbia University Press, 2010).

33   Nancy Hewitt, *No Permanent Waves: Recasting Histories of U.S. Feminism* (New Brunswick, N.J.: Rutgers University Press, 2010).

34   De Waal, *Age of Empathy*, 106–7.

35   For more recent calls for animal liberation, see Paola Cavalieri, *The Death of the Animal*, with Matthew Calarco, John M. Coetzee, Harlan B. Miller, and Cary Wolfe (New York: Columbia University Press, 2009).

36   See Con Slobodchikoff, *Chasing Doctor Dolittle: Learning the Language of Animals* (New York: St. Martin's Press, 2012), for the argument that other species communicate and that human language is not an exception in the animal world.

37   *Ape Genius*, dir. John Ruben (Public Broadcasting System, 2009), http://video.pbs.org/video/1200128615.

38   Michael Tomasello, *Why We Cooperate* (Cambridge, Mass.: MIT Press, 2009), 19.

39   Malini Suchak confirms this via e-mail communication to the authors, April 20, 2013.

40   G. A. Bradshaw, *Elephants on the Edge* (New Haven, Conn.: Yale University Press, 2009), 29.

41   Bradshaw, *Elephants on the Edge,* 11. The primary source on elephant hippocampus morphology is Atiya Hakeem et al., "Brain of the African Elephant *(Loxodonta africana)*: Neuroanatomy from Magnetic Resonance Images," *Anatomical Record Part A 287a* (2005):1117–27. The elephant hippocampus pretty much puts the primate brain to shame in terms of proportional size and structural complexity, according to neuroscientist Katherine Bryant (e-mail correspondence to authors, April 2, 2013). She would amend Bradshaw's statement to say that the hippocampus is responsible for mediating long-term memory—especially the spatial organization of things ("place cells"), but also social memory. On the hippocampus and place cells, see Elizabeth Marozzi and Kathryn J. Jeffery, "Place, Space and Memory Cells," *Current Biology* 22 (2012): 939–42. Bryant notes that it is difficult to distinguish social information from other kinds of information, and that there may be no such thing as nonsocial information. She adds the caveat that the exact function of the hippocampus probably varies from species to species, and it is likely that the elephant hippocampus might focus on social memory. For a discussion of whether the hippocampus encodes only spatial information or also social relationships, see Dharshan Kumaran and Eleanor A. Maguire, "The Human Hippocampus: Cognitive Maps or Relational Memory?," *Journal of Neuroscience* 3 (2005): 7254–59.

42   Tomasello et al, *Why We Cooperate,* 63, 72.

43   Zanna Clay and Frans de Waal, "Bonobos Respond to Distress in Others: Consolation across the Age Spectrum," *PLoS One* 8 (2003), https://doi.org/10.1371/journal.pone.0055206.

44   Bekoff, *Emotional Lives of Animals,* 13.

45   Bekoff, *Emotional Lives of Animals,* 6–7.

46   Jaak Panksepp and Lucy Biven, *The Archaeology of Mind: Neuroevolutionary Origins of Human Emotions* (New York: Norton, 2012), 371.

47   Tomasello et al, *Why We Cooperate,* 116.

48   Stefan Lovgren, "Animals Laughed Long Before Humans, Study Says," *National Geographic,* March 31, 2005, http://news.national geographic.com/.

49   Jesse Bering, "The Rat That Laughed: Do Animals Other Than Humans Have a Sense of humor? Maybe So," *Scientific American* 307 (2012): 76.

50   Bering, "Rat That Laughed," 44.

51   Bering, "Rat That Laughed," 44.

52 Bering, "Rat That Laughed," 60.
53 Vicki Hearne, *Adam's Task* (New York: Vintage, 1986), 62.
54 Provine, *Laughter*, 94–95.
55 Bekoff, *Emotional Lives of Animals*, 87.
56 Bekoff, *Emotional Lives of Animals*, 89.
57 De Waal, *Age of Empathy*, 198.
58 Suchak, e-mail communication to authors, April 20, 2013. This is in contrast with "despotic" rhesus monkeys, where a higher-ranking individual will take the food right out of the mouth of a lower-ranking individual—a behavior that would violate the social norms of chimpanzees.
59 De Waal, *Age of Empathy*, 199, 161, 24.
60 De Waal, *Age of Empathy*, 47.
61 De Waal, *Age of Empathy*, 99.
62 This statement by George Orwell is found in Sonia Orwell and Ian Angus, eds., *The Collected Essays, Journalism, and Letters of George Orwell, Vol. 3: As I Please, 1943–1945* (New York, 1969), 184. This citation is referenced in Sandra Swart's article "'The Terrible Laughter of the Afrikaner': Towards a Social History of Humor," *Journal of Social History* 42 (2009): 899.
63 De Waal, *Age of Empathy*, 8. See also Charles Darwin, *Descent of Man, and Selection in Relation to Sex* (1871; reprint, New York: Hurst, 1878), esp. chap. 3.
64 Bradshaw, *Elephants on the Edge*, 14.
65 De Waal, *Primates and Philosophers*, 44–45.
66 Todd M. Preuss, e-mail communication to authors, July 14, 2011.
67 De Waal, *Age of Empathy*, 187.
68 De Waal, *Age of Empathy*, 59.
69 De Waal, *Age of Empathy*, 61.
70 This quotation is from Spanish writer Oriol Pi-Sunyer's "Political Humor in a Dictatorial State: The Case of Spain," *Ethnohistory* 24 (1977): 179–90, cited in Swart, "Terrible Laughter," 899.
71 De Waal, *Age of Empathy*, 72.
72 Barbara Kingsolver, *Animal, Vegetable, Miracle: A Year of Food Life* (New York: HarperCollins, 2007), 90.
73 Kingsolver, *Animal, Vegetable, Miracle*, 95.
74 Bekoff, *Emotional Lives of Animals*, 57.
75 Hribal, *Fear of the Animal Planet*, 11.
76 See Philip Caputo, *Ghosts of Tsavo: Stalking the Missing Lions of East Africa* (Washington, D.C.: National Geographic Society, 2009).
77 Hribal, *Fear of the Animal Planet*, 25–26.

78   Vicki L. Ruiz, *From Out of the Shadows: Mexican Women in Twentieth-Century America*, 10th ed. (New York: Oxford University Press, 2008); Annelise Orleck, *Storming Caesar's Palace: How Black Women Fought Their Own War on Poverty* (Boston: Beacon Press, 2006).

79   Eileen Boris and Rhacel Salazar Parrenas, eds., *Intimate Labors: Cultures, Technologies, and the Politics of Care* (Stanford, Calif.: Stanford University Press, 2010).

80   Alexander Saxton, *The Indispensable Enemy: Labor and the Anti-Chinese Movement in California* (Berkeley: University of California Press, 1975).

81   See, e.g., David R. Roediger, *The Wages of Whiteness: Race and the Making of the American Working Class* (New York: Verso, 2007); *Working toward Whiteness: How America's Immigrants Became White—The Strange Journey from Ellis Island to the Suburbs* (New York: Basic Books, 2006); and *History against Misery* (Chicago: Charles H. Kerr, 2006).

82   Prashad, *Everybody Was Kung Fu Fighting*.

83   See, e.g., Calvin Martin, *The Way of the Human Being* (New Haven, Conn.: Yale University Press, 2000); Calvin Martin, *In the Spirit of the Earth: Rethinking History and Time* (Baltimore, Md.: Johns Hopkins University Press, 1993); Calvin Martin, *Keepers of the Game: Indian–Animal Relationships and the Fur Trade* (Berkeley: University of California Press, 1982); Howard Harrod, *The Animals Came Dancing: Native American Sacred Ecology and Animal Kinship* (Tucson: University of Arizona Press, 2000); and Joel Martin, *The Land Looks After Us: A History of Native American Religion* (New York: Oxford University Press, 1999).

84   Eileen Boris, "The Gender of Labor History: The Difference It Makes," *Genesis* 15, no. 2 (2016): 147–66.

85   Upton Sinclair, *The Jungle* (1906; reprint, Hollywood, Fla.: Simon and Brown, 2012); *Modern Times*, dir. Charles Chaplin (Charles Chaplin Productions, 1936).

86   Haraway, *When Species Meet*.

87   Thomas G. Andrews, *Killing for Coal: America's Deadliest Labor War* (Cambridge, Mass.: Harvard University Press, 2008), 134.

88   Andrews, *Killing for Coal*, 130.

89   Susan Orlean, *Rin Tin Tin: The Life and the Legend* (New York: Simon and Schuster, 2011), 52. Another apparently true animal story turned into a movie tells of two lions who worked together against the British attempt to build a railroad across their territory in Africa at the end of

the nineteenth century. See *The Ghost and the Darkness*, dir. Stephen Hopkins (Constellation Entertainment, 1996).

90 Haraway, *When Species Meet*, 21.

4. A Catharsis of Shame

1 "Trump Voter Feels Betrayed after Reading 800 Pages of Feminist Theory," Onion, May 3, 2017, https://politics.theonion.com/.

2 Gary Kinsman, "AIDS Activism and the Politics of Emotion: An Interview with Deborah Gould," *Upping the Anti: A Journal of Theory and Action* 8 (2009): 72. See also Arlie Russell Hochschild, "Emotion Work, Feeling Rules, and Social Structure," *American Journal of Sociology* 85, no. 3 (1979): 551–75. On the exploitation of affective labor, see Shiloh Whitney, "Affective Indigestion: Lorde, Fanon, and Gutierrez-Rodriguez on Race and Affective Labor," *Journal of Speculative Philosophy* 30, no. 3 (2016): 278–91.

3 For more on queer camp, see Lauran Whitworth, *"Goodbye Gauley Mountain,* Hello Eco-Camp: Queer Environmentalism in the Anthropocene," *Feminist Theory* 21, no. 1 (2018): 73–92.

4 Michael Gershon, *The Second Brain: A Groundbreaking New Understanding of Nervous Disorders of the Stomach and Intestine* (New York: HarperCollins, 1999); Haidt, *Happiness Hypothesis*, 5; Haraway, *When Species Meet*, 6; Willett, *Interspecies Ethics*, 84, 113–17; Wilson, *Gut Feminism*; Shannon Sullivan, *The Physiology of Sexist and Racist Oppression* (Oxford: Oxford University Press, 2015), 66–98.

5 Carroll, *Humour*; Morreall, "Philosophy of Humor."

6 Carroll, *Humour*, 18.

7 Carroll, *Humour*, 19.

8 Krefting, *All Joking Aside*, 4, 7.

9 We are therefore not surprised to see that increasingly psychologists are beginning to question cerebral theories of humor. See Rod A. Martin, *The Psychology of Humor: An Integrative Approach* (Burlington, Mass.: Elsevier Academic Press, 2007). Martin argues that humor is defined by the emotion of mirth as he brings together research demonstrating how humor can play a role in negotiating social relationships. Note by contrast that Critchley explicitly characterizes the highest laughter as "mirthless"; *On Humor*, 49–50. We are looking at not just mirth but a range of emotions while also questioning the serious/playful binary that Martin, among others, holds to.

10 We do not deny the popularity of absurdist humor. Krefting observes

that in contrast with political and charged humor, for the most part the public prefers safe, absurdist, shock, or modern-day minstrelsy humor; see *All Joking Aside*, 104.

11   Critchley, *On Humor*.

12   Freud, "Humour," 427–33.

13   Freud, *Jokes*. In fact, Freud's updated theory of humor seems to trace back to what he considers the least tendentious and most mature mode of the comedic in this earlier text. In this updated theory, Freud believes that the achievement of humor represents the ultimate stage of maturity. In contrast, what he views as the most tendentious mode of the comedic, the transgressive joke, we return to later.

14   Critchley, *On Humor*, 94–95.

15   Critchley, *On Humor*, 109.

16   Vagianos, "Amber Rose Owns Her Sexuality."

17   Samantha Bee, *Full Frontal*, September 26, 2018; Full Frontal with Samantha Bee, "Sam Goes Full Carrie over Kavanaugh," YouTube, September 26, 2018, https://youtu.be/yqrZBfk3lv0; Matt Wilstein, "Samantha Bee Goes Nuclear on GOP for 'Slut-Shaming' Kavanaugh Accusers," Daily Beast, September 26, 2018, https://www.thedaily beast.com/.

18   Morreall, "Philosophy of Humor."

19   Ralph Ellison, "The Extravagance of Laughter" (1985), in *Going to the Territory* (New York: Vintage Books, 2011).

20   Shaftsbury, *Sensus Communis*.

21   Morreall, "Philosophy of Humor."

22   Andrew Stott, *Comedy: The New Critical Idiom* (New York: Routledge, 2014), 100–101.

23   Spencer, "Physiology of Laughter."

24   Freud, *Jokes*.

25   Morreall, "Philosophy of Humor."

26   Pennebaker, *Opening Up*.

27   Pennebaker, *Opening Up*, 100–101.

28   Stern, *Interpersonal World*; and *Forms of Vitality*, esp. 46.

29   Haidt, *Happiness Hypothesis*, 33. Note, however, that terminology for these distinctions differs across disciplines.

30   Stern, *Forms of Vitality*, 45. Stern elaborates by drawing on Antonio Damasio, *The Feeling of What Happens* (Boston: Harcourt, 1999), esp. 286.

31   Bergson, *Laughter*, 22.

32   Susanne Langer, *Feeling and Form: A Theory of Art Developed from Philosophy in a New Key* (New York: Charles Scribner's Sons, 1953).

33 Lorde, *Sister Outsider*.

34 Frye, *Anatomy of Criticism*, 181.

35 Immanuel Kant, *Critique of Judgement* (1790), trans. James Creed Meredith (Oxford: Oxford University Press, 2009), 54.

36 Edmund J. Bourne, *The Anxiety and Phobia Workbook*, 5th ed. (Oakland, Calif.: New Harbinger, 2010), 82–83.

37 Lisette Cheresson, "The Science of Laughter," Wanderlust, May 6, 2016, https://wanderlust.com/.

38 Bourne, *Anxiety and Phobia Workbook*, 83

39 R. I. M. Dunbar, Rebecca Baron, Anna Frangou, et al., "Social Laughter Is Correlated with an Elevated Pain Threshold," *Proceedings of the Royal Society B: Biological Sciences* 279 (2012): 1161–67.

40 Bering, "Rat That Laughed."

41 Critchley, *On Humour*, 8.

42 Julie Holland, *Moody Bitches: The Truth about the Drugs You're Taking, the Sleep You're Missing, the Sex You're Not Having, and What's Really Making You Crazy* (New York: Penguin Books, 2015), 71.

43 Joan Jacobs Brumberg, *The Body Project: An Intimate History of American Girls* (New York: Vintage Books, 2010), 64.

44 *When Harry Met Sally*, dir. Rob Reiner (Castle Rock Entertainment, 1989).

45 Silvan Tomkins, *Shame and Its Sisters: A Silvan Tomkins Reader*, ed. Eve Kosofsky Sedgwick and Adam Green (Durham, N.C.: Duke University Press, 1995), 218, discusses the gendering of shame as female and anger as male.

46 In fact, in certain respects, these philosophers' negative take on the irrational emotions may pose problems for psychic well-being. A certain amount of dwelling on intense negative emotions and deriving insight from them rather than moderating or rising above them can be good for us. Tori Rodriguez, "Negative Emotions Are Key to Well-Being," *Scientific American Mind*, May 1, 2013. See also Lorde's "Uses of Anger," in *Sister Outsider*, 124–33, and "Eye to Eye," in *Sister Outsider*, 145–75.

47 "Periods in Ramadan," Instagram, November 1, 2018, https://www.instagram.com/p/BjVJHffntz8/?hl=en&taken-by=mistahislah.

48 Tina Fey, "Annuale," *Saturday Night Live*, 2008, http://www.nbc.com/.

49 John McCumber, "Aristotelian Catharsis and the Purgation of Women," *Diacritics* 18, no. 4 (1988): 62.

50 McCumber, "Aristotelian Catharsis," 61.

51 McCumber, "Aristotelian Catharsis," 62.

52   McCumber, "Aristotelian Catharsis," 67.

53   Martha Nussbaum, *The Fragility of Goodness: Luck and Ethics in Greek Tragedy and Philosophy* (Cambridge: Cambridge University Press, 1986).

54   Nussbaum, *Fragility of Goodness*, 390.

55   Elizabeth Belfiore, *Tragic Pleasures: Aristotle on Plot and Emotion* (Princeton, N.J.: Princeton University Press, 1992), 336.

56   Belfiore, *Tragic Pleasures*, 336.

57   Ellison, "Extravagance of Laughter." For a similar discussion of playing the dozens, see Lorde, *Sister Outsider*, 171.

58   Mary Douglas, *Purity and Danger* (London: Routledge, 1966). According to Samuel Johnson's dictionary, first published in 1755, a dirty woman defines the slut. As the 2016 presidential campaign tactics of the pussy grabber highlights, we also know her as the nasty woman. Thousands of women fought back by sporting pink pussy hats in the 2017 Women's March after Trump's inauguration.

59   Vagianos, "Amber Rose Owns Her Sexuality."

60   Bakhtin, *Rabelais*, 6. Bakhtin's particular rendition of the carnivalesque has limits for feminism but is an important reference.

61   Townes, "Feminist 'Slutwalk' Movement."

62   Robin Hilmantel, "Amber Rose Announces Date for the Next Slut Walk," *Motto*, May 10, 2016. The comic tradition of the unruly woman traces back to classic Roseanne Barr and to Mae West's burlesque-influenced performances; see Rowe, "Roseanne."

63   Townes, "Feminist 'Slutwalk' Movement." See also Melinda Chateuavert, *Sex Workers Unite: A History of the Movement from Stonewall to Slutwalk* (Boston: Beacon Press, 2014).

64   Tomkins, *Shame and Its Sisters*, 133.

65   Willett, "Sting of Shame." See also Sandra Lee Bartky, "Shame and Gender," in *Femininity and Domination: Studies in the Phenomenology of Oppression* (New York: Routledge, 1990), 83–98.

66   Anthony J. Steinbock, *Moral Emotions: Reclaiming the Evidence of the Heart* (Chicago: Northwestern University Press, 2014), 67.

67   Tomkins, *Shame and Its Sisters*.

68   Tomkins, *Shame and Its Sisters*, 137.

69   Tomkins, *Shame and Its Sisters*.

70   J. M. Lamont, "Trait Body Shame Predicts Health Outcomes in College Women: A Longitudinal Study," *Journal of Behavioral Medicine* 38, no. 5 (2015): 998–1008.

71   Sally S. Dickerson, Tara L. Gruenewald, and Margaret E. Kemey,

"When the Social Self Is Threatened: Shame, Physiology, and Health," *Journal of Personality* 72, no. 6 (2004): 1191–16.

72 Our queasy stomach's reactions to psychopaths, aka those lacking capacities for shame and empathy, underscore the need to have a gut you can trust. See Paul Babiak and Robert D. Hare, *Snakes in Suits: When Psychopaths Go to Work* (New York: HarperCollins, 2009); Eric Barker, "5 Ways to Deal with a Psychopath," *Time*, October 18, 2016; and J. Reid Meloy and M. J. Meloy, "Autonomic Arousal in the Presence of Psychopathy: A Survey of Mental Health and Criminal Justice Professionals," *Journal of Threat Assessment* 2 (2002): 21–33.

73 Consider how "Several researchers have discussed how memory and thought processes can be viewed as external to our brains. Dan Wegner of the University of Virginia has provided fascinating examples of how partners in a marriage gradually become repositories of each other's thoughts and memories. One partner may remember restaurants; the other may keep track of movies." Pennebaker, *Opening Up*, 98. Daniel M. Wegner, Toni Giuliano, and Paula T. Hertel, "Cognitive Interdependence in Close Relationships," in *Compatible and Incompatible Relationships*, edited by William Ickes (New York: Springer-Verlag, 1985).

74 Slate, "Muslims Can't Take a Joke about Islam?"

5. Solidaric Empathy and a Prison Roast with Jeff Ross

1 Jeff Ross, *Jeff Ross Roasts Criminals: Live at Brazos County Jail*, Comedy Central, season 1, episode 1, June 13, 2015; Jeff Ross, *Jeff Ross Roasts Cops*, Comedy Central, season 1, episode 1, September 10, 2016. See also Day, *Satire and Dissent*, 21–23, where she explains that much of the impact of counterpublics in social media is not through a single isolated event but through incremental effects of multiple events gradually shifting the public discourse.

2 While hip-hop is often associated with music, comedy has also played a crucial role in hip-hop culture and its impact on global politics. See K. A. Wisniewski, ed., *The Comedy of Dave Chappelle: Critical Essays* (Jefferson, N.C.: McFarland, 2009), 153.

3 Wickberg, *Senses of Humor*. We draw on this work to trace dominant views of humor, not to endorse any assumptions of linear historical progress or to assert that there are no conflicting cultures of humor between dominant and subversive groups.

4   Wickberg, *Senses of Humor*, 66.

5   Sara Ahmed, *Living a Feminist Life* (Durham, N.C.: Duke University Press, 2017), 105; Lindy West, "Real Men Might Get Made Fun Of," *New York Times*, July 12, 2017, https://www.nytimes.com/.

6.   Wickberg, *Senses of Humor*, 66.

7   Wickberg, *Senses of Humor*, 55–59.

8   Linda Hutcheon, *Irony's Edge: The Theory and Politics of Irony* (London: Routledge, 1994), 29.

9   Hutcheon, *Irony's Edge*, 59.

10   Hutcheon, *Irony's Edge*, 61. Lintott, in "Superiority," counters prevailing assumptions that ridicule theory dominated Western philosophical texts about laughter in ancient and early modern times. While Plato, Aristotle, and Hobbes railed against ridicule, which they thought of as maliciously directed toward those who were simultaneously self-ignorant and powerless, they recognized what were considered to be the graceful pleasures and charms of wit. Note also that Hume's account of sympathy emphasizes feelings, and thus he veered away from Stoic conceptions. Yet for him too only elite cultures were thought to have the correct feelings. See the editors' introduction to Amy Coplan and Peter Goldie, *Empathy: Philosophical and Psychological Approaches* (Oxford: Oxford University Press, 2011), ix–xlvii, esp. x–xi. On the elitist pretensions of the sympathy revolution as found in Hume, see Monique Roelofs, *The Cultural Promise of the Aesthetic* (New York: Bloomsbury, 2015), 55. On the Stoic notion of rational sympathy, see William B. Irvine, *A Guide to the Good Life: The Ancient Art of Stoic Joy* (Oxford: Oxford University Press, 2009), 157.

11   Hutcheon, *Irony's Edge*, 60.

12   Hutcheon, *Irony's Edge*, 60.

13   Spike Lee, dir., *Bamboozled* (2000).

14   Hutcheon, *Irony's Edge*, 79.

15   Hutcheon, *Irony's Edge*, 94.

16   Hutcheon, *Irony's Edge*, 101.

17   Hutcheon, *Irony's Edge*, 11.

18   Hutcheon, *Irony's Edge*, 102.

19   Minoru Asada, Yukie Nagai, and Hisashi Ishihara, "Why Not Artificial Sympathy?," in S. S. Ge, O. Khatib, J. J. Cabibihan, R. Simmons, and M. A. Williams, eds., *Social Robotics: ICSR 2012—Lecture Notes in Computer Science* (Berlin: Springer, 2012), 7621:278–87.

20   Asada, Nagai, and Ishihara, "Why Not Artificial Sympathy?," 7621:94–95.

21   Asada, Nagai, and Ishihara, "Why Not Artificial Sympathy?," 7621:96.

22 Paul Bloom, *Against Empathy* (New York: HarperCollins, 2016); see also Jesse Prinz, "Is Empathy Necessary for Morality?," in Coplan and Goldie, *Empathy*, 221–29. For important concerns about selective empathy, specifically "himathy," see Kate Manne, *Down Girl: The Logic of Misogyny* (Oxford: Oxford University Press, 2018).

23 Leslie Jamison, *The Empathy Exams: Essays* (Minneapolis: Graywolf Press, 2014).

24 Coplan, "Understanding Empathy: Its Features and Effects," in Coplan and Goldie, *Empathy*, 5. Coplan offers an incisive view of the matching theory of empathy, one that avoids assuming that we can put ourselves in the shoes of others. For an overview of work on empathy, see the editors' introduction, ix–xlvii. See also Mark Fagiano, "Relational Empathy," *International Journal of Philosophical Studies*, 27, no. 2 (2019). Heidi L. Maibom, *Empathy and Morality* (Oxford: Oxford University Press, 2014), 4: "Empathy aims to match the emotion that the other experiences or could reasonably be expected to experience in her situation. By contrast, the affective quality of sympathy only matches in the broadest possible terms the welfare of the other." As these authors point out, the terms "empathy" and "sympathy" are both widely confused—and in fact have shifting definitions. Our approach is offered to locate a potential for forging solidarity across lines on a fraught social field.

25 Jamison, *Empathy Exams*, 15.

26 Jamison, *Empathy Exams*, 15.

27 Jamison, *Empathy Exams*, 6.

28 Jamison, *Empathy Exams*, 15.

29 Jamison, *Empathy Exams*, 10.

30 Jamison, *Empathy Exams*, 10.

31 On the limits of white empathy, see Janine Jones, "The Impairment of Empathy in Goodwill Whites for African Americans," in *What White Looks Like*, edited by George Yancy (New York: Routledge, 2004). On the theft of others' suffering and a careful attention to the dangers of empathy, see Saidiya Hartman, *Scenes of Subjection* (Oxford: Oxford University Press, 1997), 18–20.

32 See Ahmed, *Cultural Politics*, 30, 35, 37–39. But Ahmed seems to have in mind either a matching or a contagion theory of empathy, and so allows for our notion of radical empathy.

33 For explorations of felt resonance with others, see discussions of correspondence and affect attunement in Willett, *Maternal Ethics*, 24–30, 92–95; and across nonhuman species in Willett, *Interspecies Ethics*, 80–99.

34 Another comic who mixes various forms of ridicule with a radical empathy that can cross political lines is Stephen Colbert. When asked what he is most hopeful for, Colbert recalls wondering "what happened to socially conscious music," and how he misses "top forty songs like 'Come on people now . . . Try to love one another right now.'" His hoped-for aim, he says, is that his "nightly comedy show . . . is also about love." See his podcast with Oprah Winfrey, "Stephen Colbert: Finding Your Stride," *Oprah's SuperSoul Conversations*, March 6, 2018, https://www.stitcher.com/podcast/own/oprahs-supersoul-conver sations/. On the eros figure, see Frye, *Anatomy of Criticism*, 173ff.

35 Rowe, "Roseanne," 68.

36 See Mel Watkins, *On the Real Side: Laughing, Lying, and Signifying the Underground Tradition of African-American Humor that Trans-formed American Culture, from Slavery to Richard Pryor* (New York: Simon and Schuster, 1994).

37 Haidt, *Happiness Hypothesis*, 12.

38 Tomkins, *Shame and Its Sisters*, 55.

39 Dan Zahavi explains both views with great clarity while developing the latter. See "Empathy and Social Cognition," in *Self and Other: Exploring Subjectivity, Empathy, and Shame* (Oxford: Oxford University Press, 2015), 153–87. But there are other rich variations of these views. Lori Gruen offers an analysis of empathy as a caring type of moral perception, one that can draw on reflection and more infor-mation for greater accuracy. See *Entangled Empathy: An Alternative Ethic for Our Relationships with Animals* (Brooklyn: Lantern Books, 2015), 39. Martha Nussbaum's analysis of empathy as perceptual dis-placement counts on correction from impartial reason and is guided by compassion; see *Political Emotions: Why Love Matters for Justice* (Cambridge, Mass.: Harvard University Press, 2013), 145ff. Our ac-count shares aspects of these but centers empathy not on percep-tion but on emotional engagement, and fully within underlying power dynamics.

40 Jamison, *Empathy Exams*, 5.

41 C. Wright Mills quote cited in Wickberg, *Senses of Humor*, 109.

42 "Johnny Cash—San Quentin (Live From Prison)," YouTube, March 4, 2006, https://www.youtube.com/watch?v=1zgja26eNeY. Krefting, *All Joking Aside*, provides a rich history of stand-up from its origins in post–World War II U.S. culture, especially in chap. 2. She traces how political satire or what she calls charged humor precedes and prepares for the open rebellion of the 1960s with such figures as Mort Sahl, Lenny Bruce, and Dick Gregory. She also explains how

the 1980s became a time of safe comedy and staid Reagan conservativism. Since the 1990s, we have begun to cycle through a similar phenomenon with comics charging the political climate, and feminist along with other marginalized voices more prominent.

43 Alexander, *New Jim Crow*; Tricia Rose, *The Hip Hop Wars: What We Talk about When We Talk about Hip Hop—And Why It Matters* (New York: Basic Books, 2008).

44 Tom LoBianco, "Report: Aide Says Nixon's War on Drugs Targeted Blacks, and Hippies," CNN, March 23, 2016.

45 Thomas Frank, *What's the Matter with Kansas? How Conservatives Won the Heart of America* (New York: Henry Holt, 2005).

46 See Julie Willett, *Oink! Feminism, Humor, and the Rise of the Chauvinist Pig* (unpublished).

47 Ross, *Jeff Ross Roasts Cops*.

48 In 2017, Ross takes on the hot issue of immigration and roasts the proposal for a border wall in Brownsville, Texas. Jeff Ross, *Jeff Ross Roasts the Border*, Comedy Central, season 1, episode 1, November 16, 2017.

Conclusion

1 Tig Notaro, *Live*, 2013, Spotify, https://open.spotify.com/; Melissa Leon, "How Comedian Tig Notaro Found Love after Cancer," Daily Beast, July 20, 2015, https://www.thedailybeast.com/. We expand elements of this conclusion in "The Comic in the Midst of Tragedy's Grief with Tig Notaro, Hannah Gadsby, and Others," *Journal of Aesthetics and Art Criticism* (forthcoming).

2 Hannah Gadsby, *Nanette* (2017 stand-up show released on Netflix in 2018).

3 Gadsby, *Nanette*.

4 Gadsby, *Nanette*.

5 Gadsby, *Nanette*.

Index

abortion, 30–31
absurdities, 13–14, 18, 100, 101;
    absurdist humor, 128n10
Abu-Wardeh, Jamil, 51, 58
Adams, Reginald, 13
affects, 6, 56, 59; as contagion,
    58–59; versus emotion, 49–50;
    negative, 60, 102; theory of,
    49–50
Ahmed, Sara, 50
Alcaraz, Lalo, 68
Allen, Gracie, 24, 26
allopathic. *See* catharsis
alpha male, 73, 88, 91, 83
Andrews, Thomas, 95–96
anxiety, 45, 52, 63, 69, 106, 108,
    117, 146; post-9/11, 13, 49, 63,
    142
Ape Genius, 83–86
Arab Spring, 50, 59
Aristotle, 106, 109–10, 111–12
arrogance. *See* hubris
asshole, 9, 160n33. *See also* humor
Axis of Evil Comedy Tour, 12–13,
    51, 52, 58, 61
Azmanova, Albena, 160n25

Bakhtin, Mikhail, 10–11, 16, 115
Ball, Lucille, 26
Bamboozled. See Lee, Spike
Barr, Roseanne, 12, 21, 24–26
Barreca, Gina, 27
Barrett, Lisa Felman, 159n18
Bee, Samantha, 12, 24, 118, 140,
    142
Bekoff, Marc, 17, 86–88, 92, 133
Belfiore, Elizabeth, 112–13
Bentham, Jeremy, 75–76, 78
Bergson, Henri, 105
Berlant, Lauren, 157n4
Big Mama Jo, 135–36
Bilge, Simra, 3, 9, 41
biosocial, 24; desires, 118; field,
    120; force, 102, 112. *See also*
    climate; network
birthers, 49, 52–54
blackface, 81
Black Lives Matter, 139, 140, 141
Black Panthers, 40, 65, 66
Bloom, Paul, 129
bond, 82, 96; bonding, 15, 86, 107,
    134–35
Bono, 10, 140

CYNTHIA WILLETT is Samuel Candler Dobbs professor of philosophy at Emory University with affiliated positions in women's, gender, sexuality studies; religion; the psychoanalytic studies program; and African American studies. Her authored books include *Interspecies Ethics, Irony in the Age of Empire: Comic Perspectives on Democracy and Freedom, The Soul of Justice: Social Bonds and Racial Hubris,* and *Maternal Ethics and Other Slave Moralities*. She edited *Theorizing Multiculturalism*.

JULIE WILLETT is associate professor of history at Texas Tech University, with an affiliated position in women's and gender studies. She is author of *Permanent Waves: The Making of the American Beauty Shop* and editor of *The American Beauty Industry Encyclopedia*.